Real Estate Rainmaker®

Also by Dan Gooder Richard

REAL ESTATE RAINMAKER®: Successful Strategies for Real Estate Marketing

To my mother,
Adrienne Gooder Richard,
who is an inspiration, as are her novels,
nonfiction books, and poetry.

Contents

Foreword by Allen F. Hainge   xi

Acknowledgments   xv

Introduction   xvii
    20 New Rules of Online Marketing

PART ONE

ESSENTIAL STRATEGIES TO HELP YOU TAKE YOUR MARKET BY STORM

1 **Eight Technology Truths That Could Kill Your Business**   3
    Old Rule: The Internet changes everything.
    New Rule: The Internet changes everything except the
       rules of business.

2 **Eight Proven eRainmaker Strategies for Success**   15
    Old Rule: The Internet will change real estate as we
       know it.
    New Rule: Your business is your business and the
       Internet is a tool to be used.

PART TWO

WEBSITE TECHNIQUES THAT WORK BIG FOR LITTLE COST

3 Selecting Domains to Brand Your Retirement   29
Old Rule: Your name is your brand.
New Rule: Your brand should never be your name.

4 Planning a Customer-Centered Website   43
Old Rule: Your website is all about you.
New Rule: Your website is all about the customer.

5 Driving Traffic to Your Website: 75 Ways to Promote Your Site   59
Old Rule: Online advertising will surpass offline advertising.
New Rule: Integrated offline and online promotion wins every time.

6 Driving Traffic to Your Website: Strategic Linking   83
Old Rule: If you link out to other websites, prospects will never come back.
New Rule: If you're not networking on the Internet, you're not working.

7 Driving Traffic to Your Website: Search Marketing Basics   99
Old Rule: Optimizing your site for search engines is the key to traffic.
New Rule: Offline promotion, strategic links, and search marketing combined maximize traffic.

8 Capturing E-Leads from Your Website   113
Old Rule: Delivering leads is the only job for a website.
New Rule: The best websites deliver leads *and* customer service.

9 Buyer Follow-Up: Converting Website Visits into Contracts   131
Old Rule: A picture is worth a thousand words.
New Rule: A website is worth a thousand pictures.

10 Seller Follow-Up: Turning Online Leads into Listings   145

Old Rule: The Internet will disintermediate real estate professionals.

New Rule: The Internet makes personal service even more priceless.

11 E-Loyalty: Keeping Customers for Life   157

Old Rule: Market share is paramount.

New Rule: Lifetime share of customer is even more valuable.

PART THREE

E-MAIL MARKETING TO CAPTURE AND KEEP CUSTOMERS

12 Planning Your E-Mail Marketing Strategy   171

Old Rule: The Internet works best as a direct marketing medium.

New Rule: The Internet helps you generate transactions *and* build relationships.

13 Creating E-Mail That Gets Response   183

Old Rule: Spam will be the death of e-mail.

New Rule: Permission marketing will survive after spam is outlawed.

14 Converting Prospects with E-Mail Follow-Up   195

Old Rule: Content is king.

New Rule: The right customer-focused content is king.

15 Using E-Mail to Build After-Sale Referrals and Repeat Business   209

Old Rule: The dot-com era was the peak of the Internet.

New Rule: The Next Wave Internet boom is here—and it's going to last.

16 Building a Trophy E-Mail Database   219

Old Rule: Internet games are diversions for kids.

New Rule: Kids who first played Internet games are now prime first-time buyers.

PART FOUR

DEMYSTIFYING INTERNET MARKETING

17 **E-Marketing Plan: Six Steps to Effective
    Online Marketing**   233
    Old Rule: Internet users aren't like you or me.
    New Rule: Internet users are you and me.

18 **E-Operations Plan: Streamlining with
    Virtual Assistants**   249
    Old Rule: All this tech-talk is just Geek to me.
    New Rule: You should definitely hire a virtual assistant.

19 **E-Action Plans: Becoming an eRainmaker**   257
    Old Rule: Best practices are the best practices.
    New Rule: Best practices are the ones that work for you.

20 **Exit Strategies: Branding an E-Practice to Sell**   273
    Old Rule: Retirement means declaring victory and
        turning out the lights.
    New Rule: Retirement means selling your e-practice to
        the highest bidder.

Resources   291
    Online Resource Center   291
    Shelf Help   293

Index   297

About the Author   309

Foreword

Some real estate professionals make full use of technology. Most don't. Now that the roaring 1990s and the dot-com bubble are behind us, I see in my personal coaching and seminars that real estate professionals face three challenges where technology can help:

1. *Make more money.* This means use technology to increase market share and close more transactions.
2. *Keep more money.* If you can cut expenses, do it. E-marketing can be hugely cost effective. Take my weekly e-newsletter "Technology News & Views." I send it out four times a month to 16,000 subscribers. The cost to me for those 64,000 impressions a month is only $50.
3. *Save time.* Many heavy hitters are working seven days a week, which they shouldn't. Technology can help you get a life.

Every e-marketing strategy starts with a website. Probably the number one flaw I see most often—the one topic that takes up 85% of my personal coaching sessions—is that real estate websites are not customized. Consider Alice Held (Come2AZ.com), for example. You may have never met Alice, but visit her website and you feel you know her. Today, real estate websites need to be a reflection of your business style, a refection of your area or your services or your target customers. Too many agents today bought a website years ago and let it sit while new agents leap-frogged ahead of them with more effective sites. Old, noncustomized sites are sterile. Often the sites have links they shouldn't have. These sites are not aimed at customer's needs or customized in the agent's style.

Using what you have—or knowing what technology to get—is another challenge. Some agents are afraid of technology, so they never buy it. Others buy it but don't think they can use it—so they don't. Still others, who are using technology, shouldn't, because it drains too much time away from their true business of listing and selling. For example, many have database software. But what are many agents doing to follow up within their sphere? Very little. Today many practitioners need action plans, a system, and a clear step-by-step e-marketing road map.

The third need is getting somebody else to do your technology tasks for you. One of the simplest and best solutions to e-marketing is to use a virtual assistant or transaction coordinator. VAs have all the software already and know how to use it. Hainge's Rule of Computing #4 is that, ideally, you should never touch a keyboard—except for e-mail. Have someone else do it for you. All too often real estate professionals are wasting time and not making as much money as they could.

The secret to e-marketing today is not to let technology take time away from face-to-face customer time and your personal life. Today, every real estate agent needs to know how to market using the Internet. Once you understand the integrated **REAL ESTATE RAINMAKER®: Guide to Online Marketing** system, this book walks you through the practical steps of building an e-practice brand with web domains, websites, and e-mail marketing systems complete with a trophy e-mail database of consumer and business contacts. Ultimately your e-marketing system becomes so valuable to other eRainmakers that you can sell your branded practice whenever you want.

In **REAL ESTATE RAINMAKER®: Guide to Online Marketing,** Dan Gooder Richard brings over 25 year's of experience generating real estate sales leads to focus on successful strategies for our industry. Dan's solution is a model e-marketing system *any* real estate agent can use to put the power of the Internet to work generating more leads and more sales at the lowest cost. In his practical style,

Dan tells you *how* in simple, straightforward language and then makes it easy to *do* with one real-world example after example. I'm confidant this ***Guide to Online Marketing*** will work for you.

ALLEN F. HAINGE
Founder of Allen F. Hainge CYBERSTARS®
Author of *Dominate! Capturing Your Market with Today's Technology; Secrets of the CyberStars®: Making Money with Today's Technology*

Acknowledgments

My career in real estate marketing began in 1979 when Laurie Moore-Moore and Wes Foster hired me as a young journalism school graduate to be the first director of marketing for Long & Foster Real Estate in the mid-Atlantic region.

In the decades to follow, Long & Foster has grown to be the largest diversified brokerage in the country, and I've grown for more than two decades publishing marketing materials for real estate professionals. In all those years, one immutable truth has risen above all the changes: In every market area and in every business cycle, individual real estate professionals find a way to outperform their competition. This book is enriched by those techniques from all the numerous professionals who shared with me their own ideas about e-marketing. Without their help, this book would not have been possible. To all those who took time from their busy businesses and shared their ideas in person, in writing, and in seminars, thank you. Among those I want to thank specifically are:

Russell Arkin
Antonio Atacan
Cindy Andrade
PJ Babcock
Jim Bass
Bob Bohlen
Alexis Bolin
Bruce Jay Breger

Stacy Brice
Jay Burnham
Steve Chader
Carol and Jim
 Chamberlain
Ken and Mary
 Deshaies
Gary Ditto

Pete Doty
Kathy Drewien
Vern and Audrey
 English
Blanche Evans
Pete French
Greg Frost
Matt Greene

Paulette Greene
Galand Haas
Allen F. Hainge
Alice Held
Kellee Heldoorn
Ron Henderson
Dave and Sally
  Herries
Richard and Brooke
  Hiers
David Huey
Kim Hughes
Darrell Hutson
Mike Hyles
Frank Jacovini
Gary Keller
Jerry Keller
Scot Kenkel
David Kent
Don King
Tim Kinzler
Roger Lautt

Rob Levy
Michelle Margetts
Gary Marshall
Dick Mathes
Ethel Mayer
Judy McCutchin
Leslie McDonnell
Peter McGarry
Rick Miner
Heidi Mueller
Stephen O'Hara
Kathy O'Rourke
Nic Paley
Zac Pasmanick
Jack Peckham
John Pinto
Tom Randall
Bill Renaud
Thierry Roche
Margaret Rome
Michael J. Russer
Walter Sanford

Ed Sears
Ira and Carol Serkes
Gary Shade
Linda Soesbe
Reese Stewart
Ron Street
Dianne Sutton
Sandy Teller
Michelle Thornton
Steve Tryggeseth
Beth Tyler
Joe Valenti
Dave Wallace
Todd Walters
Mollie Wasserman
Bob Webster
Barbara Weismann
John F. Williams
Adrian Willanger
Tom and Patti Wilser
Gary and Laury
  Woods

No project of this size is possible without invaluable support. I would also like to thank my wife, Synnöve, whose love and support make it all possible—and worth it; our staff at the Gooder Group, who kept the business running while I worked at home most days for half a year; my Tech Diva, Amy Hausman, whose research focused a laser beam on details beyond measure; my agents at Altair Literary Agency, Nicholas Smith and Andrea Pedolsky, whose steadfast guidance shaped this project every step of the way; my comanaging editor at Gooder Group, Deb Rhoney, whose insightful edits make me look good; my production staff at Publications Development Company; my brother, Randall Richard, whose technical edits kept me on track at every turn; my permissions and research assistant, Sydney Royal; my production manager at John Wiley & Sons, Linda Indig; and my patient senior editor at John Wiley & Sons, Mike Hamilton, whose outside jump shot is still a thing of beauty. Many thanks; I couldn't have done it without you.

DAN GOODER RICHARD

Introduction

20 New Rules of Online Marketing

1. **Old Rule:** The Internet changes everything.
   New Rule: The Internet changes everything except the rules of business.
2. **Old Rule:** The Internet will change real estate as we know it.
   New Rule: Your business is your business and the Internet is a tool to be used.
3. **Old Rule:** Your name is your brand.
   New Rule: Your brand should never be your name.
4. **Old Rule:** Your website is all about you.
   New Rule: Your website is all about the customer.
5. **Old Rule:** Online advertising will surpass offline advertising.
   New Rule: Integrated offline and online promotion wins every time.

6. **Old Rule:** If you link out to other websites, prospects will never come back.
   New Rule: If you're not networking on the Internet, you're not working.

7. **Old Rule:** Optimizing your site for search engines is the key to traffic.
   New Rule: Offline promotion, strategic links, and search marketing combined maximize traffic.

8. **Old Rule:** Delivering leads is the only job for a website.
   New Rule: The best websites deliver leads *and* customer service.

9. **Old Rule:** A picture is worth a thousand words.
   New Rule: A website is worth a thousand pictures.

10. **Old Rule:** The Internet will disintermediate real estate professionals.
    New Rule: The Internet makes personal service even more priceless.

11. **Old Rule:** Market share is paramount.
    New Rule: Lifetime share of customer is even more valuable.

12. **Old Rule:** The Internet works best as a direct marketing medium.
    New Rule: The Internet helps you generate transactions *and* build relationships.

13. **Old Rule:** Spam will be the death of e-mail.
    New Rule: Permission marketing will survive after spam is outlawed.

14. **Old Rule:** Content is king.
    New Rule: The right customer-focused content is king.

15. **Old Rule:** The dot-com era was the peak of the Internet.
    New Rule: The Next Wave Internet boom is here—and it's going to last.

16. **Old Rule:** Internet games are diversions for kids.
    New Rule: Kids who first played Internet games are now prime first-time buyers.

17. **Old Rule:** Internet users aren't like you or me.
    New Rule: Internet users are you and me.

18. **Old Rule:** All this tech-talk is just Geek to me.
    New Rule: You should definitely hire a virtual assistant.

19. **Old Rule:** Best practices are the best practices.
    New Rule: Best practices are the ones that work for you.

20. **Old Rule:** Retirement means declaring victory and turning out the lights.
    New Rule: Retirement means selling your e-practice to the highest bidder.

I'm Dan Gooder Richard.

In college I was a history and journalism major. As publisher of Gooder Group, I've learned how to use the Internet and technology as a marketing tool to grow our business and to grow the practices of thousands of real estate professionals. That's why *REAL ESTATE RAINMAKER®: Guide to Online Marketing* is a marketing book, not a tech manual.

REAL ESTATE RAINMAKER®: Guide to Online Marketing is not for a limited audience of advanced power users. It is filled with hands-on tips and techniques designed for novices and experts alike. This book was written for the tens of thousands of real estate professionals who want to make sense of the Internet and online real estate marketing. It is indispensable for real estate marketers who need new solutions and more profitable ways to use the tools the Internet provides in combination with time-tested offline marketing techniques. *REAL ESTATE RAINMAKER®: Guide to Online Marketing* is the perfect solution for real estate people at all levels in the industry that want to build a profitable Internet strategy.

To get the full benefit of *REAL ESTATE RAINMAKER®: Guide to Online Marketing,* it is not necessary for you to have read my previous book, *REAL ESTATE RAINMAKER®.* Since I wrote the first book—primarily about offline marketing—the Internet has arrived on the scene. *REAL ESTATE RAINMAKER®: Guide to Online Marketing* is the natural extension of those proven offline marketing principles into online marketing. Both books deliver practical, workable guidelines and strategies, plus tested action steps for those wanting to sharpen their real estate marketing skills.

Over the years, I've seen technologies arrive—and many fade away—and realized there will always be new tech tools to add to our marketing toolbox. Almost every e-marketing conversation includes a "Hey have you seen this?" comment about a new (or old) tool you've never heard of before. Take heart. Remember, people who know more than you just got started before you. Ultimately learning about e-marketing is simply exposure. Everyone learns technology by doing, by repetition. Nobody gets it the first time. The secret is spotting e-marketing tools that make you money, trying them out, and tossing old marketing techniques that no longer work, which is the purpose of this book.

The Internet has proved it can power any real estate business. More than 71% of consumers use the Internet during their home search, according to the National Association of REALTORS®. Yet, only 6% of buyers and 2% of sellers say they found their real estate agent through the Internet. Today, only a small segment of top-sales agents have taken full advantage of the Internet. Most traditional, solo practitioners are still feeling their way without a complete grasp of the opportunities offered by the Internet and e-marketing.

Every real estate agent needs buyers *and* sellers. Yet, most agents primarily use the Internet to generate only buyers. A huge untapped opportunity exists for every agent to generate the most lucrative Internet prospects of all: home sellers. To take full advantage of the web today, real estate professionals need to know which e-marketing strategies work—and which don't. Non-Internet practitioners need to step up to a level playing field—or step aside. For the hundreds of eRainmakers surveyed and interviewed for this book, the Internet has not "changed real estate as we know it," as the Wall Street analysts pitched. Instead, these eRainmakers have learned—sometimes the hard way—in the real world trenches of generating more leads and more sales online that e-marketing is another slice of the whole marketing pie. It is a big slice and a growing slice, but still just a slice.

Simply put, **REAL ESTATE RAINMAKER®: Guide to Online Marketing** shows you exactly how e-marketing fits into real estate and how to develop (or makeover) your personal e-strategy to make more money for your own e-practice.

How to Use This Book

REAL ESTATE RAINMAKER®: Guide to Online Marketing is really two books in one: a guide to your *thinking* and a guide to *doing*. The book is divided into four parts. In *Part One* you will discover how to avoid having your practice drowned by the growing wave of Internet e-customers and e-competitors. *Part Two* outlines tested website techniques that produce big results for little cost. *Part Three* shows you how to use e-mail to capture customers and keep them for life. In *Part Four,* we get down to nuts-and-bolts, and you will be guided step-by-step through essential exercises to write your own e-strategy road map—complete with action plans, budget, and shopping lists. Finally—and many eRainmakers say they read the last chapter first— you will learn how to build e-practice assets of such value you will be able to sell your practice to another eRainmaker when you want to move on.

At our essential companion website, **eRainmaker.com,** we have brought together for the first-time anywhere virtually every available real estate e-marketing tool and product into one Online Resource Center. In it you will find a unique Website Buyers Guide, Link Index, Resource Guide, Great Websites, GeekSpeak Glossary, and much more. Information is constantly updated and intuitively organized with powerful links direct to providers' sites. New entries and resources are added regularly in response to reader requests and the ever-changing marketplace.

No matter what your past experience with online real estate marketing, this book was written for you . . . the real estate professional who wants to become an eRainmaker and profit from the next Internet wave. In the Guide, the online novice and intermediate real estate professional will find an easy-to-grasp, comprehensive view of e-marketing to build a new, more-profitable practice. The Guide is also designed for the advanced "power user" who needs the hard-won, invaluable little secrets to e-marketing that will take an existing e-practice to the next level. *REAL ESTATE RAINMAKER®: Guide to Online Marketing* is designed for you.

Make it Rain!®

DAN GOODER RICHARD
Fairfax, Virginia

Real Estate Rainmaker®

PART

ONE

ESSENTIAL STRATEGIES TO HELP YOU TAKE YOUR MARKET BY STORM

1

Eight Technology Truths That Could Kill Your Business

OLD RULE

The Internet changes everything.

NEW RULE

The Internet changes everything except the rules of business.

Truth #1: Most Customers Contact Only One Real Estate Agent

Online or offline, there is one fundamental truth about the real estate industry: Most customers use the first salesperson they contact. Readers of my previous book, **Real Estate Rainmaker®**, will recognize how this fundamental truth has not changed over the years. In 1997, my company, Gooder Group, sponsored a question on the bi-annual National Association of REALTORS® (NAR) survey of thousands of recent home buyers and sellers, *Home Buying and Selling Process*. The question was: "How many real estate agents did you contact before you selected one to help you buy (or sell) your house?" Every two

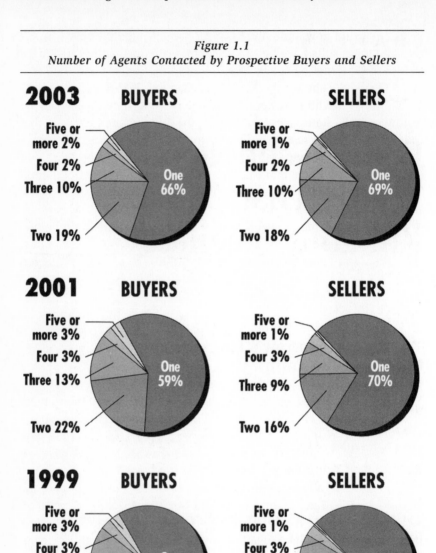

Figure 1.1
Number of Agents Contacted by Prospective Buyers and Sellers

2003   **BUYERS**

Five or more 2%
Four 2%
Three 10%
Two 19%
One 66%

SELLERS

Five or more 1%
Four 2%
Three 10%
Two 18%
One 69%

2001   **BUYERS**

Five or more 3%
Four 3%
Three 13%
Two 22%
One 59%

SELLERS

Five or more 1%
Four 3%
Three 9%
Two 16%
One 70%

1999   **BUYERS**

Five or more 3%
Four 3%
Three 11%
Two 22%
One 61%

SELLERS

Five or more 1%
Four 3%
Three 8%
Two 14%
One 74%

Source: NATIONAL ASSOCIATION OF REALTORS®, *Profile of Home Buyers and Sellers,* various years. Used with permission.

years since and now annually, the NAR has repeated the survey question and the results have been consistent, even during the early adoption of the Internet by consumers.

As Figure 1.1 shows, the amount of agent shopping varies slightly among buyers, who shop more, and sellers, who shop less, when selecting a real estate salesperson. Yet, the fundamental truth is that *consumers view all real estate professionals as pretty much the same.* We know there is a wide variance in competence and experience, but consumers don't know that—until after they're under contract. A consumer's needs are most often serviced by the first real estate salesperson they contact.

Two out of three times if you are the real estate professional prospects contact first, you will get the customer. Conversely, if customers contact your competition first, two-thirds of the time you're left out of the deal. The secret is to build a marketing system that *guarantees* customers contact you first.

Truth #2: Tomorrow's Internet Customer Will Drive the Train

Much hand wringing occurred in the late 1990s about the coming "cyber-customer." This unknown—and thus scary—creature was going to click a mouse and buy a house. This was to be a new breed of customer—young, tech-savvy, hands-off—who was the direct opposite of the "average" real estate professional—age 49, tech-averse, hands-on. Reports came in about the first home sales done completely over the web. Then Bill Gates published *Business@ the Speed of Thought* in 1999 and predicted the Internet would "disintermediate" real estate professionals by bringing together buyers and sellers directly . . . eliminating the middleman.

Yikes!

Now that the postbubble dust has settled on the dot-com era, the reality for real estate professionals is less dire but still dramatic. Today's real estate customers have not mutated into separate species—traditional versus cyber-consumer. Instead, the reality is a convergence into a hybrid customer that I call a *Tech-and-Touch* customer (TnT). In the final analysis, TnT customers use the Internet for real estate the same way they use it for other purchases:

68% research online, buy in store (or use in-store pickup);

54% research in store, buy online;

47% research by catalog, buy online;

38% research online, buy over phone,

according to Jupiter Research/NFO, May 2000, *American Demographics,* December 2000.

In their groundbreaking book *Convergence Marketing,* authors Jerry Wind and Vijay Mahajan give an example that clearly defines the hybrid customer. "Charles Schwab found that while about 90% of all trades are handled online, 60% to 70% of new accounts are set up in branch offices," they wrote, quoting from remarks by Neal Goldstein, Wharton Fellow in e-Business program, San Francisco, January 2001.

Just like the stock brokerage customer, today's real estate brokerage customer is a hybrid who uses the Internet to gather information about process and properties and often appreciates e-mail as the preferred channel of communication. When TnT customers are ready, they turn to a real estate professional in person for specialized expertise to find property, negotiate a contract, and close the transaction.

The new convergence customer *will not kill your business.* But now that the TnT customer can drive the real estate train, if you don't know how to get them on *your* train, competitors who do know how could leave your train stranded and empty at the station.

Truth #3: Only 6 Percent of Customers Find Their Real Estate Agent on the Internet

Only 6% of home buyers and 2% of sellers in 2003 *found* their real estate agent through the Internet, according to the National Association of REALTORS *2003 Profile of Home Buyers and Sellers.* Yet, that same survey reports 71% of consumers *used* the Internet to gather information during their home search. (The previous time the NAR published the survey in 2002 the figures were 3% for lead generation and 41% for Internet use.) Why do the NAR figures put the Internet near the *bottom* as a lead-generator? How can this be when the Internet is near the *top* as a widely used property resource during the home search?

What are our prospects telling us? Put simply, most consumers have adopted the Internet as a home-finding tool faster than real estate

Table 1.1
Method Used to Find Real Estate Agent

Method	Buyers (%)	Sellers (%)
Referred by friend, neighbor, relative	44	40
Used agent previously to buy or sell house	14	27
Visited open house and met agent	7	4
Walked into/called office and agent was on duty	6	5
Internet/website	**6**	**2**
Yard sign	6	3
Personal contact by agent (telephone, etc.)	5	7
Referred through employer/relocation company	5	3
Referred through another real estate broker/agent	4	3
Newspaper/Yellow Pages/home book ad	4	3
Direct mail (newsletter, flier, letter, postcard, etc.)	1	2
Advertising specialty (calendar, magnet, etc.)	1	1

Note: Detail may not add to 100% due to multiple responses.
Source: National Association of REALTORS®, *2003 Profile of Home Buyers and Sellers.*

professionals have adopted the web as a marketing tool. Table 1.1 gives the raw numbers of how consumers report they found their agent.

Today, there is a tremendous untapped opportunity to capture home buying and selling prospects—before they contact the competition—by effectively fishing in the same website and e-mail channels prospects are already using. Now that the dot-com meltdown has cleared the 1990s hype of online marketing versus traditional marketing (read: old fashioned), real estate professionals need to know what is *really* working in today's e-marketplace. One answer is clear: If your website doesn't capture them on the first visit and your e-mail follow up doesn't lock them in as a satisfied prospect, don't be surprised if they are forever lost as customers to the competition.

Truth #4: Brokerages and Mega-Teams Have Declared War on Your Customers

In the late 1990s, when the Wall Street analysts and media stories panicked the real estate industry into a mad rush to "get on the Internet," real estate professionals fretted over how to get something—anything— up on the web and into e-mail. *Brochureware* websites mushroomed and locating any technology that sent mass e-mails was the order of the day.

Since Y2K, with the proliferation of websites and the flood of mass e-mail, what was novel in the 1990s is passé today. Most important, e-marketing brought results—some dumb luck, some first-adapter cherry picking. Successful results spawned sophistication built on experience and trial-and-error experiments.

Savvy eRainmakers moved on to the next level and asked themselves how they could get more for their e-marketing dollars. What exactly did they want their e-marketing investment to deliver and increase? Image? Services? Sales? Efficiency? Profits?

In today's environment of a gazillion websites and inbox clutter, only the best thrive. Many of the successful eRainmakers now run mega-agent sales teams (two licensees) or company-size groups (three or more licensees). They have declared war on the customers of less sophisticated practitioners and brokerages. Today, your customer is someone else's prospect. After all, in a marketplace where every customer is served, the only way to increase market share is to steal clients from another real estate practitioner. Thriving eRainmakers have gone beyond asking themselves "How do I get on the Net?" and beyond "What do I want to increase?" They now ask themselves "Where can the Internet take my business?" and "How can this tool improve my bottom line?"

The outcome is a growing gap in production among real estate practitioners between the "Haves" and the "Have-Littles."

Truth #5: Six Mythunderstandings That Stand between You and High Achievement

In his best-selling book *The Millionaire Real Estate Agent,* Gary Keller outlines the six most common myths that keep real estate professionals from achieving success. Keller, founder and CEO of Keller Williams International, understands the false barriers to success that can kill a real estate practice. He also understands the reality that lies behind these perceived barriers. Here are Keller's Six Myth Understandings from the first part of this must-read book:

1. *Myth:* I can't do it.

   Truth: Until you try, you can't possibly know what you can or can't do.

2. *Myth:* It can't be done in my market.

   Truth: Yes it can, but you may need a new approach.

3. *Myth:* It would take too much time and effort—I would lose my freedom.

   Truth: Time and effort are not the deciding factors in success.

4. *Myth:* It's too risky. I'll lose money.

   Truth: Risk is in direct proportion to how well you hold your incremental costs accountable to producing incremental results.

5. *Myth:* My clients will only work with me—only I can deliver quality service.

   Truth: Your clients aren't loyal to you; they are loyal to the standards you represent.

6. *Myth:* Having a goal and not fully realizing it is a negative thing.

   Truth: Having a goal and not trying to achieve it is a negative thing.

Every one of Keller's truths applies double to e-marketing. First, because e-marketing is a "new trick for an old dog" for many real estate professionals who have been on the scene longer than the Internet. Second, because online marketing is a dynamic new aspect of real estate marketing that has an emerging track record but hasn't been around the track enough times to wear comfortable ruts.

Ultimately, the secret to learning about technology is *exposure.* This fact is so important, it's worth repeating. Everyone learns about e-marketing by doing, by repetition. Nobody gets it the first time. People, who know more than you, just got started before you. Take heart. Avoid Keller's six "mythunderstandings." You can take your e-practice to the next level and leave much of your competition— whether intermediates or comfortable top producers—hopelessly behind in the eyes of today's demanding consumers.

Truth #6: The Internet Pressures Every Website to Be Better Today than Yesterday

Online competition is tough—and relentless. As of this writing, more than 30 million web domains have been registered worldwide. Google continuously searches more than three billion web pages—and counting. Gone are the early days of brochureware websites and classified ads online. Gone is the effectiveness of superficial content and "I'm the Greatest" personality websites. In May 2003, the National Association of REALTORS' Center for REALTOR Technology reported almost all real estate professionals use e-mail in their business and more than 60% of all REALTORS have a personal website, either their own or through their brokerage.

As more and more agents launch e-marketing, real estate professionals need ever-more sophisticated website content, more appealing "look and feel," and smarter presentation to stay ahead of the competition—and stay up with today's consumer. All these choices make online consumers savvy comparison shoppers. Today, as more and more consumers shop online for properties as a first step, real estate professionals who were early adopters of online marketing in the 1990s—but haven't kept pace—risk having uncompetitive websites that underwhelm prospects, risk declining search engine rankings, and risk losing their Internet business market share. Online marketing is changing and, to be successful, every real estate professional must change with it.

As Satchel Paige, the great Hall of Fame baseball pitcher, once said, "Don't look back; something may be gaining on you." It is. In fact, competitors in the rearview mirror *are* closer than they appear. The next real estate downturn will weed out those who have not learned to be smarter e-marketers than they were yesterday.

Truth #7: The Honeymoon Is Over—E-Mail Is Not for the Unsophisticated Anymore

The dramatic increase in e-mails has created a fundamental challenge for real estate professionals. Jupiter Research, which tracks Internet activity, claims the average e-mail user received 2,200 spam messages over the past year, according to *PC Magazine* February 25, 2003. On average, consumers in one study received 254 e-mails in their inbox each week in 2002, compared with 159 per week in 2001—an increase of 60% (*2002 Consumer E-mail Study* copyright DoubleClick, Inc., a New York-based online marketing firm). Today real estate professionals are faced with a double-edged sword.

On the one hand, e-mail is the "killer" application of the Internet:

☑ 75% of consumers who receive permission-based (opt-in) e-mail say that it is their preferred method of communication, compared with 25% preferring postal mail and 0% who prefer telemarketing (*2002 Consumer E-mail Study*, copyright DoubleClick, Inc.).

☑ Low cost of delivery (compared to printing and postage for direct mail) can minimize marketing expenses and maximize worldwide reach.

☑ E-mail is fast, convenient, leaves a written record, and is interactive like no other communications tool even the telephone.

☑ Successful open rates, click-through rates, and sales figures prove permission-based e-mail is a powerful and effective tool.

On the other hand, the honeymoon for e-mail is over:

☑ 90% of consumers in one study said unsolicited promotional e-mail is their number-one consumer concern (*2002 Consumer E-mail Study*, copyright DoubleClick, Inc.).

☑ About 60% of all e-mail in 2004 (up from 40% in 2002 and 8% in 2001) and 40% of all direct mail is business marketing messages (Gartner Group, *USA Today*, October 2, 2003; Brightmail, Inc., *Washington Post*, March 12, 2003).

☑ Consumers have 2.63 e-mail addresses on average, using personal and work accounts to separate legitimate offers and private e-mail from unsolicited e-mail (*2002 Consumer E-mail Study*, copyright DoubleClick, Inc.).

☑ Between 20% and 40% of all e-mail addresses go bad or "churn" every year (Assurance Systems, *Avoid the Spam Filter Trap*, October 2002; NFO InDepth Internative, *Business2.com*, July 30, 2001; NFO WorldGroup, *ClickZ.com*, March 28, 2001).

☑ Of all sent e-mails, 12.5% bounce back undeliverable (*Q1 2003 E-mail Trend Report*, copyright DoubleClick, Inc.).

☑ E-mail filters (also, "spam killers") block more and more e-mail from being delivered. That includes desktop software filters that block 2% to 8% of all e-mail and Internet Service Providers (ISP) that filter 6% to 8% of all e-mail sent (*PC Magazine*, February 25, 2003, and Assurance Systems, *Avoid the Spam Filter Trap*, October 2002, respectively).

☑ The nondelivery rate of legitimate e-mail falsely identified as spam (false positives) to permission-based lists was at least 17% in first half 2003—up from 15% in Q4 2002 and 12% in Q3 2002 (Return Path, *First Half 2003 E-mail Blocking and Filtering Report*).

Today, just because you sent e-mail—and did not receive a bounce-back—doesn't mean your e-mail was delivered or read. Simply put, mass spammers with unwanted e-mails are soiling the e-mail inbox for genuine e-marketers with true messages for their legitimate opt-in customers and contacts. After all, what is spam? Not just unsolicited e-mail, but e-mail you didn't ask for *and* you don't want. That distinction is critical. Our contacts, prospects, and customers may want the real estate information we send, even though they don't "ask" for it.

The e-mail challenge facing every real estate professional is two fold: First, how do you build a permission-based opt-in e-mail database that welcomes your messages? Second, how do you penetrate the inbox clutter of annoying spam with valuable information sent at an optimal frequency that your customers read? The alternative is bleak. If you do not use sophisticated e-marketing that meets the expectations of increasingly sophisticated customers, your legitimate messages will be irretrievably lost in the deluge of aggressive mass marketers. Thankfully, there are proven techniques for doing this.

Truth #8: The Rules of the Online Marketing Game Are Constantly Changing

You are no longer in the real estate industry. You are in the marketing business. Your first job is marketing—generating leads, capturing customers with follow-up, cultivating clients for life—not sales. Do your marketing job right, and sales will follow. In fact, marketing done properly will produce all the sales you can handle.

Never has the need to market effectively been greater thanks to the Internet. Not only must real estate professionals be technologically savvy to work with Internet customers, but now you also must add value to the experience by bringing *knowledge* to the customer, not just information. As a group, real estate professionals have adapted steadily to technology—computers, faxes, cell phones, digital cameras, PDAs—and adjusted from an information gatekeeper role that controls access to the transaction to a knowledge provider who negotiates and makes sense out of the real estate jigsaw puzzle.

Yet the rules of the online marketing game continue to change. How can anyone *keep up* with the Internet ocean where you can drift forever and not reach any destination? Who has *time* to figure out every available product and service for online marketing that seem to change as fast as a mouse click? How do you *adapt* quickly enough to make your marketing do what it never had to do before and maintain a competitive edge online?

Today, real estate professionals are in the marketing business where the key to success in online marketing is:

1. A website,
2. An e-mail database, and
3. Technology assistance.

That much is straightforward. The *real* secret to success is exactly *how* these things are assembled to satisfy today's online customers.

Busy prospects size you up and form lasting judgments within a few seconds of opening your website or scanning your e-mail. That means within a few seconds your marketing must create a positive reaction—or you may never get a chance to close the sale in person. What's more, today's comparison shoppers test you to determine if you can provide the *knowledge* they need to save them time, money, and headache—or they turn to one of your competitors hovering in the wings. In short, real estate marketing today needs new solutions to the ever-changing technology truths that can kill your practice.

Fortunately, proven strategies to success have emerged.

2

Eight Proven eRainmaker Strategies for Success

OLD RULE

The Internet will change real estate as we know it.

NEW RULE

Your business is your business and the Internet is a tool to be used.

What *Has* the Internet Changed?

We are still in the same real estate industry. We still work in the same market area. Many of the players are still the same people. We are still matchmakers bringing sellers and buyers together. Clearly, many aspects of the real estate world "as we know it" haven't changed.

What the Internet has revolutionized—changed or evolved may be better words—is our customers' habits and expectations. Prospects examine property features and view virtual tours online, but still want the human hand holding and personal negotiating skills of the real estate professional to close a transaction. To stay focused on customers, customers' needs must be mirrored in eRainmakers' websites and in the services delivered by technology. Technology is a tool. The Internet itself has added some specific new tools to our marketing toolbox. Yet, we still tote a toolbox, like carpenters who have added pneumatic nail guns but haven't thrown away their hammers.

In the 1990s, dot-coms failed because they used the Internet as a platform, as an island invented by pure technology. Today, eRainmakers use the Internet as a tool, as a means to an end. The Internet is not a place or platform to do business, as the dot-com meltdown revealed. The Internet is a tool to be used for doing work. Your real estate practice cannot be judged by your website or the technology you use. Your practice is bigger than its technology. That's why the web is now part of our strategy, not the strategy itself. The Internet is part of our marketing, part of our transaction management, part of our customer relations. We are real estate professionals and, by the way, we use the Internet. What has changed is our *attitude.*

Websites not only must work, they must also do work. eRainmakers who have adopted web-based software have discovered they can better serve their customers, boost sales, maximize the possible number of transactions, streamline operations, and create unexpected efficiencies.

eRainmaker Strategy #1: Focus on the Customer, Not Your Ego

Sophisticated yet consumer-focused e-marketing invites prospects to interact with you. Effective websites and e-mail compel visitors to request information, study and compare listings, and drill into a number of pertinent links, all in the privacy of their homes. Web-smart pros report that specific features attract potential clients and keep them coming back—financial calculators, virtual tours, links to MLS, and, the winner of them all, free updates by e-mail of new listings that match the buyer's search criteria.

Experienced eRainmakers know, however, you can offer any number of helpful services and attractive materials, but if potential clients become impatient with your website, they'll fly off into cyberspace. If they have trouble getting past self-centered biographies and chest-beating profiles or if they must agonize watching photos download block-by-block, or if they need a teenager to navigate to their goal, your prospects will jump to something better, just one easy click away—and they won't come back.

Reese Stewart, a Broker/Manager with RE/MAX Central Realty in the Orlando area (ReeseStewart.com), credits his lead-capture success to his easily navigated website and his easy-to-complete Home Search Form that redirects prospects to his Internet Data Exchange (IDX) site where they can search area listings. "I recently wrote an offer which was accepted for a $1.1 million home. This was a direct result of a lead I received from my website form," Stewart said.

Another fan of customer-centered websites is Gary Marshall, a top producer with Assist 2 Sell Realty in Newnan, Georgia (GaryMarshall .com). Marshall says his most successful lead-capture technique is offering a free, over-the-Net home evaluation that often captures as many as three prospective sellers a day. "A site that gives clear instructions, lets potential buyers and sellers register easily, and gives me the details I need to expand my lead file" is his key to success.

eRainmaker Strategy #2: Understand the Endless Loop of E-Marketing: Website–E-Mail–Website

Now that the first Internet wave of innovation and wild claims has receded back into the marketing ocean, the next customer-driven Internet wave is building offshore. Soon, as high-speed Internet access reaches a critical mass and is installed in a growing majority of consumer households, the promise of e-marketing for real estate will arrive. It is later than expected—too late for some who dove head-first into the cyber-shallows of the late 1990s—yet eagerly awaited by a savvy band of real estate eRainmakers who learned from experience which e-strategies actually work and which costly mistakes to avoid.

Endless E-Marketing Loop

Courtesy of Gooder Group.

As marketers, we call the Internet a "pull" technology. Websites fundamentally pull in visitors looking for information, value-added services, and convenience. (Anyone who has ever surfed the Internet knows how easy it is to be pulled in!) In contrast, e-mail is a "push" technology. E-mail requires a recipient's address, which allows marketers to push the delivery of well-crafted multiple-message targeted campaigns designed to reflect the specific interests of permission-based contacts.

eRainmaker Strategy #2 is a straight-forward model to move your entire e-marketing strategy forward throughout your career. Simply put, e-marketing is a never-ending loop that cycles continuously between your "destination" website and your e-mail marketing. The destination website is the repository of all your information, response offers, and services. Once reached, prospects can relax and need go no further. Your e-mail—especially an automated "drip" marketing system of continuous e-mail—is designed to follow-up prospects and drive traffic back to the website. When prospects are ready to buy or sell or refer someone, they will already be captured in the loop.

eRainmaker Strategy #3: Maximize Results with an Integrated Online and Offline E-Strategy

E-marketing does not stand alone. The most effective e-strategy is to integrate and coordinate all your marketing efforts offline and online—what marketers call *convergence* or *cross-channel marketing.* By making all your marketing work in tandem, each effort will work better because today's hybrid "tech and touch" customers respond to the entire media mix.

Real estate practitioners can take a lesson from what non-real estate marketers have learned. Customers who receive offers in multiple ways (direct mail, e-mail, print ad, web ad, etc.) also purchase—sometimes much later—in multiple ways (i.e., cross-channel). After receiving an e-mail or visiting a website, consumers may buy in a retail store, from a catalog, over the phone, from another website, or through an affiliate. In fact, 59% of consumers have purchased offline as a result of receiving a permission-based e-mail, according to the *2002 Consumer E-mail Study,* copyright DoubleClick, Inc. that surveyed 1,000 consumers in September 2002. In short, there is no online, mouse-only cyber-consumer. Instead, today's consumers respond in as many ways as they receive your offers.

One of the best ways to converge your overall marketing into one powerful stream of business—like channeling several creeks into one powerful river—is to build your own integrated e-strategy (more on planning this critical technique in Part Four). Richard Hiers takes an integrated approach as the top producer behind the Real Estate Help Desk with First Team Real Estate in Seal Beach, California

(RealEstateHelpDesk.net). "I continue to promote my website by putting the URL everywhere else that I can—business card, letterhead, mailing envelops, monthly mailings—even a sign on my car," said Hiers, but he stopped buying print ads in early 2002. "I rely heavily on Overture and Google to drive traffic to my website. This has allowed me to reduce my marketing costs from $1,500 per month to $800 per month, while greatly increasing the results. I am now experiencing about 3,000 (up from 1,000) unique visitors per month, with 75 to 80 (up from 35 to 40) per month accepting the invitation to register."

Hiers added some "high touch" follow-up to his "high tech" marketing. Specifically, he mails a hand-written note to website registrants within two days and follows with a phone call immediately to prequalify them on the basis of move-date motivation and financial ability. Using information gleaned during the phone calls, he assigns each buyer to one of three priority levels for follow-up attention. "All potential buyers receive some form of consistent follow-up over the next few months, either by phone, e-mail, or regular mail." Hiers reports he has a 100% success rate getting prospects to sign a buyer-broker representation before he begins to work for them.

Another example of convergence marketing is using e-mail to make your direct mail more effective. One eRainmaker technique you can put into practice immediately is the *Bookend Technique.*

Bookend Technique

Next time you come back from the post office after dropping off your printed newsletter, send e-mail to everyone with an e-mail address on your direct mail list, alerting them to the stories coming out in your latest issue. We call this first e-mail a "teaser" or "softener" because the recipient will see it *before* the newsletter is delivered. The day after you receive your newsletter copy (always be sure to include yourself in your mailing list), send a second e-mail that repeats the response offer from the coupon inside your newsletter. We call this *after* e-mail a "closer" because it is designed to elicit response from people sitting on the fence.

By coordinating your offline and online marketing, the multiple exposures will make all your marketing work better. Best of all, this powerful e-mail technique is virtually free! Remember, the Bookend Technique is a good assignment for a staff member or virtual assistant or whoever addresses the newsletter. Now, maximize your results.

Apply the before-teaser and after-closer e-mail approach to boost results from *all* your mailings, such as Just Listed, Just Sold, Open House invitations, Broker Opens, seminar announcements, even fulfillment mail-outs such as relocation packages, prelisting kits, and free reports. You will reap incredible results with this one eRainmaker technique alone.

eRainmaker Strategy #4: Attract Prequalified Customers with Direct-Response E-Offers

eRainmakers have learned that by selecting the right response offer they can select the type of customer who responds. Response offers of real value to the customer can cover a wide range of tangible premiums and intangible services. Free services, such as online home price evaluation, virtual tours, or a direct link to financial calculators and the multiple listing service database, attract serious home buyers. Rich content of practical assistance can include community information, demographic profiles, school scores, mortgage interest rates, and relocation assistance. Printed brochures and e-reports are popular, especially those that address a buyer's or seller's particular concerns.

Ron Henderson (CharlestonExpert.com), CRS and a top performer with Century 21 Properties Plus in Charleston, South Carolina, favors offering a wide variety of quality content on his site. Henderson said, "There is something on my website for everyone in any stage of the home buying, selling, relocation, or move-up process. In 2001, I averaged 1,674 weekly hits with 3.6 page visits. After upgrading my site with links to interesting and relevant sources of real estate facts and figures, my average steadily increased. For the first eight months of 2003, I averaged 12,263 hits per week with 6.98 page visits. My biggest problem is handling and screening the 15 to 25 inquiries per day. I use an automatic drip system to establish and maintain contact."

Internet-savvy consumers turn to real estate sites early in their buying cycle to gather information to help them make educated decisions down the line. "My website is a one-stop resource center," said Frank Jacovini (Philator.com), a leading associate broker with DiGennaro Real Estate, Inc. in Philadelphia. "I pack my site with tips and tools to provide as many answers as there are questions."

Once real estate professionals learned consumers are not some dreaded cyber-customer, buying and selling their homes with the click of a mouse, we also realized online customers still want direct human service. That's when eRainmakers began to add value to their services, and turned those value-added solutions into compelling direct-response offers on the Internet.

Direct-response eRainmaker value-added offers capture prospects from websites using free E-Reports, free New Listing Updates, free Estimates of Value, free Sweepstakes ("pay no mortgage for a year"), free Interest Rate Alerts, and other service offers (more on these website offers in Chapter 8). And a funny thing happened. Early adapters of these e-marketing techniques flourished, capturing lifetime share of customer largely at the expense of the part-timers and offline agents who didn't grab a slice of the new "marketspace" pie.

The result was eRainmakers jumped on the opportunity to generate self-qualified customers using proven direct-marketing techniques repurposed for the Internet. By picking their response offer, eRainmakers discovered they could pick their customers. This ability to direct the path of growth in their practice—more listings, higher priced properties, more dual-sided transactions, greater volume overall—gave eRainmakers increased income, and they rode the crest of increased home prices in the early 2000s to give themselves a tidal raise.

eRainmaker Strategy #5: Automate Your E-Mail for More Sales and More Referrals

Consistent prospect follow-up online and offline is essential. Every successful practitioner knows consistent follow-up is the key to converting a large lead file into a profitable large *closed* file. What's new is the Internet gives real estate professionals new ways to automate the follow-up process. Putting the automated tools in place to generate, cultivate, and capture a continuous stream of leads *without* needing undue human attention—until the customer asks—is a fundamental e-strategy for becoming a high-volume eRainmaker.

Rapid response to inquiries is the critical first step no matter how you obtain the lead. Internet buyers and sellers who make instant requests via a website have come to expect instant replies. Top producers comply. Bill Renaud (RenaudOttenTeam.com), with The Renaud Otten Team, one of Canada's top real estate teams based in Ottawa, Ontario, uses their "High Energy Home Buyer Program" to respond to online leads. The program is a free service for buyers who complete a profile listing their home preferences and requirements. Renaud Otten's program continually searches the MLS for matches to a buyer's profile. Any property match is instantly sent by e-mail, fax, or phone, according to the buyer's preference. "This program was put into place in 1997," Renaud reported, "and it continues to be our #1 lead generation source. It provides us with approximately 10 to 20 buyer leads a week. It's incredible."

Joe Valenti (CBSHOME.com), president and CEO at CBSHOME Real Estate in the Omaha area, stresses the importance of providing real value and added, "But information alone is not enough. The consumer wants a rapid response to an inquiry." CBSHOME uses the ShowingTime program that allows consumers to schedule showings 24 hours a day. "Our company has the highest conversion rate for this program—13%," Valenti said.

The website for The New Generation of Realtors in Philadelphia receives more than 20,000 hits a month, according to Antonio Atacan (CenterCityRealEstate.com), a top agent with Prudential Fox & Roach. Atacan believes Center City's ability to provide accurate information quickly is the key to their success. He explained, "The site is updated daily, and potential clients receive immediate responses. Approximately 40% of our business is generated from our website. In 2001, for example, my team closed over $35 million in sales."

eRainmaker Strategy #6: Start and Finish by Cultivating a Permission-Based E-Mail Enhanced Trophy Database

In 1995, for the first time, more personal computers were sold than television sets. That same year, e-mail messages sent exceeded the number of regular stamped letters mailed. Also in 1995, Netscape's new web browser (software to display and navigate the Internet) and Netscape's spectacular initial public offering (IPO) on Wall Street launched the dot-com boom by unleashing the commercial potential of the Internet. From the beginning of the Internet Age, e-mail has been the "killer application" that was adapted first and used by the greatest number of consumers. In 1996, Microsoft went online with Hotmail, the first web-based e-mail site. During the late 1990s, collecting e-mail addresses was an obvious marketing objective. Today, that simple objective is not enough.

Today's eRainmaker objectives must be more sophisticated because of the proliferation of e-mail addresses (most e-mail users maintain multiple addresses for multiple uses), the constant erosion of your list (bounce-backs from bad addresses average 10% to 12% worldwide), the fact that not *everybody* in your database has an e-mail account (or will tell you) and because genuine e-mail can easily get lost in the clutter of spam. Successful eRainmakers practice two strategies. First, they strive to enhance their direct-marketing Trophy Database with e-mail (without a postal address and phone number it's difficult to refresh bad e-mails). Second, eRainmakers get *permission* to send e-mail announcements about items of *interest* and on a *frequency* that are valued by their customer database.

The key to creating a permission-based Trophy E-Mail Database that will become a core business asset worth selling is to enhance its quality until the Trophy Database can be used to add value to the customer relationship in the customer's terms, not just a mailing list. The most successful strategies are to identify exactly what your clients' value, then deliver that value-added information and service with integrated offline and online marketing. (More hands-on tips are included in Chapter 13.)

eRainmaker Strategy #7: Delegate Tech Tasks to Virtual Assistants so You Don't Touch a Keyboard

Real estate professionals will never become techno wizards—and they shouldn't. They shouldn't because they have better things to do with their time—like list and sell or manage those who do list and sell. Few top-producing eRainmakers know how the Internet works— or care—and even fewer real estate professionals have the time or inclination to give what it takes to become a technology specialist. Face it: Technology is complicated, time consuming, and best delegated to someone else, just like coordinating marketing and processing, which are not core responsibilities of the successful eRainmaker. Now there is a better way.

Over the last 20 years, organizations have resized and downsized, until today the ideal eRainmaker organization is stripped down to its core function (listing and selling), while outsourcing (or delegating) all other less productive functions. That's why eRainmaker Strategy #7 is to hire a virtual assistant (hourly contractors who work remotely by computer) to do the tasks that require technology. Not only has a group of real estate virtual assistants (VAs) emerged across the country that specializes in helping leading eRainmakers build their practices (with an eye toward selling it someday), but now these real estate VAs are also specially trained and certified. Most VAs are technologically savvy and extraordinarily detail oriented.

Virtual outsourcing has arrived as a strategic solution. Naturally, you need to know how to find, evaluate, hire and work with a VA. After all, some tasks still require physical presence and hard-copy documents. Both for the technologically clueless and for the forward-thinking eRainmaker who knows what to let go—and what to keep in house—using virtual assistants is a hugely profitable strategy. Best of all, whoever buys your practice, can keep the VAs doing the job without your clients falling through the cracks. (More on this VA e-strategy in Chapter 18, E-Operations.)

eRainmaker Strategy #8: Build a Self-Sustaining E-Practice Another eRainmaker Will Buy for Cash

The chapters that follow show you how to use the proven principles of successful e-marketing to build a self-sustaining e-practice another eRainmaker will buy for cash. You will learn how to:

- ☑ Build thousands of trusting and appreciative customer relationships that maximize your percentage of captured business.
- ☑ Create websites that generate prospects, schedule showings, capture listings and channel a deluge of new prospects to your practice.
- ☑ Capture the relocation market by nurturing local relationships and out-of-town networks that send a constant stream of business to you at little cost.
- ☑ Send thousands of newsletters, postcards, fliers, and letters with no cost for printing and postage so you keep more of what you make by reducing expenses.
- ☑ Use *permission marketing* to minimize feast-and-famine market fluctuations by cultivating an endless stream of referrals virtually free.

☑ Build a "barrier to exit" that maximizes loyalty, eliminates agent switching and creates a cost for doing business with your competition—at little cost to you.

☑ Close more deals in less time leveraging team productivity by coordinating onsite staff and virtual assistants for minimal cost and maximum results.

☑ Brand your practice so your system stands above the competition and you become the only logical choice in your market.

We've Met the Future and It Is Now

Clearly, the Internet is here to stay. It has not "ended real estate as we know it," as the hype predicted in the last decade. The Internet has, instead, added a powerful new tool to our marketing mix. Perhaps the future is best summarized by the success of Tom and Patti Wilser (Real-Estate-Portland-Oregon.com), a top husband-and-wife team with RE/MAX Equity Group in Portland, Oregon: "Out of our last 38 inquiries, 18 have been web-form requests, nine were phone calls for additional information on properties viewed on the Internet, and 10 were requests to be automatically updated as properties came up for sale. One inquiry was for general information about the real estate process." Put simply, online marketing works.

The path to being a successful eRainmaker today is three simple strategies:

1. Create a branded, customer-focused, destination website and promote it.

2. Build a permission-based, e-mail enhanced Trophy Database and automate the system.

3. Delegate technology tasks to virtual assistant(s) or staff so you rarely touch a keyboard (except for e-mail).

In the following chapters, you find the proven principles behind these straightforward strategies as well as essential references to our *eRainmaker.com Online Resource Center* to guide those you assign to implement specific tasks. Buckle up.

~~~~~~~~~~~~~

WEBSITE TECHNIQUES THAT WORK BIG FOR LITTLE COST

Selecting Domains to Brand Your Retirement

Keep Your Eye on Your Exit Strategy

The Internet *has* changed some things. Today's customers expect
"tech and touch" services. Buyers research homes for sale online *before* they call us in person. Sellers want their homes promoted on
the Internet after they list with us. Long-distance referral sources
have added unexpected new revenue streams. *Technology* and *Communications* have become permanent line item costs. Part of every
work day is spent reading and writing short e-mail notes. A whole
set of new technology skills are needed—or we must find people
who have them.

Experienced real estate professionals who embrace the Internet's
potential reinvent their practices with fresh approaches. Newbie
licensees leapfrog ahead to become top producers by embracing

technology. Local practices become regional, national, and even global. Veteran agents move across country, then set up shop and snatch market share away from born-and-bred locals. Innovative eRainmakers make money in new ways from their websites and e-mail.

Today, technology matters. Websites and e-mail matter. And customers matter more. New technologies will always be arriving. The job of the successful eRainmaker is to reflect the customer's needs by using technology to solve customer problems and deliver superior service—not to be a technology junkie adapting the latest technology for technology's sake. As I've said, most savvy eRainmakers don't know how the Internet works and don't care. What they do care about are their customers: How to create customers, how to convert customers, and how to keep customers—online and offline.

Ultimately—after all the dust settles—every successful eRainmaker wants to move on—and bank a tidy sum after years of investing in their practice. That investment begins with your brand—a desirable asset—easily transferred and worth serious money to the eRainmaker who buys your practice. Begin with your exit strategy in mind—begin with your brand.

Plan Ahead When Selecting a Destination Domain

Selecting a destination domain—your address on the Internet—requires planning because your domain will become a significant asset in your brand. Brands are one of those things that get better with age. Great brands gain familiarity and power with each passing year. Someday, you will want to move on and sell your practice to another real estate professional. If that buyer can assume your corporate identity without missing a deal, then you have added significant value to your practice. You will spend years and tens of thousands of dollars promoting your brand and your brand experience (that is, the services prospects can expect from your business system). Don't waste that investment.

A brand is not a novelty theme (such as, playing cards) or a target customer (buyers) or a property type (waterfront) or a market area (Fairfax, Virginia). Your brand is the sum total of your practice, including your services, your systems, your corporate identity, your customer database, and your unique positioning statement. Everything you do—online and offline—contributes to your brand. The experience your customers have when they work with you and your team or group is your brand.

These experiences—the brand experience—is what a buyer of your practice will someday take over and strive to continue to deliver to your customers. Just like when you order a Big Mac at a McDonald's restaurant, no matter who owns the store franchise, a Big Mac tastes the same. That experience is McDonald's brand.

Experience shows the Internet is not an alternate universe with its own brand rules. Your brand or corporate identity (not to be confused with your personal identity) includes your business name, website domain(s), e-mail address(es), logotype (your business's "signature" using words, symbols, or props), slogan(s), toll-free number, and more. The corporate identity will appear on every promotional and business item you produce from website to e-stationery to ads and signs and from business cards to vehicles and vanity license plates to advertising specialties. To make your brand memorable, consistently use the same logotype, typeface, color palette, and design. Online consistency will impact customer's offline perception of your brand—and vice versa. For a real estate Universal Resource Locator (URL, or web address) example, visit 888TheSign.com, which says it all, including the sign company's toll free number (888-The-Sign or 888-843-7446).

Eight Best Practices for Creating a Brand Domain

If you are a student of marketing, you know Al Ries. Ries is one of the world's best-known marketing strategists. His books with Jack Trout, *Positioning: The Battle for Your Mind*, *The 22 Immutable Laws of Marketing*, *Bottom-Up Marketing*, *Marketing Warfare*, and *Horse Sense*, have become a definitive body of work that contributes to the core of almost every marketing curriculum.

Al Ries and Laura Ries, his daughter and president of their Atlanta, Georgia, consulting firm Ries & Ries (Ries.com), wrote *The 22 Immutable Laws of Branding*. The book also includes *The 11 Immutable Laws of Internet Branding*. In the Internet section, the authors outline "The Law of the Proper Name," which is immutable law #4 and includes their eight best practices for creating a brand domain. As the subtitle reads, "Your name stands alone on the Internet, so you'd better have a good one." Ries and Ries recommend that a brand name should:

1. Be short.
2. Be simple.
3. Suggest the category.
4. Be unique.
5. Be alliterative.
6. Be speakable.
7. Be shocking.
8. Be personalized.

For a complete in-depth treatment of the laws of brands, don't miss this outstanding book by Ries and Ries.

Select a User-Friendly Domain That Serves, Rather than Sells

Your *brand* should never be your name. Ultimately, a buyer of your practice will pay you more for a brand or corporate identity if he or she can (1) assume the brand and (2) avoid spending big bucks transforming the brand from a personal identity into a corporate identity (most common mistake). Remember, your corporate identity is separate from your personal identity. Your corporate identity is designed to attract customers (marketing). Your personal identity convinces prospects to use *you* (sales). Prospective future buyers of your practice will have their own personal sales style. What your ultimate buyer *will* pay for is the corporate identity, brand experience, and customer database you have carefully cultivated over years in the marketplace.

Imagine trying to carry on the "Dan Richard Team" if your name isn't Dan Richard. This does not mean you should not register your name as a domain. A name URL is a helpful tool for out-of-town customers and agents to find you easily. (Be sure to register your "published" business name, like DanGooderRichard.com, not a formal variation or nickname that is not intuitive, such as DanielGRichard.com or DannyR.com.) Redirect your name URL to your branded, destination website. (For more on Brand Value, see Chapter 20.)

One major first step toward a brand name is selecting your destination website domain. To find available domain names, visit NetworkSolutions.com, Register.com, and other domain registry services (eRainmaker.com: Domain Registration).

Select a domain that is consumer-centric, not ego-centric. Domains that relate to the consumer, not to the personality of the real estate professional, are more effective because they *attract* the consumer. If the domain is also short, catchy, and to the point, then you have a winner. For example, BuyInVA.com is centered on the consumer's interest in Virginia property (or Come2VA.info, Move2VA.info, VaHomesR.us, BuynVA.com, all actual domains available at press time) and captures prospects *before* they have heard the name of a real estate professional (it even follows the "keep-it-short" rule). Compare that brand domain to a personality domain name, such as RichardTeam.com (or DanRichardTeam.com, TheDanRichardTeam.com, also all available), which is about me personally, not my customer's interest in property for sale. Personal domain names have little intuitive recognition for market strangers and less value to a future practice purchaser.

Domain names that are geographic or property type-specific are very successful for Dave Wallace (VenturaRealEstate.com), a leading producer with Keller Williams Realty in Ventura, California. "By using a name that identifies the areas or types of properties we service," said Wallace, "we seem to increase the number of visitors to

---

GeekSpeak

Pointing: (Also, "redirecting") Technique of having domain registrar assign the same internet protocol (IP) address to any number of domain names in an "all-roads-lead-to-Rome" approach.

Parking: Tactic of temporarily pointing a domain to an existing site or web page until a new active site is developed. Parking allows you to register the domain today and reserve its use for tomorrow.

Protecting: Practice of registering multiple domains with slight variations to keep copycat competitors from using similar domain, such as different extensions (MySite.com, MySite.us, MySite.biz, MySite.info).

our sites. A person on the Internet is far more likely to visit a site named VenturaRealEstate.com (one of our sites) if they are looking in our area or VenturaCondoKing.com (not one of our sites) if they are looking for a condo or another specific type of property in our area."

One early mistake Wallace will not repeat: "Using my own name for my first site. The consumer could not care less who we are. If they are not from this immediate area, they most certainly *don't* know who we are!" Wallace added, "The Internet is a valuable tool to help people with their real estate needs. We can capture far more leads if our sites (and we) provide value when visited rather than trying to 'sell' them or focus the content of our sites on ourselves!"

Multibranding Puts More Hooks in the Water

Top eRainmakers don't stop with only one domain, once they have a branded destination website. Take for example, Dick Mathes (RelocationIowa.com, HomeRealtyGroup.org, DickMathes.com) who dominates the Mason City, Iowa, area personally averaging 10% market share of active listings as one of 85 members of the local realty board. Mathes has registered more than 80 domains linked to landing pages but only maintains one primary website. "Every domain has its own cover sheet which is a mirror of my destination site home page," Mathes said. "That allows me to present a unique collection of keywords and descriptive metatags that boost that domain's placement in search engines. Yet, prospects can click-through every multibranded landing page to our primary destination site at RelocationIowa.com."

Mathes' traffic statistics (he publishes them behind a "Thank You" graphic right on his site) indicate he averages more than 7,500 unique visitors a month to his destination site with about half the traffic coming from his local market area of only 30,000 people in North Central Iowa. For all his websites and domains, Mathes invests an annual budget of $10,000 to gross more than $150,000 from web leads alone. About 60% of his consistent 125+ annual transactions are touched directly or indirectly by his website. "Prospects either find me on the Internet or see my offline marketing and say 'I checked you out on your website before contacting you,'" Mathes said.

Another variation of effective multibranding is to use unique "promotable" domains for specialty subpages in your website.

John F. Williams (MO-RE.com, HireMyTeam.com), a top agent with The MORE Company, a real estate marketing firm in the St. Louis area, does this very effectively. Williams has assigned unique domains to specialty subpages within his principal site. Each domain, such as HelpMeFindAHouse.com, HotListingsDaily.com, PrepareToMove.com, SuccessfulRelocation.com, and so on, does double duty as (1) a descriptive address that is used in offline advertising and (2) as navigation links within the website itself. Williams maintains more than 100 domains in his online real estate arsenal. "Technology should not cost you money. Technology should make you money," said Williams. "If I spend one dollar on technology I expect ten dollars in return."

Yet another outstanding example is the destination site of Galand Haas (GalandHaas.com), an innovative market leader in the Eugene and Springfield, Oregon areas, Allen F. Hainge CYBERSTAR® and Howard Brinton Star with RE/MAX Integrity (see Figure 3.1). The navigation links on Haas's award-winning site point to special URLs, such as Property Search (GotListings.com), Automated Home Finder (ForHomeInfo.com), Homesellers Info (ForHomesellers.com), Free Real Estate Reports (HomeReport.org), that can be promoted in print and direct mail to increase site traffic.

Multibranding works wonders for Gary Marshall (GaryMarshall .com), a "Broker/Rainmaker" with Assist 2 Sell Buyer & Seller Realty Center in Newnan, Georgia. "First of all I have four domain names: GaryMarshall.com, Assist2SellRealty.com, CowetaCountyHomes.com and FayetteCountyHouses.com," said Marshall. "They all go to the same website. I have my name as a web address in case anybody looks me up that way. Same thing for the company website."

After 12 years of owning an accounting firm, Bruce Jay Breger (HomeTeamExpert.com) went into real estate, and now is with RE/MAX Gold Coast in Thousand Oaks, California. Breger is one of a new breed of "Young Lions" who have put e-marketing center stage in their real estate practice. "My website is my business in computer form on the Internet," said Breger. "Several years ago I began to buy domains for Conejo County, such as ThousandOaksRealEstate .com, SimiValleyRealEstate.com, NewburyParkRealEstate.com, because I knew everyone in my market would be using computers to shop for real estate."

After registering a new domain, HomeTeamExpert.com, in January 2003, Breger spent four months developing his HomeTeamExpert.com site. To top off the project, he developed a unique domain logo to brand

Figure 3.1
Multibrand Your Website with Promotable URLs

Source: Courtesy of Galand Haas (GalandHaas.com), RE/MAX Integrity, Eugene, Oregon.

the site. In April 2003, Breger added four traffic-builder domains when he purchased MoorParkRealEstate.com, CamarilloRealEstate.com, OxnardRealEstate.com, and FillmoreRealEstate.com. To drive traffic to his branded site, Breger turned his car into a traveling URL billboard, with whole-car decals, and invested in pay-per-click links. "In the first five months of 2003, I've already doubled my production for all of 2002," Breger said.

Quick Checklist of Brand Mistakes to Avoid

☑ Avoid using your personal name as the corporate name.

☑ Avoid using someone else's trademark in your web address, such as REALTOR (permitted if you are member of NAR, but *not* permitted if "realtor" is used with descriptive words or phrases; see Realtor.org for Trademark Manual), CENTURY 21, RE/MAX, your brokerage company, BY REFERRAL ONLY, and so on.

☑ Avoid using your photo as the corporate identity. (Use your photo or team photo to help prospects remember your "name and a face," but not as a corporate brand name because your image is of no interest to a business buyer once you leave. You'll also avoid costly makeovers as you age or change team members in a group photo.) Most important, a corporate brand relieves you of being the only one personally to deliver all the services of your practice.

☑ Avoid identifying your entire practice with a narrow restriction that limits brand value, practice expansion, or ability to relocate brand, such as:

- *Too small an area name* (large regions, metro areas, or states are okay, keep community, subdivision, neighborhood as sub-specialties of identity).

- *One gender* (The Home Guy, Ms. Real Estate, The Property Man, Lady of the House, Condo King, Queen of First-Time Buyers).

- *One type or style of home* (condo, waterfront, resort, new homes, townhouse; keep these as subspecialties).

- *Restrictive customer type* (seniors, first-time buyers, transfer-ees, military—keep these as subspecialties).

- *Limited team or group description* (husband-and-wife, mother-and-daughter, mom-and-pop, sisters—your buyer won't be able to relate to your brand).

☑ Avoid a corporate identity logotype and brand name that doesn't reproduce in black-and-white (newspaper), has illegible type when reduced to very small size, or reads awkwardly as a type-written word in a letter, e-mail, or news story.

Ten Great Domains with Brand Value

Great domains have tremendous brand value and are invaluable to the eventual buyer of your practice. Notice how you could step into many of these top brands. Interestingly, these generic names (listed alphabetically) begin to read almost like a Yellow Pages directory under the "Real Estate" heading. Check out Yellow Pages in telephone books from other cities for inspiration, gather ideas from the real estate sections of online directories such as REALTOR.org, Google or Yahoo, or experiment with variations at domain registries such as NetworkSolutions.com:

- ☑ *BestAgent.com:* Judi Wolfson, RE/MAX Associates, Doylestown, Pennsylvania
- ☑ *Our-New-House.com:* Michael Ferguson, Century 21 First Class, Schaumburg, Illinois
- ☑ *RealEstateHelpDesk.net:* Richard and Brooke Hiers, First Team Real Estate, Seal Beach, California
- ☑ *REALST8.com:* Joe Molnar, RE/MAX Connection, South Bend, Indiana
- ☑ *SellaHome.com:* Tom Donegan, RE/MAX Premier, Fairfax, Virginia
- ☑ *SuburbanHomes.com:* Jon and Mary Beth Perkins, RE/MAX Results, Minneapolis, Minnesota
- ☑ *TopAgents.com:* Ted and Mary Macy, RE/MAX Greater Atlanta, Roswell, Georgia
- ☑ *YourHappyHome.com:* Tim Anderson and Pat Mancuso, KELLER WILLIAMS Premier Realty, Woodbury, Minnesota
- ☑ *YourHouseHunter.com:* Steve Werley, COLDWELL BANKER Landis Homesale Services, Wyomissing, Pennsylvania
- ☑ *WickedGoodHomes.com:* Peter Bohush, KELLER WILLIAMS Realty, Westboro, Massachusetts

Ten Regional, State, and Area Domains with Sellable Brand Value

Often a powerful brand name and domain can have a regional or corporate slant. Every eRainmaker should have a domain that contains their city, state, or market area that points to their main website. Check out these samples. Imagine the value to other eRainmakers who want to merge your practice into theirs, which can be done with nothing more than a redirection of the domain to their website. Be sure not to select an area that is so small it could restrict your growth.

- ☑ *AZHomeSales.com:* Craig Sapp, REALTY EXECUTIVES, Phoenix, Arizona

☑ *CarolinaRealEstate.com:* Ron Henderson, CENTURY 21 Properties Plus Charleston, North Charleston, South Carolina

☑ *ISellChicago.com:* Roger Lautt, RE/MAX Exclusive Properties, Chicago, Illinois

☑ *HomesInStCroix.com:* Lad Concepcion, Farchette & Hanley, Christiansted, St. Croix, U.S. Virgin Islands

☑ *MankatoHomes.com:* Dar Vosburg, RE/MAX Dynamic Associates, Mankato, Minnesota

☑ *NewJerseyHomeInfo.com:* Frank Fidell and Irene Gaffigan, CENTURY 21 Apex Properties, Metuchen, New Jersey

☑ *OKCHomesellers.com:* Bill Wilson and Heather Herzel, Paradigm Realty, Edmond, Oklahoma

☑ *Portland-Homes.com:* Bill Willis, RE/MAX Equity Group, Portland, Oregon

☑ *SoldOnReno.com:* Bob Clement, PRUDENTIAL Nevada Realty, Reno, Nevada

☑ *StartPackingIdaho.com:* Kevin Hughes, RE/MAX West, Boise, Idaho

Twelve Short URLs Ideal as License Plates or Phone Numbers

What does it look like to cross-market a corporate identity from web address to vanity license plate to phone number (ideally, toll-free)? Here are some real URLs I have converted to vanity license plates (maximum seven characters) and phone numbers. The secret is coming up with a brand identity that has seven characters or less, and is available from domain registries, your state DMV, and the telephone company. Keep looking. They are out there! (Following are real domains, imaginary phone numbers.)

☑ AREAHOM and 273-2466 (Area-Home.com)

☑ BUYAHOM and 289-2466 (BuyAHome.com)

☑ BUZZ X2 and 280-0092 (BuzzBuzz.com)

☑ CRZNHOM and 270-6466 (CruisinHome.com)

☑ HAPPYHM and 427-7946 (HappyHome.com)

☑ KEY2HMS and 539-2467 (Key2Homes.com)

☑ MOVE2ME and 668-3263 (Move2Maine.com)

    ☑ RE4LIVN and 734-5486 (RealEstateForLiving.com)

    ☑ RLTYSLS and 758-9757 (RealtySells.com)

    ☑ SELAHOM and 735-2466 (SellAHome.com)

    ☑ SOLDING and 765-3464 (Solding.com)

    ☑ TOPRLTY and 867-7589 (TopRealty.com)

Domain Names: What They Mean, What's Allowed, and How to Pick a Winner

An extension, or Top Level Domain (TLD), is the highest level category of Internet names. The extension choices you see here include all unrestricted global extensions, as well as unrestricted extensions that are available from specific countries. The extensions .COM, .NET, .ORG, .BIZ, and .INFO are examples of global Top Level Domains (gTLD). The extensions .U.K. (from Great Britain), .FR (from France), and .CA (from Canada) are examples of country code Top Level Domains (ccTLD).

If the domain you want isn't available with one extension (for example, .COM), try another extension, such as .BIZ. Just be aware, lazy prospects may type .COM out of habit and go to somebody else's website by mistake. Take care to make your domain different enough to be memorable and unique—and avoid confusing your prospects with "extension misdirection":

    ☑ *.BIZ:* recommended for small business sites; .BZ is alternative if .BIZ is not available.

    ☑ *.COM:* to be used for commercial and personal sites.

    ☑ *.INFO:* to be used for both commercial and personal resource sites; fourth most popular extension after .COM, .NET, .ORG.

    ☑ *.NAME:* to be used for personal sites. Must be composed of first and last name, for example: DanRichard.name. First name (Dan) must have at least 1 character and no more than 63 characters. Second name (Richard) must have at least 3 characters and no more than 63 characters. You cannot start or end a domain name with a dot (Dan.Richard.name which is interpreted as Dan.Richard—an unrecognized extension).

    ☑ *.NET:* recommended for companies involved in Internet infrastructure or intranet websites.

Your website address is called an URL (Universal Resource Locator). Every address can contain several parts: Protocol, Subdomain, Domain, Extension, and Subfolders.

Here is the anatomy of a "fully qualified" (complete) web address:

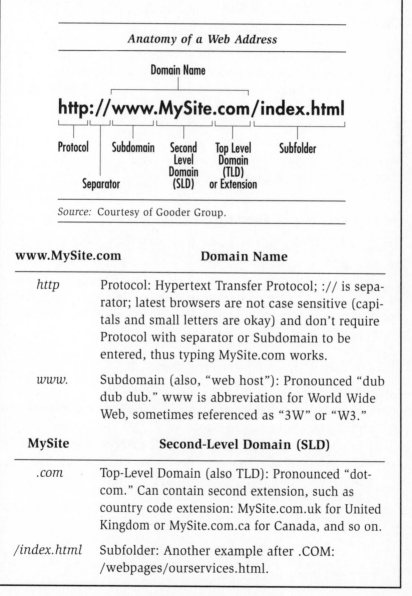

Source: Courtesy of Gooder Group.

www.MySite.com	Domain Name
http	Protocol: Hypertext Transfer Protocol; :// is separator; latest browsers are not case sensitive (capitals and small letters are okay) and don't require Protocol with separator or Subdomain to be entered, thus typing MySite.com works.
www.	Subdomain (also, "web host"): Pronounced "dub dub dub." www is abbreviation for World Wide Web, sometimes referenced as "3W" or "W3."

MySite	**Second-Level Domain (SLD)**
.com	Top-Level Domain (also TLD): Pronounced "dot-com." Can contain second extension, such as country code extension: MySite.com.uk for United Kingdom or MySite.com.ca for Canada, and so on.
/index.html	Subfolder: Another example after .COM: /webpages/ourservices.html.

☑ *.ORG:* recommended for nonprofit organizations or trade associations.

☑ *.TV:* recommended for rich content/multimedia sites, especially entertainment and media industry.

☑ *.WS:* (WebSite) to be used for commercial and personal sites. .WS domains registered through Register.com™ must have between 4 and 59 characters, not including the .WS extension.

For more information on domain registration, visit the public information site at Internic.net where they maintain an Accredited Registrar Directory of hundreds of sites that register domains. Registrar prices vary, especially for multiple year registrations or multiple domain registrations. To reduce your annual domain registry costs, consider bulk registration (multiple domains), low-cost registries (GoDaddy.com, EasyHost.com, NetworkSolutions.com bulk registration, etc.) or lower prices for multiyear registration.

Quick Checklist of Domain Syntax Rules

Although domain extensions are recommended for specific types of organizations, to my knowledge there are no validating mechanisms to enforce compliance, beyond the practical effect of being listed among other URLs with the same extension—which could put your URL in the wrong section of some search directories. Here are some basic rules of syntax for domains:

☑ Use only letters, numbers, or hyphen ("-").

☑ Cannot begin or end with a hyphen or period.

☑ Generally, must have more than 3 characters and less than 63 characters, not including extension. (.COM, .NET, and .ORG domain names exceeding a total of 26 characters are supported by most web browsers. However, certain web browsers, e-mail programs, and other Internet-related applications may not support domain names more than 26 characters.)

4

Planning a Customer-Centered Website

Striking It Rich with a Few Simple Strategies

Your website is one of your greatest e-business assets along with your e-mail database and your domain. The players who build websites at first glance look similar to the people who produce a printed brochure. In fact, early websites were called *brochureware* because they simply published printed marketing materials on the Internet— typically an old personal brochure. The critical difference between a personal brochure and a website is the unique interactivity and functions the Internet offers. There are three skills needed to produce a website:

1. *Copywriter (writer/editor):* Ability to translate the uniqueness of your practice into words and organized concepts.

2. *Web Designer (graphic designer):* Layout, images, icons, navigation links; responsible for "look and feel," typically works with a software program called an HTML editor (Hypertext Markup Language) such as Dreamweaver, Front Page, or Hot Metal.

3. *Web Developer (programmer):* Functionality, such as e-mail, response forms, database features (listing, transaction or link managers, etc.), often works in PERL program to write code in CGI (Common Gateway Interface) that is hosted by a UNIX server or ASP (Active Server Page) that is processed on a Microsoft web server typically accessing a database such as Sequel (SQL).

One talented person may wear all three hats, but a sophisticated website requires a team of specialists. Typically, for your first personal website, you provide the words (and probably photos) and the website service provides the design and programming skills. You'll soon discover there is a fourth role. That role is the job of making routine revisions (site maintenance), which may be done by a specialist at an hourly rate or by a staff member or virtual assistant at a lower cost, sometimes using a *Control Panel* tool with subscriber-only access.

To Buy or Build a Website, That Is the Question

"Where do I start?" The short answer is: Don't reinvent the wheel. Never build your first website. Always buy.

Template Pages

Think of a web page as a single page in a chapter of the book that is your website. Web designers put up a single web page as a placeholder for a new URL (web address) to point to temporarily while the website is under construction. A placeholder presence with a handful of pages—called a *template website*—often is the first website for beginners, typically containing a photo, contact information, and basic "About Us" text. If the template pages are provided by a franchise or brokerage, the template pages may have links to the umbrella organization site and its property listings. Typically, you get minimal options to personalize or change a cookie-cutter template site. Today, the main thing a template website accomplishes is to drive disappointed prospects to the competition.

Personal Websites

Ready-made sites are easily personalized and soon take on a unique identity that reflects your style and approach. Yet, much of your work is simply picking and choosing because real estate websites share many common features. To fill the need, a growing list of providers has emerged that provide outstanding personal websites virtually off the shelf. Another list of providers specializes in providing company brokerage-level websites (eRainmaker.com: Personal Websites or Company Websites).

With ready-made websites, the price is right. Your first-year budget will include setup (initial design) and annual operating costs (hosting) ranging from $500 to $5,000 or more. Be sure to ask about pricing for changes and site maintenance once you have published your website. To make your personal website search easier, we have provided an updated Website Buyers Guide at eRainmaker.com that lists many specialized real estate website providers who offer scores of website packages combined. Websites are grouped by first-year cost (initial design and operating expense) in four categories: Under $1,000, $1,000 to $2,500, $2,500 to $5,000, $5,000+. As you ascend the price scale, you generally get what you pay for and come away with a more sophisticated website.

Custom Websites

As your online practice grows, and you ramp up your webcentric loop of website—e-mail—website, you will want to invest in a truly customer-oriented, custom website—what e-marketers call a "Destination Website" because once prospects get there they don't have a need to leave. You may also discover you want several websites (multi-branding) for different audiences, specialties, or communities, or to redirect traffic from lesser "parked" domains to your principal brand-name site. These custom websites—developed for you from scratch—are an ongoing "work in progress" and require a custom website designer. Leading custom-site designers have specialized in real estate and have multiple sites in their portfolios (eRainmaker.com: Custom Websites). Prices for custom sites begin at $2,500 for design only and go up, reaching $50,000 or more, depending on the extent of your project (and size of your budget)—and that does not include the hours of your time to be involved in the project. Developing a custom destination website is the ultimate goal of many master eRainmakers.

Quick Checklist of Top 10 Reasons to Buy Your First Website

- ☑ You don't know your online customers yet.
- ☑ Modest budget.
- ☑ Fixed cost.
- ☑ Covers basics easily with minimal learning curve.
- ☑ Build your custom site using material from personal site experience.
- ☑ Learn what works from first site—and what doesn't—to use in custom site.
- ☑ Develop staff, procedures, software tools, and hardware infrastructure to handle web leads and follow up.
- ☑ Ask for customer feedback and use it.
- ☑ Find web designer who listens and makes changes you want.
- ☑ Give yourself time to create new marketing tools to promote new site.

Know How to Talk to Web Designers to Get What You Want

Developing a destination website from scratch requires a carefully outlined plan. Working with prospects and customers online is different than doing work offline—but different doesn't have to be harder. Ultimately, your online goal is to get a face-to-face appointment with your prospect because that is the only way to close—just like offline. Like developing your e-strategy, there are six basic steps:

1. *Budget.* Begin with an annual budget that makes you comfortable. Regardless of the amount, this figure—which will include initial design, annual operating expenses, and site maintenance—will keep you and your web designer on track. Our categories of Under $1,000, $1,000 to $2,500, $2,500 to $5,000, $5,000 or more for the first year including initial design and one-year operating costs are good guidelines. The website world of dazzling additional features ("bells and whistles") is a heady environment. Without a firm budget, you risk the frustrating eyes-bigger-than-your-stomach syndrome that can only be cured with a look-but-don't-touch budget. Save those features for next year, or the year after.

2. *Benchmark your success.* To paraphrase the renowned management consultant, Peter Drucker, "What is measured can be managed." Establish benchmarks for your new website or a revised website. By counting your unique visitors, return visits, referrer sources (other sites where visitors click links to your site) and response rates for e-mail registrations and web inquiries, you can know tomorrow if compared to yesterday you have improved. (More on website tracking statistics in Chapter 5.)

3. *Brand your position.* Differentiate your practice by developing a unique slogan—what marketers call a Unique Selling Proposition (USP) or mission. Reinforce this position with a logo, site design, link labels, and featured services. Everything on your site should support your core strategy. As leading technology trainer Michael Russer says, your USP "causes prospects to immediately and viscerally: (a) recognize your value; (b) perceive you are the best; (c) want to contact you." An example of a USP is: "With a combined experience of more than 81 personal moves, our team knows relocation!" More USP examples: "We sell over 150 homes a year with 98% customer satisfaction. We can sell your home fast . . . and get the best price." "Our goal is to turn every client into a raving fan." "Your One-Stop Real Estate Resource Center." For the tech-and-touch customer: "Traditional Values, Today's Technology" (Nadine Richardson, 1st Signature Homes/GMAC Real Estate, Naperville, IL).

4. *Organize by target customer.* Select every customer type you want to capture and develop a section of your website to match each target customer. Focus the section only on that type of consumer: waterfront property, luxury homes, first-time buyers, second homes, investors, homes in a geographic area, outbound relocation, and so on. If

you want buyer and seller categories, avoid a one-size-fits-all approach by using subpages within the category so you don't treat all buyers and sellers alike. If you have a broad practice, you may develop different entry points into your website (1. MySite.com, 2. MySite.com/condos, and 3. MySite.com/newbuyers) for different target customers. Remember, there's no requirement to have your home page be the only initial page prospects land on to enter your site.

5. *Solve prospect's problems.* Answer the question every consumer unconsciously asks: "What's in it for me?" What would make them say "Wow!"? What do they need to learn? Worst fears? Highest hopes? What information is a must have? The short answer is unique up-to-date content, highly valuable to that consumer's needs and problems. Brainstorm the solutions to these problems. Put the solutions (content) on your website and have links to those pages in your e-mail.

6. *Close with calls to action.* Speak to your target prospects in conversational language that often uses "you" (rewrite every "I/We" sentence into a "You" sentence). Use direct-response emotional headlines ("Avoid the 10 Costliest Mistakes Even Smart Buyers Make"). Indicate clearly what you want prospects to do and what they will get if they act ("call to action"), such as "Click here to get a computerized printout of recent sales that affect your home's value—without talking to an agent." Use real-world testimonials from past clients with permission.

Five Musts to Create a REAL ESTATE RAINMAKER Great Website

1. *Customer focus:* Centered on consumer and service, not the real estate professional's personality.

2. *User friendly:* Easily understood, easy-to-locate information, ideally practices the *Two-Click Rule*—two clicks to reach desired information from any page. (Most visitors click on Homes for Sale, Buying, Selling, Relocating or About Us buttons in that order.)

3. *Rich content:* In-depth information that is valued and useful to customer, from articles and services to virtual tours and maps.

4. *Extensive forms:* Uses numerous lead-capture response forms. Forms can have the additional benefit of hiding your e-mail address from automated harvesters.

5. *Branded:* Domain and website easily transferred to new practice buyer with minimal makeover, customized but not heavily
personalized.

Critical Strategies for Making Money with Your Website

Allen F. Hainge, a national real estate technology speaker, has brought
together the Allen F. Hainge CYBERSTARS®, a group of market-leading
agents with significant web presence from all over the United States,
Canada, and Australia. By studying the CYBERSTARS, Hainge says, he
has learned what technology makes money—and what doesn't—when
it comes to real estate e-marketing today. Hainge's insights come chock-
full of practical tips and real-world advice.

"The main thing these top agents taught me," Hainge said, "is that
their personal websites have formed the heart and soul of their businesses. Top agents have, almost without fail, superb websites. When
it comes to the CYBERSTARS themselves, when I last surveyed them,
I found they earned from $20,000 to over $700,000 from their websites alone in the past 12 months. Twenty-two percent of them
earned in excess of $100,000 in closed gross commissions from their
sites alone."

The difference between a CYBERSTAR website that makes money,
and an "also ran," Hainge believes, is that top sites have three essential
ingredients the others don't. The first three strategies below come from
an article (#104: "Making Money With Your Website") Hainge wrote
for the Marketing Tips section of the AdvancedAccess.com site, which
features an excellent real estate tip every week that's well worth a
bookmarked regular visit. Here are Hainge's three website essentials—
and four more follow from my experience. (eRainmaker.com: Great
Websites has direct links to notable websites worth visiting.)

eRainmaker Strategy #1: Be Consumer Oriented, Not Agent Oriented

"Everything about the site is geared toward the consumer, not the
agent," Hainge says. If all you have on your site is a bunch of listings
and information about you (that is, your basic template site), you're

not making much money—if any. The consumer will click off your site and go find one that's geared toward his or her needs.

eRainmaker Strategy #2: Have a Wealth of Information for the Consumer

Look at your website as a consumer would. What would you want to know about your area? What would you want to know about buying and selling a home? What would you want to know about selecting

---

Figure 4.1
Blend Custom Content with Plug-In Pages for Maximum Value

Source: Courtesy of Alice Held (Come2AZ.com), RE/MAX Excalibur, Scottsdale, Arizona.

---

and working with an agent? What would you want to know about hiring an agent? What would make you feel good about an agent? The most effective approach is a complete custom site, naturally. The easiest and least expensive way to get a lot of consumer-oriented information on your site, of course, is to link to content providers or get a good personalized site that comes with hundreds of pages of tested content, advises Hainge. (See Figure 4.1.)

eRainmaker Strategy #3: Add Your Own Content . . . without Being a "Techie"

Add "stuff" to your site on a regular basis, things that would appeal to the consumer who visits your site, Hainge teaches. Here are a few ideas used by the CYBERSTARS and other successful agents:

- ☑ Local school information.
- ☑ Virtual tours for every listing.
- ☑ Local tax data.
- ☑ Sample forms used for buying or selling.
- ☑ Community information for visitors.
- ☑ Real estate statistics and market updates.
- ☑ Links to your "business partners" (attorney, title company, lawn service, carpet cleaning company, moving company, etc.).
- ☑ Testimonials from satisfied clients and customers (consider using photos and audio files for them), concludes Hainge.

eRainmaker Strategy #4: Take Your Site beyond "Sticky"

Having the right customer-focused content is king (New Rule #14) because prospects are searching for a real estate practitioner who is a knowledgeable, experienced, specialist. Yet, not just any content will meet the need. Content that makes visitors stick around the site is key—and specific, targeted customer content makes your website the "stickiest." Two content-rich sites worth a visit are published by Jerry Keller (JerryKeller.com and PorterRanchHomeseller.com), a leading agent with RE/MAX Olson & Associates in Northridge, California, whose website provider is Advanced Access.

Once consumers stick around to view your content and they start to realize how knowledgeable you are, they are more likely to share their private information in a web form to you and become a prospect. More examples of sticky customer-oriented content or links to content, include:

- ☑ Floor plans of home models.
- ☑ Recent area home listings with addresses and prices.
- ☑ Subdivision site maps.
- ☑ Golf course information for area.
- ☑ Local movie guide.
- ☑ Aerial photos of area.
- ☑ Local history.
- ☑ Special nearby attractions.

eRainmaker Strategy #5: Make a Good First Impression

We all know how important first impressions are. That's why agents dress professionally, drive a great car, and encourage home sellers to keep their properties in showcase shape. Your website must make a good first impression, too. Prospects come and go with rapid mouse clicks, so you must instantly grab the attention of every visitor to your site. The key, as it always is online, is content. Be sure the first page visitors see is full of information rather than circus-like clutter or wasted "white space." Visitors need to know and trust who is behind the site (you would be surprised how often sites don't place address, phone, fax, or e-mail information in easy-to-find places) and what they can find on subsequent pages. You don't need to tell your life story right off the bat.

eRainmaker Strategy #6: Savvy Sites Say It Simply

Speaking of good web design, fast is good (Figure 4.2). Resist the temptation to overload your site with super-large photos and graphics. Sure, it's easy to paste photos and clip art and neat logos all over your site.

Figure 4.2
Make It Easy to Find by Presenting It Simply

Source: Courtesy of Jim Bass (JimBassRealEstateGroup.com), Jim Bass Real Estate Group, Real Estate Teams, LLC, Frederick, Maryland.

But those items slow down the functionality of your site—especially for visitors with slower home-computer dial-up connections—and slow download can detract from your message. The function of your site is always first; cosmetics come second. Some of the most effective sites are clean and simple, often on a plain white background. To see how powerful simplicity can be, take a look at AT&T's home page: ATT.com.

eRainmaker Strategy #7: Seven Techniques to Give Your Site "Web Appeal"

Just like "curb appeal" for an active listing if prospects don't get out of the car, you're dead. If your website doesn't get prospects "off their mouse," you're toast. Emphasize the first things visitors see when they come to your website. This first moment is when you must capture their attention and lead them into your site. Most people don't want to wait for a Flash intro to play or read long text or scroll down a home page trying to decipher the site to find what they want.

Here are seven successful techniques to get website visitors from your home page to the inside of your site:

1. *Inventory:* Emphasize the most important things visitors need when they come to your website: homes for sale, real estate information, and area facts.

2. *Offers:* Use your home page to offer free items that help you capture information and provide services. The word "free" is still the most powerful word in response marketing, especially in the Internet world (followed closely by "click here").

3. *Bookmarks:* Most of the time less is more when trying to capture the attention of your web visitor, less clicks, less to read, less to scroll. Enhance your website's curb appeal with simple, direct navigation labels or make a list of interesting items and "bookmark" them (link to another page or location on same page to go there quickly, like a physical bookmark). Don't forget to add a bookmark that sends them back to the top.

4. *Feedback:* Ask clients, who became clients after first visiting your website, what they liked and didn't like about your site. Constant feedback is the best way to make sure your site provides the services consumers want and that those services are easy to find on your website. Consider adding a survey (multiple questions) or poll (single question) to your website, or in a pop-up after they submit a web-form.

5. *Simple:* A clean, organized, and helpful website can really give you an edge over the competition. Creating one is easier than you think, but you need the right tools. Webmasterfree.com is a great place to find resources, especially free software you can put to work right away.

6. *Printouts:* Checklists are a great "free gift" you can provide your online visitors. Make buying, selling, packing, moving, and re- modeling checklists. Present them in a printer-friendly format so visitors can make hard copies to keep. (Don't forget to add all your contact information and logo on these printouts.)

7. *Enhancements:* Once you have your site up and running, keep improving it. Nothing turns visitors away like stale informa- tion. The latest market statistics, buyer and seller tip of the week, dated real estate trends and featured new listings—all of these are fresh, effective content hooks. To learn more about web design and HTML (Hypertext Markup Language) go to HTMLGoodies.com for basic tutorials and advanced sugges- tions. Better yet, ask your tech staffer, virtual assistant, or web designer to add new content or components.

GeekSpeak
Making Sense of Web Pages

Browser page: Also, "default home page," "starter page." First page displayed when starting web browser like Microsoft's In- ternet Explorer or Netscape's Navigator.

Entrance page: First page where visitor enters website, often from link in e-mail or another website. Entrance page doesn't have to be home page.

Exit page: Last page where visitor leaves website. Entrance and exit page statistics can indicate visitor hot buttons and turn-off pages.

Home page: First page presented when user selects a website address (URL).

Landing page: Any page presented when visitor clicks on a link.

Splash page: Initial page used as a lead-in prior to home page. Often contains Flash animation or multimedia effects.

Welcome page: Also, "doorway page," "jump page," "cover sheet." Temporary page that opens before a home page. Often used for multiple domains and special timed promotions or events.

Making Your Website Better and Different with Customer Service Tools

Once the website basics of direct-response content, listings with virtual tours, and automated e-mail follow-up are in place, successful eRainmakers make their websites even more useful with customer service tools. These special tools (what e-marketers call "interactivity") allow visitors to accomplish a purpose or do work or simply entertain themselves. The more visitors participate in your site, the more likely they will respond, return, or remember your domain. Today's customer service web tools make an enhanced eRainmaker site stand out above run-of-the-mill static websites.

Beyond these interactive tools are still more optional add-ons (what web designers call "bells and whistles") that are consumer pleasing but not essential. One caution: If you put all these customer service tools *and* bells and whistles on one page, it's like being in a Fourth of July parade during a tornado—your visitors will leave shell-shocked and airsick. Be prudent. Don't pull out all the stops—unless you want to crash and burn (eRainmaker.com: For suppliers search by italicized category following).

Interactive Service Tools

☑ *Autoresponders:* Automatic and virtually instant prewritten e-mail replies to predictable requests received by a specific e-mail address inbox. Ideal for specific response forms. Ask your web designer or ISP, too.

☑ *Bulletin boards:* Electronic version of real-world bulletin boards that allow visitors to enter messages organized by subjects ("threads") to be read by other users. Can be moderated and live chat. Typically offered as an online community service.

☑ *Calculators:* Payment and prequalification calculator tools, seller cost analysis, relocation planners, net proceeds, or just mortgage interest rates can keep buyers on your site.

☑ *E-cards:* Allow visitors to select from huge collection of postcards and greeting cards and send from your website. Some capture sender and recipient e-mail address for you.

☑ *E-mail links:* A basic link to compose a preaddressed e-mail. Instead of labeling the button "e-mail us" or "Contact us," use

"More Information" as the display text because experience shows more people will respond, according to Bill Tarter at Homes.com, one of the leading providers of real estate websites.

☑ *E-mail this:* Also, "Forward to a Friend." Sends another recipient a hyperlink to your page by e-mail. Typically sends you a notice with sender's *and* recipient's names and e-mails. Sometimes called "viral marketing," this tell-a-friend "word-of-mouse" technique generates another possible customer from an existing customer.

☑ *Internal site search engine:* Lets visitors search your site by keywords they enter, and lets you learn what keywords visitors use (for your metatags, discussed in Chapter 7).

☑ *Live chat:* Real-time text-based conversation ("online chat") similar to instant messaging allows visitor to exchange live dialog anytime real estate professional (or staff member) is online. Requires floor time staffing. Big advantage is ability to work with more than one prospect at once because one can talk on phone during pause in text exchanges or handle multiple text conversations simultaneously. Ultimately, the more you can replace one-on-one phone calls with e-mail and text chat, the more business you can handle with the same staff.

☑ *Mapping:* Links to local maps are invaluable for prospects to locate properties or learn the lay of the land (especially for out-of-town relocation customers) or even find your office or open house.

☑ *Translation:* Machine translations aren't perfect, but for non-English speakers who would be lost without a translated site this tool presents a real estate professional with a global mindset and outstanding service.

☑ *Web forms:* Also, "e-mail forms." Faster than typing a message and visitors can maintain anonymity. Form-based e-mail encourages response because visitors stay on your site (instead of opening their e-mail software). Also forms can protect your inbox from spam by hiding your address from harvesting bots.

☑ *Website phone calls:* Customer enters name, phone number, and e-mail into pop-up form. Service calls customer to "hold for connection," then calls you and you speak to customer—or service plays "unavailable message" for customer. One variation

forwards e-mail from your website to your phone as a synthe-
sized voice message.

Bells and Whistles

☑ *Calendars:* Simple calendar you can update easily, especially for
Open Houses, local events.

☑ *Day and date:* Makes your site appear to be refreshed daily.

☑ *Favorite icons:* Also known as *Favicons.* These graphics files acti-
vate a program ("script") that saves ("bookmarks") a link to
your site in the visitor's favorites and inserts an icon link to your
site on their computer, or sets your page as the visitor's browser
starter page.

☑ *Slide shows:* Virtual tours that showcase your area, communities
or services.

☑ *Video:* Flash player presents pictures of you or a presentation.

☑ *Weather:* Local weather is ideal for your "relocating" pages, along
with hotels, airports, commuter highway cams, schools, utility
hookup, voter registration and other useful newcomer features.

5

〰〰〰〰〰〰

Driving Traffic to Your Website: 75 Ways to Promote Your Site

〰〰〰〰〰〰〰

OLD RULE

Online advertising will surpass offline advertising.

NEW RULE

Integrated offline and online promotion wins every time.

〰〰〰〰〰〰〰

How to Become a Household URL

The difference between a top-ranked website and an ad in the Yellow Pages is that folks know how to find you in the phone book.

How will buyers and sellers track you down on the Internet, if they don't even know you exist? *You have to drive folks to your destination site.* Internet visitors reach websites in three basic ways: direct navigation, strategic links, and search engines, according to WebSideStory (WebSideStory.com), a leading provider of web traffic tracking tools (what marketers call "web analytics"). *Direct navigation* means visitors typed your URL directly into the address bar of their browser; also included are links in e-mail, bookmarks, favorites, and using the drop-down history of previous visited sites. *Strategic links* represent click-throughs from links on other sites such as reciprocal link partners (also "affiliates"), directories, banner ads, or sponsored links. Finally, *search engine* referrals come from known search sites where users enter search terms; selection program compares terms to the site's indexed database, and returns results to searcher, as well as relevant paid links.

What is stunning about WebSideStory's analysis (see Figure 5.1 for Jan.–June 2003 and Table 5.1 for three-year trend) is that two-out-of-three website visitors (66%) in the United States found the websites they wanted through direct navigation while strategic links and search engines only generated 18% and 16%, respectively, of all Internet visitors.

The StatMarket data by WebSideStory was collected from visitors to more than 125,000 sites using WebSideStory's Hit Box analysis tools in 2003 that record "referrer" sources (where a visitor came from, or where you return if you click the "back" button). The figures represent the surfing habits of about 12 million Internet users globally on a given day. To the degree return visitors use direct navigation or strategic links on subsequent visits after initially finding your site through a search engine, search engine percentages may be somewhat underreported in StatMarket figures.

Figure 5.1
How Visitors Find Websites

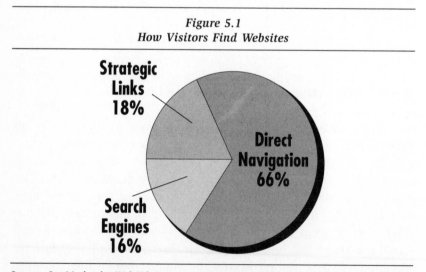

Source: StatMarket by WebSideStory.com January to June 2003. Used with permission.

Table 5.1
Three-Year Trend of U.S. Internet Use

Referral Source	2003 (%)	2002 (5)	2001 (%)
Direct navigation	66	61	60
Strategic links	18	26	30
Search engines	16	13	10

Source: StatMarket by WebSideStory.com. The 2003 figures are for January–June. Used with permission.

Why did strategic links lose ground and search engines gain importance in recent years? "The thrill of meandering around the Web is gone for many users," said Geoff Johnston vice president of product marketing for WebSideStory's StatMarket. "They now tend to know where they want to go and they get there directly to do their business. The days of huge numbers of visitors randomly tripping across sites are gone."

Branding may be the most important single factor. "Direct navigation continues to grow," Johnston said, "which means the gap between [branded] haves and have-nots on the Web is likely to grow. Search engines remain crucial to allow users to find a site the first time (or for one-time uses) but if the site is not worth returning to, the search engines won't help forever. Users are tending to find sites they like and returning regularly more now than ever."

The big "Aha!" is clear. Every eRainmaker needs a three-part e-strategy in today's environment to put marketing dollars *first*— and mostly—into promoting direct navigation, then *second* into strategic links (Chapter 6), and *third* into search marketing placement (Chapter 7).

The best initial e-strategy is to use low-tech means to promote your website. Offline marketing works wonders, from direct mail, homes magazine ads, newspaper classifieds, television and radio spots to your license plate and bumper stickers. Even more fundamental is simply printing your site address everywhere your phone or street address appear—from your business cards and letterhead to your for-sale signs— to build site traffic. Make every direct mail piece, print ad, sign, e-mail, and more serve a dual purpose to drive visitors to your website *and* generate leads. In short, put your website address everywhere you are spending marketing dollars.

Top technology trainer Allen F. Hainge (AFHSeminars.com) said it very well in his recommended book, *Dominate! Capturing Your Market with Today's Technology:*

> Web Centric™ is a term I've coined to sum up what top sales associates nationwide are doing to dominate their market: *their website forms the core of their business, and all their marketing efforts point the consumer to their website* . . . in other words, they realize their website has depth far beyond any other medium they can use, and they use every means to get prospects to their site.

Leading website designer Sandy Teller (SizzlingStudios.com) in Naples, Florida, has illustrated web-centric marketing in one picture that is worth a thousand words. All promotions must point to your branded destination website (Figure 5.2).

Here are 75 of the most successful offline and online techniques to dramatically boost your website traffic:

1. *Advertising specialties:* Every promotional item you distribute should feature your site address. Branders.com is an excellent source for promotional specialty items from apparel to tradeshow giveaways. Include your web address on promotional items such as calendars, notepads, magnets, pencils, coffee mugs, Frisbees, and so on.

2. *B2B:* Contact your business partners (lenders, title reps, home inspectors, appraisers, attorneys, etc.) and give them your web address. Propose a strategic link exchange.

3. *Badge of honor:* Include your web address on your name badge at all conventions and meetings, or bring stickers or ribbons to attach. Put your web address on your permanent name badge and wear it at all public functions.

4. *Balloons:* Buy balloons printed with your web address to inflate from your open house and directional signs. Give inflated balloons to sellers to promote their yard sale.

5. *Broadcast ads:* Use your web address in electronic ads that require remembering your contact information such as radio, TV, cable.

6. *Brochure boxes:* Include your website address and a reason to visit on your brochure boxes, such as "Search All Area Homes

Figure 5.2
Web-Centric Marketing

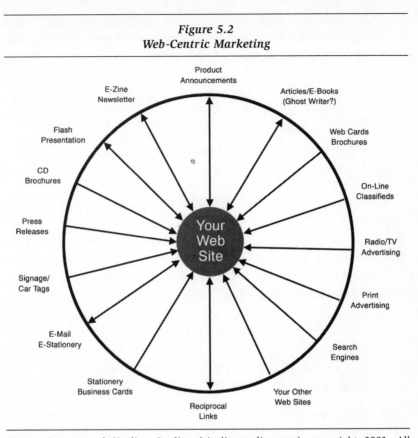

for Sale Anytime." Inside the box (if the last brochure is taken) put a sign "Visit MySite.com for complete information on this property."

7. *Bulletin boards:* Think of other places to distribute your web cards (see #51) or business cards, such as community bulletin boards. Include simple tear off tabs printed with your web address and small headline: "To Visit Every Listing, Visit . . ."

8. *Bumper stickers:* Print peel-n-stick bumper stickers to promote your web address. "Honk if you want to sell your home."

9. *Bus benches:* Keep it simple (URL, name, phone) and a fast read. Benches on slower traffic streets work best (easier to read at 20 mph than 40 mph). Select neighborhoods that match your target customer profile.

10. *Business cards:* Include your web address on your business cards. Sounds obvious, but most agents don't. Take, for example, the more than 12,661 real estate business cards my company has collected at tradeshows over five years between 1999 and 2003. In 1999, 78% did not have a website address on the card. In 2003, 51% of the cards did not have a web address. Getting better, but still no cigar. (E-mail is a different story. In 2003, only 18% did not list an e-mail address.)

11. *Car talk:* Tie-in your offline marketing with your website by including a photo of decaled vehicle or vanity license plate on your website. "You may have seen us around town," would be a great postcard headline.

12. *Child's play:* Create a "Kids Only" section of your website with unique URL, ideally with photos of the fashions local kids are wearing in school. Print address on handouts for relocation prospects to take home to kids, such as kites with your web address or yo-yos or glider planes.

13. *Coat hangers:* Local dry cleaners may give you a nice discount to advertise your web address on the paper covers of coat hangers that the cleaners would otherwise have to pay for themselves. Literally, great shelf life: "Closet too small? Contact us about selling your home at www.MySite.com."

14. *Co-brokers:* Send e-mail to all local co-op brokers in your network who have agreed to receive early notice of new listings with a link to virtual tours. Include your web address.

15. *Community flyers:* Print flyers for distribution in your farming neighborhoods and areas near you. Tell people what's in it for them to visit your site. Ideally have a section of your site devoted to community news, school info, and local services of importance, including helpful links to other area publications or sites such as schools, local government, continuing education, parks and recreation, homeowners association directories, and so on.

16. *Computer connections:* Hand out advertising specialties for computer users with your web address, such as mouse pads, monitor calendar strips, monitor cleaners, glare screens, wrist rests, and so on.

17. *Contests:* Feature a sweepstakes or contest (if legal in your state) where prospects can go to the website to enter. Promote the contest everywhere in ads, direct mail, e-mail signature, brochure box fliers, and so on.

18. *Conversations:* Mention your website whenever you have the opportunity upon meeting new acquaintances. Hand them something with your web address on it.

19. *Coupons:* Include your web address on printable coupons sent to prospects as PDF files.

20. *Credit line:* Put your web address in your biographical credit line in all articles you write.

21. *Designations:* Contact any organizations you belong to and give them your web address and e-mail, especially NAR at Realtor .org and other professional groups such as: SRES, WCR, RS Council, and so on.

22. *Diskette and CD:* Publish your website (or most useful parts, such as printable checklist forms) on CD or diskette and provide to prospective clients. Have a technical person include programming that will open a web browser and download your site with a single click.

23. *Door magnet:* Put your web address on both front doors of your auto with a removable door magnet from a local sign store.

24. *Door hangers:* Add your website on door hangers that you leave behind when canvassing, putting out open house invitations, and as "Sorry to miss you" notes when owners are not home. Offer the reader a reason to visit your site ("Learn how to drive up the value of your home with fix-ups and makeovers").

25. *Dream home:* Ask prospects what they want in a dream home— and offer to find it for them when they visit your website and tell you exactly what they want ("Free Home Finder Service").

26. *Duty desk:* Mention your web address to every prospect that calls when you are on floor duty or opportunity time, as permitted by office rules.

27. *E-newsletter:* Encourage contacts who receive your e-mail newsletter to bookmark the e-newsletter URL and forward issues to friends.

28. *E-mail signature:* In your e-mail "signature" (4 to 5 lines about you, what you do, where you do it), insert how they can contact you and your site address at the bottom of every e-mail. Many e-mail programs allow you to create a signature and add it automatically. At minimum, the signature can contain your contact information. Many eRainmakers use their imaginations and maintain multiple signatures for different situations.

Here are some example signatures:

☑ CYBERSTAR® Ira Serkes (BerkeleyHomes.com) with RE/MAX Executive in Berkeley, California, uses one of the longest and

---

eRainmaker Tips

Create Signature Signatures:

☑ Create unique signatures for different groups (buyers, sellers, investors, past clients, B2B referral contacts, business network, reciprocal link network, and so on).

☑ Include your photo and logo, even your handwritten signature, in a JPG or GIF file.

☑ Add links to inspirational quotes or homeowner tips or "Go to Home Page."

☑ Change the content regularly for variety (sometimes easier than changing the links themselves, which may be saved with previous e-mail in a customer's inbox).

☑ Remember signatures are simply prepopulated documents. That means signatures can be entire letters. Prewritten signature "letters" are an excellent way to respond quickly with a few clicks to routine inquiries, perhaps with a personal first sentence or two. Then you or your assistant can respond in-depth later (more on this powerful "first-response" technique in Chapter 14).

most creative e-mail signatures (too long to reprint here) that he can easily cut and edit as needed for specific clients (ira@BerkeleyHomes.com).

☑ Ethel Mayer is a top-producing agent in Long & Foster Realtors' leading Bethesda Gateway office in Maryland. Note Mayer's e-mail signature "P.S.":

> Ethel Mayer
> Long & Foster Real Estate
> Bethesda Gateway
> ethel.mayer@longandfoster.com
> www.homesdatabase.com/ethelmayer
>
> (301) 907-7600 (ext. 4737)

Oh, by the way . . . should you come in contact with anyone who is considering buying or selling a property anywhere, I would be delighted to help them. Please don't hesitate to give me a call with their name and number or e-mail address. I'll follow up right away, and I'll be happy to provide them with information and/or answer any questions that they might have.

☑ Top agent Margaret Rome (HomeRome.com) tells it all in her e-mail signature. Notice how Rome has registered her phone number as a URL.

> With admiration and appreciation,
> Margaret
> Margaret Rome
> http://www.HomeRome.com/HTML/brokeragent/broker.html
> ABR, CRS, GRI, LTG, RECS, RRC
> Floyd Wickman Master Sales Academy
> An Allen Hainge CyberStar®
> Coldwell Banker Residential Brokerage
> Baltimore, Maryland
> www.HomeRome.com
> MRome@HomeRome.com
> Internet or Phone www.410-358-3375.com
> SELL YOUR HOME WITH MARGARET ROME
> Send FREE greeting cards from www.HomeRome.com

29. *Field days:* Giveaway sun visors at sports events with your web address on visor. Water bottles filled with sports drinks.

Have peel-n-stick labels printed with your web address that stick on individual-size water bottles.

30. *Forward to a friend:* Use "viral" marketing or stealth marketing to have visitors forward a link to your site to a friend via e-mail by making it as easy as word-of-mouse.

31. *Friends and family:* Ask your friends and family to help promote your website to their friends. Give them business cards and website postcards to hand out or mail. This pass-along technique is critical for your tell-a-friend viral marketing.

32. *Grocery carts:* Target neighborhood prospects with an ad on supermarket carts. Go bold, simple, big with your web address, and one headline such as "Our website eats the competition for lunch" or "The one address our competitors don't want you to visit."

33. *Great content:* Install good, deep content on your site. Without content, search engines don't find you, and prospects don't find reasons to "stick" to your site and, eventually, contact you. When all sites have the same IDX listings, the only difference between sites is content.

34. *Hindsight:* Turn your rear window into a sign with a see-through clear label with your web address. Place high or low on window for maximum visibility.

35. *Homes magazines:* Place your web address prominently at the top of every homes magazine ad you run. In place of a property photo, insert a screen shot of your home page with URL boldly printed above the image. Consider a call-to-action headline such as "The only address you need to know" to see all the latest area listings.

36. *Invitations:* Send out invitations by e-mail and send direct mail to your family and friends asking them to visit your website. Ask directly for referrals to help you spread the word to others. Use the same copy for your client appreciation party invitations.

37. *Just listed:* Send new-on-market information (your listings and company listings) to your sphere of buyers via e-mail and include hot links to virtual tours on your website. Zac Pasmanick (TheZacTeam.com), a top Howard Brinton Star with RE/MAX Greater Atlanta, calls this traffic-building technique

"Sneak-a-Peek" because his buyers receive the e-mail before the property is advertised, shown in an open house, or hits the MLS.

38. *Key chain:* Order key chains as a giveaway that includes your web address ("Your link to area real estate").

39. *Letterhead:* Print your web address on your letterhead, envelopes, and under your return address on postcards.

40. *License frame:* Buy a custom license plate frame advertising your website.

41. *Listserv:* Establish an e-mail distribution list for a particular target neighborhood or price range or house style and send news specific to their interest including a link to your site in every bulletin.

42. *Logotype:* Have a URL logotype created and put your web logo at the top of your stationery, both printed and e-stationery, print it on your literature, as well as on top of every web page (Figure 5.3). The logotype could become your brand.

43. *Market Conditions Report:* Consider subscribing to an innovative service from Realty Times (RealtyTimes.com), one of the real estate industry's leading news services. You write a short description of your local market conditions and update it monthly (with staff help), including rating trends toward a

---

Figure 5.3
Promote Your Website with Logo

Source: Courtesy of Heidi Mueller (sfrelo.com), Prudential California Realty, San Francisco, California.

buyer's or seller's market and prices. Each report categorized by city and state includes links to your website,
newsletter (optional), and e-mail contact form. Major portals
(AOL, Homestore, Yahoo, MSN, etc.) and website providers
publish the reports on their sites which attracts consumer
traffic back to your personal site. Annual fee.

44. *Model cars:* Buy miniature toy cars of your rolling billboard
    vehicle with decals of your web address and give to kids of
    past clients.

45. *New listing business cards:* Give all your home sellers a stack
    of customized business cards featuring a photo of their home
    on the back with your site address to hand out to all their
    friends, neighbors, relatives, and coworkers (Pagemaker, Pub-
    lisher, or similar desktop publishing software).

46. *Newsletter name:* Use your web address as the name of your
    newsletter or custom newspaper. For example, top producer Tom
    Randall (AmesRealty.com), a Howard Brinton Star with RE/MAX
    Real Estate Center in Ames, Iowa, titles his newspaper by Cus-
    tom House Publishers: "*amesrealty.com*municator."

47. *Newspaper classifieds:* Feature your web address for virtual
    tours, property listing, area information, and so on. Cross-
    promote your site in your print ads to drive more traffic than
    the standard ad showcasing only one home.

48. *Online groups:* Participate in discussion forums and news-
    groups, especially if they are focused on your local area or for
    real estate professionals who may be referral sources. You can
    post messages—make sure you have something valid to say—
    and at the bottom of your post add your URL. Beware: Groups
    can be time consuming and may have marginal return.

49. *Pages of Interest:* Advertise specific points of interest and spe-
    cialty sections in your site that provide value to the consumer,
    such as condos, second homes, seniors, investors, and so on
    (Figure 5.4). Put the ads in newspapers, homes magazines,
    radio spots, postcards, and even banner ads on other sites.

50. *Past clients:* Drop a note or leave voice mail for all past buyers
    and sellers to give them your web address, offer answers to any
    questions, and ask for their e-mail address so you can reply
    with yours. Add your domain on all your closing gifts.

Figure 5.4
Advertise Services with Specialty Domains

Source: Courtesy of Russell Arkin (NorthernVAHomeInfo.com), RE/MAX Distinctive Real Estate, McLean, Virginia.

51. *Postcards:* Create custom postcards (Figure 5.5) or buy postcards that come printed with a screen shot of your website in color. Take this idea a step further by creating a series of cards each featuring a different section in your site for different target customers, and launch a 6-month to 12-month mailing campaign. If you leave some cards blank on the address side, you can use the cards for thank-you notes, just listed/just sold cards, and so on.

52. *Presentations:* Put your web address on all your listing presentation folders and documents, forms, checklists, CMAs, and other office supplies, including a Homeowner's Book.

53. *Print Ads:* Instead of your URL being at the bottom in your ads, place it big, bold, and prominent to make your website the focus of the ad. The Corcoran Group (Corcoran.com) in New

---

Figure 5.5
Use Postcards to Retrieve Big Results

Source: Courtesy of Kellee Heldoorn (TheHeldoornTeam.com), Keller Williams Realty, Southlake, Texas.

York City has produced some of the best award-winning ad campaigns for many years (Figures 5.6 and 5.7). "Every print campaign we run," said Lori Levin, The Corcoran Group's Director of Advertising, "from the smallest one-inch classified to a 52-foot wall promotes our website." Here are some sample Corcoran Group headlines:

- "dot.com today, sold, dot.gone tomorrow. Your home listed on real estate's leading site. corcoran.com"

- "one click. thousands of apartments. Updated daily. Where do you want to live? corcoran.com"

- "Exceptional Real Estate, super human resources. Thousands of listings with photos and floorplans, in real time. corcoran .com"

Figure 5.6
"Where Do You Want to Live?" Corcoran.com Campaign

Source: Courtesy of The Corcoran Group, owned and operated by NRT Incorporated.

54. *Publicity:* Announce a newsworthy new feature of your site to the media with a press release, such as automatic listing updates, one-stop resource hotline, virtual tours, or website award. Encourage editors to think of you as a news source available for comment. Consider writing a regular column about real estate (or purchase a ghost-written column, often more cost effective in smaller markets than metro areas where newspaper display ads can be prohibitive).

55. *Radio show:* Superstar Thierry Roche has made his mark in his Northern Virginia market telling everybody who would listen about his business—literally. For years, Roche (InsideRealEstate .com), an all-star agent with RE/MAX Premier in Fairfax, Virginia, has hosted a radio show on a local business talk radio station (Figure 5.8). WRC 1260AM station sells him the airtime and Roche resells advertiser spots and sponsorships—usually for a little more than it costs him for the entire show. A simple telephone connection allows Roche to broadcast every Saturday at noon from his broker's office. One of the principal benefits is increased traffic to Roche's website, which is designed to capture leads and has the same branded URL as the easy-to-remember radio program: Inside Real Estate.

Figure 5.7
"Follow the leader." Corcoran.com 52-foot Billboard

Source: Courtesy of The Corcoran Group, owned and operated by NRT Incorporated.

56. *Restaurants:* Offer local restaurants free listings on your site. Include the restaurant's theme or menu, prices, and photos of specialties. In return, the restaurant may allow you to leave business cards or a tent card featuring your website at their restaurant. Ask if the restaurant has a discount offer you can add to your site. Works for many other merchants, too. Keep eyes open for a cash-register or window sign opportunity to advertise your website where customers can logon and print a discount coupon for a return to the merchant.

57. *Rolling billboard:* Feature your site on your vehicle. VW beetle, a Chrysler PT Cruiser, or a moving truck make a great mobile sign with full-car vinyl decal or custom painted sign.

Figure 5.8
Maximize Website Traffic with Radio Talkshow

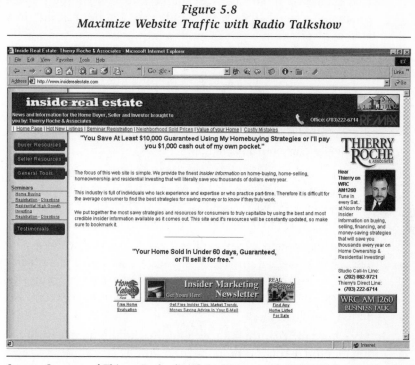

Source: Courtesy of Thierry Roche (InsideRealEstate.com), RE/MAX Premier, Fairfax, Virginia.

58. *Seminars:* Use your website (and a response web form) for registrations for your home buyer, seller, investment, and second-home seminars. "Register at MySite.com Now for Upcoming Seminar. Seats limited."

59. *Showing feedback:* Forward showing feedback to your clients from showing agents and office colleagues, and include link to your web address.

60. *Sign posts:* Order a glow-in-the-dark self-adhesive strip featuring your web address to be applied to the vertical post of your yard signs.

61. *Sign riders:* Feature your website or virtual tours on your sign riders. Include the wording, "For a Virtual Tour Visit MySite .com." Consider assigning a number to each virtual tour for

easy reference. Have local sign shop create a vinyl "sold" cover to slip over metal signs with the phrase "We did it again! Just sold at MySite.com."

62. *Signage techniques:* Along with your name and phone number, add your URL to for-sale signs and riders. Tips:

   • Internet domain names are not case sensitive; upper case, lower case, or mixed title case are all okay.

   • Capitalize the first letter of each word for easy readability (MySite.com, not mysite.com).

   • Drop the "www" subdomain prefix; URLs work with and without prefix for most browsers. Consider typesetting the extension (.COM) vertically at end of domain, or underneath domain in smaller type to reduce width of URL.

63. *Site upgrade:* Send e-mail notice to your "e-farm" when a new feature is published on your site. You can even give visitors the ability to receive e-mail notice any time a part of your site changes (for any page the button is on). (eRainmaker.com: Internal Search)

64. *Slide margin:* Feature your web address in the border of slides on a laptop listing presentation and PowerPoint slide presentations to groups.

65. *Sold homes:* Post photos of homes you've sold on individual pages on your site. Suggest buyers invite their friends and relatives to see their new home on your site. You can also use an expanded virtual tour for this technique, using nearby neighborhood features, photos, and map links.

66. *Staff:* Make certain your staff knows your website address. Practice visiting the site as a consumer would to train staff on how to coach callers to use the site, especially during office hours when callers may be at work. Encourage staff to ask, "Do you have Internet access? Can you go there now?" while on phone with callers to walk visitor through site.

67. *Stickers:* Avoid waiting until your supply of old business cards is used up to add or change your new web address (or e-mail). Print stickers the size of a return address-change label that says: "Visit my new website! www.MySite.com." Stick them everywhere—on the back of old business cards, property flyers,

presentation folders, note pads, envelopes, old stationery—until the old materials are reprinted.

68. *Surveys:* Use an e-mail or offline ad to announce polls on your website. Polling software is available that posts results instantly on your site in attractive bar charts. (eRainmaker .com: Survey/Polling)

69. *Tear sheets:* Staple your web address (or use self-adhesive labels) to homes magazines and mail magazines to relocation prospects. "Visit our site to see ANY home advertised inside." Insert your full-page ad tear sheets into a Plexiglas stand for display at open houses or in listings with an "As Seen In" including your web address to "See a virtual tour."

70. *Thank-you notes:* Preprint your thank-you note stationery with your web address. Then, every time you write a note, no matter if it is to family, friends, or business contacts, you'll promote your site. Don't be shy. Many times friends and family are unaware of your website and your current offerings.

71. *Transit ads:* From shelter posters to side-board bus panels and shopping mall kiosks to taxi placards, keep your message short, simple, and quick to read: your web address and unique positioning statement ("Your Dream Home Finder").

72. *Trunk tag:* Put your URL on the trunk of your car with a special tag, similar to the dealership or manufacturer trunk plate—chrome or gold.

73. *Vanity plate:* Order a vanity license plate with your URL if the address is within the 6 to 7 character limit in your state (Figure 5.9).

74. *Voice mail:* Include your website address in your voice mail announcement message. It's free. Sample message: "Hi, this is [your name]. I'm away from my desk right now or on another call. Please leave a message and I'll get right back to you. After the beep, visit our website at MySite.com for every home for sale in our area and answers to any real estate question. That's MySite.com."

75. *Youth events:* If you have children or grandchildren in youth events (sports, church groups, school activities, etc.), attend the event with your digital camera, recommends Allen Hainge. Take

---

Figure 5.9
Vanity License Plates

Our License Plates

Honk to say "Hi!" If you see us around town!!

Source: Courtesy of Richard and Brooke Hiers (RealEstateHelpDesk.net), First Team Real Estate, Long Beach, California.

---

plenty of photos—especially group shots, create a page for them, then let every parent know where to see the photos . . . at your website. Send e-mail with a link to the page. If the event is regular (soccer league, etc.), do it every week during the season. Better yet, create a link on your website to a photo printing service such as Ofoto.com or SnapFish.com. Post the event photos in an album at those sites where parents can view and buy prints (optional).

How to Really Know If Your Advertising Is Driving Traffic to Your Site

Philadelphia department-store magnate John Wanamaker (1838–1922) once said: "Half the money I spend on advertising is wasted, and the trouble is I don't know which half." That problem applies to offline advertising for your website. To make the most of your marketing dollars, there are several unique ways you can track the source of your traffic and determine what works and what doesn't.

☑ *Use a website traffic log service.* The service logs and reports the URLs that visitors call to download your web pages. (See eRainmaker Tip.)

☑ *Add a subfolder to your URL in print ads* (MySite.com/ HomesMagazine or MySite.com/ext123). Create a special index page (also, "landing page," "welcome page," "doorway page") that is a copy of your regular home page to greet those ad readers (e.g., MySite.com/index-promo01.html, instead of regular page: MySite.com/index.html). Register this unique index page with the traffic log service to count visits prompted by the specific ad.

☑ *Use a hyperlink identification code.* In strategic links on other websites, after your domain add "?" followed by a unique source code (Example: MySite.com/Traffic?SourceX001). Develop standardized code format, such as E001-E999 for e-mails, A001–A999 for print ads, B001–B999 for banner ads, and so on. Because the link is hidden "behind" the display text, your log service can count the click-through source, but display text reads normally and is not confusing or revealing to the visitor.

☑ *Create a unique e-mail account.* Establish a special account (Example: HomesMagazine123@MySite.com), and set rules in your e-mail software to direct those e-mails to a folder. Periodically tally the e-mails generated by your ad or e-marketing activity.

☑ *Register multiple domains.* Advertise the multibrand domains we learned about in Chapter 3 only in specific publications or direct promotions. Register the traffic log service to count the click-throughs to know which advertisements work best. You can also

---

eRainmaker Tip

Track Your Traffic: You (or your web master) can insert a special tracking code in your website pages, and a traffic analysis service will produce revealing statistics for an annual fee. Use this intelligence to gauge how well your site is performing and, most important, how to improve its weaknesses. Task your web master, tech staffer, or virtual assistant to make the most of these revealing statistics. (eRainmaker.com: Statistics)

redirect the domain to land on your destination website home page or a specific interior page.

Why Tracking Unique Visitors, Referrers, Page Views, and Clickstreams Is Critical

Reserve the right to be smarter today than you were yesterday, to paraphrase a favorite saying of President Harry S Truman. The same holds true with your website. Websites are a work in progress. They are never complete. Every website can be better today than it was yesterday. That doesn't mean you have to redesign your website just for the sake of a makeover. But it does mean you *must* track visitor behavior to learn how to make your site better.

Quick Checklist of Essential Website Tracking Statistics to Monitor

- ☑ *Unique visitors (counts visitors with unique address entering first time that day or other specified period):* Most basic traffic measure, contrasts with "page views" which give an inflated "hits" count.

- ☑ *Referrers (strategic links used by prospects to visit your site):* Tells you where traffic comes from and what website a visitor was at prior to your site, such as your sponsored banner ad, a directory listing, or search engine.

- ☑ *Search engines (reports known search engines where visitors found the link to your site):* Tracks how well search engine registration and site optimization is working.

- ☑ *Entrance page (first landing page):* Eye opener, especially if visitors arrive at pages other than your home page. May show other sites have linked to specific content in your site instead of your home page. This statistic often indicates how critical it is to have your contact information visible on every page of your website.

- ☑ *Exit page (last page visited before visitor leaves):* Can reveal pages or navigation that are turn-offs to visitors.

- ☑ *Many other statistics are useful:* Return visitors, time on site, page path (also, "clickstream"), date, and time (typically reflects publication of offline advertising or e-mail marketing) gives you sense if visitors are at work or late-night users.

Remember, terms used for measuring website traffic are different from terms used for measuring results of Internet advertising. Internet ads measure results by impressions (also, "ad views"), priced in cost per thousand (CPM, where M is the Roman numeral for thousand), click-throughs, and conversions. (More on measuring web advertising effectiveness in Chapter 17.)

CHAPTER

6

Driving Traffic to Your Website: Strategic Linking

Leveraging the Online Search Channel

Strategic linking is the second most powerful technique for driving visitors to your website, after promoting your website offline. As marketers, we describe search marketing as "leveraging the search channel." Because your prospects are purposely visiting other related real estate websites for information, having links through to your website is a natural fit.

Think of strategic linking as a virtual referral network. As in the real world, referrals can be one of your largest sources of business. In fact, web statistic logs that count the number of click-throughs to your website use the term *referring URLs* as the source of traffic. Just like generating offline referrals, to nurture relationships with online link partners the partners must value referrals (educate them), they must endorse you (ask for link), and they must keep the hyperlink active (stay in touch).

There are three basic approaches to strategic links and search marketing:

1. *Reciprocal links* (mutual link swap, typically free).
2. *Pay-per-performance* (paid advertising).
3. *Search engine placement* (directory registration; more on Search Marketing Basics in Chapter 7).

Whichever approach you use, the result is the same: Self-qualified prospects discover your link and click-through to your website from another link partner site. The importance of having other sites agree to add your link in their site is so significant that some search engines calculate your site's *link popularity* to determine your rank in their search results lists.

eRainmaker Strategy #1: Lay the Foundation for Strategic Links

Here are your first steps to prepare implementation of your strategic links campaign:

1. *Publish relevant content.* Offer good content and features that provide real value to your mutual audience. The chance of exchanging links increases as other real estate compatible sites discover your website and recognize its benefits.
2. *Create pages to add strategic links.* You'll need to create pages or locations on your site to display your strategic links. Consider organizing them by geography or by business category. Successful eRainmakers have labeled these pages variously: Useful Links, Community Info, Professional Services, Locator, Service Directory, and so on.
3. *Automate your reciprocal links.* Want to make adding reciprocal links to your website hands-free? Follow the example of top agents Gary and Laury Woods (SantaBarbaraProperties.com) in Santa Barbara, California, who use the Local Partners service from their website provider, AdvancedAccess.com (Marketing Tip #126). In their "Partners" section, the Woods have posted a simple form where other websites can add themselves to the Wood's

"Links Page" directory. It's free and in return the Woods ask to be added to the partner's website. The Woods make it even easier by supplying graphics and HTML code for the reciprocal partner to add to the partner's website.

Separate from identifying and sending link swap requests is the management of your link pages. Some of the best web-based applications that manage your link partners can fully automate the time-consuming task of swapping links with other sites and maintaining your link pages. (eRainmaker.com: Link Management.)

4. *Delegate task to staff or virtual assistant.* It is work to develop new link partners over the phone and in e-mail exchanges, plus adding links and monitoring the links to be sure they work takes time. Once you have ramped up the process, consider delegating the job to staff or to a virtual assistant, or hire a virtual consultant. After all, that's why top-producing eRainmakers make the big bucks. You can also hire services to do the labor-intensive work of locating and developing link partners. Not only do they seek out quality link partners but they also manage the needed notifications and assist with posting reciprocal links on your links pages. Consultants and some applications already maintain valuable categorized directories of websites that trade reciprocal links with other sites (eRainmaker.com: Link Management).

eRainmaker Strategy #2: Promote Link Popularity

Search engines consider the number of links on other websites that link through to your website as an endorsement of your site: the more through links to your website, the more relevant and popular your site is with others. Link popularity—the number of websites that link to your website—is one of the factors search engines use to determine how well your site matches a search term, in addition to content, title, description, and metatags (Chapter 7). Some search engines also give weight to the importance of the sites that link to you. This means when heavily trafficked major portals, such as REALTOR.com or HouseandHome.MSN.com (formerly HomeAdvisor .com) link to your site, your credibility is higher than if your local homeowners association links to your website.

GeekSpeak

Link Popularity Analysis: For a free analysis of your site's link popularity—an eye-opening comparison with up to three competing websites—go to MarketLeap.com/publinkpop or LinkPopularityCheck.com. (For link counts but no comparison visit LinkPopularity.com.) Be sure to have your competition's URLs handy.

Leverage the Existing Network of Link Partners

Would you like a list of other websites that accept links to sites like yours? Here's how to do it free in five easy steps:

1. *Go to your favorite search engine.* For example, in Google.com > Advanced Search > Page-Specific Search, enter your website in "pages similar to your pages" to find competitor sites that have similar Google search criteria. You can also enter a regular Google search phrase that prospects would typically use to find your site, for example, "Northern Virginia real estate." Print list of sites returned by your search.

2. *Go to LinkPopularity.com or return to your search engine and enter those competitor URLs one-by-one to see what similar link partner sites link to the competitor sites.* You now have a list of similar sites (link partners) that accept strategic links to sites like yours.

3. *Contact the prospective link partners by e-mail and propose they link to your site or that you both publish mutual reciprocal links to each other.*

4. *Repeat Steps 2 and 3 for all the strategic link partners you found in Step 1.* As you can see, this is an excellent project for your tech consultant or virtual assistant (eRainmaker.com: Link Management).

5. *Monitor your progress toward building your own link partner network.* Regularly return to Google.com to do an advanced search of your site in "pages that link to your pages" to find existing link partners that Google has logged. You can also track your link

popularity growth by recording how many sites link through to your site at LinkPopularity.com or LinkPopularityCheck.com.

eRainmaker Strategy #3: Open More Doors and Close More Deals with Reciprocal Link Partners

You know the old adage, "Scratch my back and I'll scratch yours." That saying describes reciprocal linking, where you add a link to someone else's website in return for them adding a link through to your site. Any business with a website that shares the same purpose and attracts the same prospects is a possible link partner.

Tee-up the process with phone calls, followed by an e-mail request. Eventually, you may simply e-mail potential partners and propose a reciprocal link. Be sure to invite your link prospect to visit your site by including a hyperlink in your e-mail. Make it easy to respond. To agree to a reciprocal link, all candidates need to do is reply to your e-mail, include their web address and perhaps identify the category where they want to be listed.

How much will this cost? Why not make it pay for itself? Consider following the *zero-based budget* technique of top producer Matt Greene (IowaHomes4U.com) with Iowa Realty in Des Moines, Iowa. Greene offers a three-tiered program on his Advanced Access site. Greene swaps reciprocal links with businesses in his simple Favorite Links section for free but charges $25 per year for a link on his Community Links page that displays the partner's site on Greene's site in a frame. He charges $100 per year for a paid advertisement on his Local Partners page with more information and an e-mail link to the advertiser so the partner doesn't have to have a website to get business from Greene's site. Greene puts a list of all Local Partners into every relocation and first-time buyer packet he mails out.

How to Build Link Popularity for Your Website

Start with the website owners you already know or have linked with and expand the list. The more visible you are to the community (on-line and offline), the more visible your site will be to prospective link partners in the same search channel who share similar target customers and link-popularity search engines. Here are seven ways to find prospective link partners:

☑ *Target real estate professionals.* A real estate network of out-of-market links can be a huge traffic builder because exchanging links is a win-win for both sides. Request a reciprocal link on other real estate professionals' sites if they have a resource or helpful links section. Start with agents who have sent you direct referrals in the past. Then add agents outside your market area, associates in your franchise or relocation referral network, fellow designation holders (CRS, SRES, ABR, CCIM, LTG, CLHMS [Luxury Homes], etc.), or acquaintances from conferences and meetings.

☑ *Research closing-table players.* Assemble the website URLs of local transaction-related businesses (lenders, attorneys, title representatives, inspectors, hazard insurance brokers, surveyors, closing officers, and so on). Often they are affiliates or associate members of your realty board.

☑ *Gather home-service businesses.* Collect home-service providers who have websites in your "concierge" network (remodelers, home furnishing stores, painters, electricians, floor covering shops, landscapers, appliance stores, window treatment providers, maid services, and so on). "One good referral deserves another."

☑ *Watch for trigger sites.* Trigger sites are websites visited by prospective home buyers and sellers who are searching for information related to their upcoming lifestyle transition. Link your site, for example, to sites having to do with relocation, communities or subdivisions, careers, new-child or parenting, weddings, seniors, second homes or vacation rentals, homeowner associations, school graduations, and more.

☑ *Cultivate B2B referral sources.* Ask other business professionals and referral sources who have websites to exchange links—accountants, financial planners, estate attorneys, family practice lawyers, stock brokers, and so on.

☑ *Check directories.* Links from real-estate-specific search directories dedicated to news and information are often open to a reciprocal link because the audience of your site matches their audience. (More in the "Pay-per-Performance" section that follows.)

☑ *Register with search engines.* Link to human-based search engines—such as Yahoo! and the Open Directory Project—to get

---

eRainmaker Tip

Two-from-One: One registered domain name can be used as two different web addresses at no additional cost. By using the subdomain (www.MySite.com) or dropping the subdomain (MySite.com) you create two different addresses. The addresses can point to the same or two different websites. Typically, the second site is a "welcome page" that contains referring links to your destination site to increase your main site's link popularity. Visitors simply click-through the welcome page to your main website. Be sure to make the welcome page sufficiently different to not be a direct copy of your main home page.

---

validated as a good site. Be sure to use the correct category with a good description.

Costly Mistakes to Avoid in Your Strategic Linking Campaign

Remember, the purpose of strategic links is to add value to your website visitors' experience. Strategic link pages are a very useful feature for visitors. Reciprocal strategic linking will also increase traffic to your site—as long as link partner sites attract a similar target audience. Because Internet visitors are purposeful, they will return to your site— even after clicking off to other sites—if your site gives them valuable "sticky" content beyond properties for sale. At the end of the day, increased link popularity will also enhance your search marketing placement. Yet, never forget that your primary purpose is to add value for your visitors.

Here are some mistakes to avoid:

☑ Avoid link categories generally that are in left field compared to the subject and theme of your site: real estate, housing, shelter, moving, and local area.

☑ Avoid links from partners whose sites' purpose is not related to your site or who exhibit low integrity or blast mass e-mails soliciting links ("link spamming").

☑ Avoid "free-for-all" link sites, "link farms," and unrelated "link exchanges" where the sole purpose in swapping links is to increase link popularity, not to help visitors. Even worse, avoid sites whose purpose is to harvest *your* URL or e-mail address. Hundreds of links on a page can be a tip-off.

☑ Don't be afraid to ask off-topic link partners to "link off." Share with the partner that both your sites are being penalized. Search engines compare *reputation* (what a page is known for as reflected by your link partner sites) and your site's *topic* (what your content is actually about). If reputation and topic don't match, both sites are penalized with reduced rankings.

☑ Avoid bulk submission programs that send "blanket" e-mails requesting links. Instead, individualize every link swap request as much as possible—note an appealing feature of their site or shared keywords, include their links page URL, talk about their business, ask a site-related question, anything to personalize your request.

☑ Avoid using a "parked" domain site that's directed to a copy of your main site stuffed with lots of links back to your main site. Instead, it is more effective to create unique stand-alone sites from scratch, with valuable content for visitors (not copied clones of your main site) for those redirection domains.

☑ Avoid dead links and the dreaded "HTTP 404—file not found" error messages by monitoring links on your site to be sure they are active.

eRainmaker Strategy #4: Invest in Pay-per-Performance Advertising Links

In the previous chapter, we discussed numerous techniques to promote direct navigation to your website using offline and online tactics. In the offline world, such as newspapers or homes magazines, the publication provides you tear sheets from the publication to prove your ad ran. On the Internet, there is no industrywide practice comparable to tear sheets for proof of performance.

To fill that gap, savvy eRainmakers have taken advantage of a new link advertising technique generally called pay-per-performance (PPP). In a nutshell, PPP marketers only charge you for results, not for placing the ad. Instead of paying to run an advertisement, you pay for the results the ad produces. What a concept! This is possible because both the marketer and the advertiser can track the click-throughs. It's also why PPP search marketing is one of the fastest growing promotional techniques online today.

Online PPP advertising allows you to stretch your online promotion budget with guaranteed results. Even better, performance statistics allow you to pinpoint what works—and what doesn't. With PPP you can adjust your ad or link text or location or offer or your budget until you find a mix that is profitable for you. As every eRainmaker knows, tying your e-strategy to results—not exposure—is the road to higher income. What is more, by capturing the PPP prospect in an automated e-mail follow-up program, you can turn a one-shot ad campaign into a permission-based Trophy E-Mail Database you can work for years—guaranteeing the profitable results that repetition and relationships continually provide.

Successful eRainmakers use four different online types of pay-per-performance promotions:

1. *Pay-per-view:* Typically, the business model of larger websites. These portals charge for the number of times the page containing your ad is viewed or downloaded. Marketers refer to this exposure technique as the "war for eyeballs." From the advertiser's perspective, you must accept the word of the website that their traffic statistics are valid and reflect true performance. Prices are based on a "more traffic, higher price" model and may be quoted in CPM (Cost per Thousand), where M is the Roman numeral for thousand.

2. *Pay-per-click:* You pay a certain amount for each click-through to your website. Rates vary considerably. Some sites charge higher rates because they add on some "branding value" for exposing your site to eyeballs, even though not all prospects click-through.

3. *Pay-per-lead:* In this situation, you pay for each lead the site generates; typically you pay for the information a prospect enters into a response form on the site. This prospect information

is forwarded to you, sometimes by matching your service area to the area of interest or zip code of the prospect.

4. *Pay-per-closing.* Think of this as similar to a traditional referral fee, which it typically is. You only pay for deals generated by the site when a transaction closes.

Expose Yourself to Prospects with Pay-per-View

Pay-per-view can work wonders, especially if you use eye-catching property photos or listing enhancements or banner ads (horizontal shape), skyscrapers (vertical shape) or pop-unders with dynamic graphics or direct-response animation. A powerful, customer-centered response offer can also swell results, especially when you add links to a basic biography page on the portal site. With banner ad response trending lower in recent years, however, use of the pay-per-view advertising model has declined since the 1990s, partly because additional photos and banner ads can appear costly when it's hard to track results. As time goes on more banner ad sites are converting to pay-per-click when someone clicks on your ad and goes to your site. Services have emerged (eRainmaker.com: Performance Advertising) to match website publishers and advertisers, and to provide the tracking and billing services portals need to offer an alternative to pay-per-view banner ads.

Generating Traffic Using Pay-per-Click Search Engines

With over three billion web pages catalogued by search engines globally, your site can easily get lost in the crowd.

For a fee, some search engines will place your site higher in the rankings. This can be accomplished by buying straightforward pay-per-view banner ads or top-of-page sponsored links. A budget-stretching approach is to use pay-per-click search engines (PPCSE). If no one clicks on your link, you don't pay.

Pay-per-click search engines work this way. You open an account, make a minimum deposit as a starting balance, enter your site's URL, title and description and bid on relevant keywords, such as "real estate," "realty," "homes for sale," and so on. When a visitor searches for "real estate" on the search engine where you have an account, the details of your site, including your URL, appear. Sites are typically ranked by the amount you are willing to pay per click with top bid at top of the list. When the visitor clicks on your link, your account is debited the amount you have bid on that keyword.

Ideally, visitors are "qualified" by the fact that they searched for your targeted keywords. The largest search engines accept paid and free listings. Some pay-per-click search engines only list websites willing to pay for their placement, so most if not all of the listed websites are about products or services, not informational sites such as schools, government, charities, or nonprofits. That's one reason why pay-per-click search engines tend to deliver genuine prospects.

The biggest advantage of pay-per-click search engines is you can register dozens—even hundreds—of keywords that will bring up your site at the top of different results lists. That way you can promote many minor keywords that get minimal response without having to pay for them until they perform. The downside to keyword pay-per-click is that common real estate lead-generating keywords are well known in the industry. The competition for keywords, especially from portals with deeper advertising pockets than individual real estate practitioners, tends to drive up the price advertisers will bid for an essential keyword. Also, you may get sellers and buyers interested in areas outside your market area (simply refer them to another real estate professional who services the area).

If you haven't already done so, go to Overture.com and type a market area into the "Search the Web" box, such as "Northern Virginia real estate." Next, click "View Advertisers' Max Bids." You'll see that the number-one ranked site under "Northern Virginia real estate" (as this book was written) is paying $5.01 to Overture every time someone clicks on the link to their website. Placement on Overture affects your placement on other major search engines, such as MSN, Yahoo, Lycos, AltaVista, InfoSpace. With Overture's "sponsored listings," advertisers bid for placement within search results (the highest bidder gets the highest rank). The paid listings are followed by "additional listings" that are ranked by content relevance. Only advertisers pay each time a customer clicks on their sponsored listing on the Overture website or across its affiliate network.

Many other submission services are available. To learn more, visit eRainmaker.com: Pay-per-Click.

Capturing Live Prospects with Pay-per-Lead Is Another Effective Model

Another variation of the pay-per-performance approach is the pay-per-lead model of some search engines. Prospects submit the type of service they need (buying, selling, or both) and where they are located. The request is forwarded by e-mail to a licensed real estate professional that has registered for that city, county, or zip code. The registered real estate professional responds with a proposal directly to the prospect, and the prospect decides to work with the professional or not. The agent or broker pays a flat fee (for example, buy only: $29.95; sell only: $49.95; buy and sell: $69.95) for each valid lead (i.e., valid contact information including working e-mail, truly interested in real estate and of legal age) or the subscriber gets credit back for leads that prove to be nonqualified.

Pay-per-lead advertising can be particularly effective for real estate professionals specializing in higher-end market areas. Leads are worth more if the service is provided exclusively within a zip code or territory. Be sure to ask if service charges upfront fees, monthly membership fees, or referral fees (percent of closed transaction) in addition to price per lead. Look for services where you can cap the number of leads you receive initially to test the service, or to stay within budget. Before you register, determine if you can pause your leads or cancel the program anytime. Expect the service to provide an environment that provides introductory contact with prospects, but does not cultivate or work the leads for you. For lead-generating services, visit eRainmaker .com: Pay-per-Lead.

A variation of the pay-per-response technique that doesn't cost you anything is to use a Guest Book or a giveaway offer or other response offers on your own website to capture leads from your own site visitors. The big advantage of a paid-lead service is that it expands your prospecting net to a wider circle of traffic that hasn't found your site yet.

Using Pay-per-Closing Technique from Licensed Referral Service

The fourth technique is a referral membership service that is a licensed broker and charges a referral fee for closed transactions. This find-an-agent resource e-mails you anonymous buyer and seller prospects that have requested a proposal for their specific situation. Prospects are attracted with a "no obligation, free, online" service that allows the prospect to evaluate an agent based on the agent's proposal and presentation. One of the leaders in the field is Home-Gain (HomeGain.com). Here's how it works.

Prospects register and request a proposal or enter a search for properties for sale. You send a personalized response via an online form. Prospects read the responses and make direct contact with the real estate professionals they select. Then you market your services and close the agreement. Currently, HomeGain charges a monthly membership fee to new members and a 25% referral fee upon close of escrow by a prospect to whom the member has sent a proposal. HomeGain assumes a minimum brokerage commission of 2% when calculating the referral fee amount. Visit the site for FAQs and contact members of Century Club (more than $100,000 in gross commissions from HomeGain leads) and President's Club (more than $50,000 in gross commissions) to get their take on the value of the leads.

Heidi Mueller (sfrelo.com) with Prudential California Realty in San Francisco, California, was HomeGain's Top Online Producer nationwide for 2001 and 2002, and has collected more than $310,000 in gross commissions from HomeGain transactions. "Internet customers today are very educated, sometimes over informed," said Mueller. "They have lots of information. What they need is someone to make sense out of that information. I give them context and advice and coach them about the pros and cons of each property."

Mueller builds trust with HomeGain prospects through her experience and straight-shooting advice. "I tell them what I do for them, how I work, point them to my website, and personalize the information based on their requests." Mueller's website plays a key role. "My site is just like me, very personal. People get the information they want and need, and I make the website fun. What I don't do is try to fit everybody into a pattern, into a template. Just be a real person. Be yourself. The secret is how you listen to your clients," said Mueller. "Every one of my clients is a VIP."

HomeGain is the most effective site Mueller has used to provide leads and have those leads turn into business. "When customers contact me through HomeGain they have money and they're ready. Sometimes the customers already know what home they want and need me to get it for them and close the deal." Mueller closed 60 sales in

2002. Twenty-six of those clients came from HomeGain. "I love HomeGain!" said Mueller.

Another HomeGain success story comes from Stephen O'Hara (SteveOhara.com), who is perennially in the top 100 RE/MAX United States sales teams, a Chairman's Club winner and a RE/MAX Lifetime Hall of Famer with RE/MAX Real Estate Services in Monarch Beach, California. O'Hara has been using the Internet to generate business since the mid-1990s and owns the sought-after URL: OrangeCountyRealEstate.com. "I made it a priority to check out what came down the pike," O'Hara said. "Not just what had sex appeal, but what had true functionality." O'Hara uses WebTrends to track traffic on his website that averages more than 1,000 unique visitors per month with nearly half returning multiple times for 2,500 to 3,500 total visitor sessions monthly.

O'Hara's HomeGain success comes from being open with the information he provides to HomeGain prospects, and not being secretive about fees, addresses, and prices to get a name and number out of prospects. "I don't go for the close right off the bat. Instead I use language in my e-mail that's not too 'salesy' and more relationship building." O'Hara sticks with a prospect as long as it takes. "Many agents drop a prospect after two or three e-mails and don't work the people." Gradually the e-mails go from formal to friendly until O'Hara sometimes gets a sense he can clown around with the prospect. "I once sent self-tanning lotion to a prospect in Wisconsin to use until they got here." Overall, O'Hara's team averages about 150 transactions worth $50 million a year. Part of that production is more than $55,000 in gross HomeGain commissions over time. "HomeGain more than pays for itself," O'Hara said.

Blending Online Savvy with Offline Service to Succeed

Richard and Brooke Hiers (RealEstateHelpDesk.net), a top-selling couple with First Team Real Estate in Seal Beach, California, have done just about everything right with their e-marketing from their branded domain and website to generating website traffic. "Using third-party vendors, such as Overture, to place my website at the top of search engines has been extremely helpful to drive targeted audiences to my website," said Richard Hiers. "Our site averages about

3,000 unique visitors per month, with 75 to 80 of those visitors providing accurate personal information during registration."

One unexpected lesson Hiers' learned about e-marketing came offline. "By far, the biggest mistake in driving traffic to our website actually doesn't involve getting visitors to arrive," Richard Hiers recalled. "It was a failure to get back to basic prospecting techniques with those visitors. A great website with lots of visitors can lull an agent into believing the phone will magically ring. It won't. Every visitor needs to be proactively and systematically followed up—by e-mail, U.S. mail, and the telephone—to qualify them and get them to emerge from cyberspace."

Driving Traffic to Your Website: Search Marketing Basics

Times Have Changed

Old conventional wisdom said for a website to survive, it *had* to be at the top of the search engines. Times have changed. With more than 30 million domains registered and with search engine criteria changing constantly, search engines simply are not the way most prospects (only 16%) find a website among the glut of competition. Yet, for first-time visitors and prospects with a purpose, online search engines are analogous to offline Yellow Pages—a basic reference tool if not a primary source of business. Today, web prospects act more like hunters than gatherers—even Apple's latest browser is called "Safari" compared to Microsoft's venerable "Explorer."

It has always been difficult for website owners playing the "search marketing" game to predict all the search criteria most prospects will use when they are looking for real estate information. Once you do succeed at the search-engine-placement game and rank near the top of the lists, numerous competitors surround your listing with their listings ready to take your prospects. Yet some real estate professionals swear by search engines. Others find their website at the top of search lists regularly. What's the secret? Here's how they do it.

Six Strategies to Maximize Your Search Engine Rank

Having a website that search engines can't find is like winking in the dark. You know you're doing it. But nobody else does. Still visitors can get to your site other ways—and usually do.

A search engine (also, *search directory*) is a cross between the phone book and a library card catalog on steroids. Not only can users search by title and author and subject (and other data fields), but the search engine also scans website content for key terms and can tell how many other sites are linked to yours. Because every search engine programmer has tried to invent a better "mousetrap," every search engine uses different criteria and prioritizes each factor differently.

Adapting your site to meet as many criteria of as many search engines as possible is called "search-engine optimization." You know you are doing it right when your website moves up to a higher rank (also, called placement). As you would expect, entire businesses and specialists have emerged who do nothing else but advise you how to optimize your site for search engines. Search engines themselves often make money by selling ads and sponsored links that display advertisers messages alongside matching search results. The more traffic the search engine site gets, the more it can charge for its pay-per-view ads (what marketers call the "media model," similar to newspapers and television) or pay-per-performance links.

Nielsen/NetRatings is one of the leading Internet and digital media audience information and analysis services. Table 7.1 shows the percentage of U.S. Internet users that conducted a search on a top 12 search engine site at least once during January 2003. More than 60,000

Table 7.1
Consumer Use of Top 12 Search Engines

Search Engine	Consumer Use (%)
1. Google	29.5
2. Yahoo	28.9
3. MSN	27.6
4. AOL	18.4
5. Ask Jeeves	9.9
6. Overture (acquired by Yahoo late 2003)	4.8
7. InfoSpace	4.5
8. Netscape	4.4
9. Altavista	4.0
10. Lycos	2.4
11. EarthLink	2.0
12. LookSmart	1.7

Source: Nielsen/Net Ratings, January 2003.

home and work users were measured with real-time computer meters to estimate these figures. Because a web searcher may visit more than one service, the combined totals exceed 100%. The top four search engines—Google, Yahoo!, MSN, and AOL—accounted for the bulk of all search referrals in this study.

Here are six successful eRainmaker strategies to maximize your search engine results. Use them yourself or use them to get what you want when you talk to an expert for hire.

eRainmaker Strategy #1: Use Software to Automate Registration and Reporting

Top eRainmakers have learned three critical lessons about search engines.

1. Getting your site ranked in the first 10 to 30 matches (equivalent of first three pages) in major search engines is the difference between being found and being lost in the haystack.

2. More than 90% of search engine referrals come from a handful of major search engines—not the scores or hundreds of no-name sites whose real purpose may be to collect e-mail addresses from Internet marketers to send them promotions from other marketers.

3. Adapting the pages on your website to meet search engine criteria (also, search engine optimization or SEO) requires expert advice, web designer implementation, and constant monitoring. This expertise naturally requires a significant learning curve and has spawned a need for specialists you can hire, which can be a sizable investment for delivering substantial, ongoing results.

Many eRainmakers have found an easier way: Buy a software program (some sell for about $150) that tells you in plain words what to do, then delegate the task to your virtual assistant or tech staff. Several excellent search engine optimization software packages are on the market (eRainmaker.com: Search, General).

Checklist of Search Engine Placement Tools Your Software or Specialist Should Provide

☑ *Analyze traffic.* You'll need a traffic log that counts and delivers reports to determine what keywords or phrases people use to search your site and which search engines send your site the most and least traffic.

☑ *Critique pages.* You'll want expert advice that tells you exactly how to optimize each web page—either existing or new pages—to match the unique personality of each major search engine index criteria.

☑ *Generate pages.* Using keywords, phrases, and descriptions of your business, you or staff or web designer must create optimized pages. Experienced eRainmakers know some of the most popular pages will become alternate entrances to your website—giving targeted prospects (and search engines) even more opportunities to find your site.

☑ *Upload pages.* Once an optimized page has been created on a local computer, the file will be transferred (uploaded) to the Internet server computer that maintains your site at an internet protocol (IP) address or domain name that visitors open. Files can be transferred using the file transfer protocol (FTP) program in the software or your own FTP program.

☑ *Submit pages to search engines.* Your web pages will be submitted to search engines. In some cases, search engines accept automated registration. Others require manual submissions. It can be a plus to have a "slow submit" program that emulates manual submissions.

☑ *Schedule uploads and submissions.* You will want to repeat the process regularly of analyzing traffic logs, generating re-optimized pages, uploading pages, and submitting pages to search engines. Ideally you'll want the software to be able to automatically schedule this process, whether it is daily, weekly, monthly, or quarterly. Have your virtual assistant keep on top of this important task.

☑ *Multiply results.* As time goes by, you may want to use this process for multiple websites, unlimited major and minor keywords, unlimited pages, and numerous search engines. Having the ability to grow as your e-strategy grows often makes your initial software shopping criteria pay off.

eRainmaker Strategy #2: Content, Content, Content

Search engines usually read the first 500 words from each page and use that text to create a relevance index for a particular search term. Weave your keywords into your content (remember, humans are your primary reader, not the search computer) to make your web pages more likely to be relevant for keyword searches. By focusing on quality content, your website naturally becomes more attractive for other sites to link to without having to request a reciprocal link. For example, visit the website of top producer Ron Henderson (CharlestonExpert.com) with Century 21 Properties Plus Charleston in North Charleston, South Carolina, and scroll down to the Site Map section at the very bottom of every page that's chock-full of keywords blended into the content, a standard feature of sites provided by Best Image Marketing (BestImage.com) (see Figure 7.1).

COSTLY MISTAKE TO AVOID

You cannot trick the search engines. Flooding the engines with multiple versions of the same page, or repeating the same term over and over, can actually hurt your rating—and possibly get your site banned from being listed in a search engine.

Figure 7.1
Site Map Posts Keyword Collection on Every Page

Source: Courtesy of Ron Henderson (CharlestonExpert.com), Century 21 Properties Plus Charleston, North Charleston, South Carolina.

eRainmaker Strategy #3: Use Metatags, Title, and Description

In the source code at the top of most web pages, the web designer places HTML *metatags* to help describe the document. In the 1990s, these metatags were the primary way to attract search engine traffic. Today, metatags no longer dominate search engine results now that content, link popularity, and link structure have joined the mix. Yet, metatags are still important.

Title, description, and keywords are the three most important metatags that search engines focus on to help them determine the relevance of a website for a particular search phrase. Experienced eRainmakers use an internal site search engine to determine what keywords

---

eRainmaker Tip

Inside Specs: Titles should be less than 80 characters; contain words and phrases that accurately describe your page; be unique and relevant; and use every title-tag word somewhere in the page itself. Dick Mathes (RelocationIowa.com) with Home Realty Group in Mason City, Iowa, is a master of titles, tags, and domains. Mathes uses this simple but effective title line: "Mason City Iowa Real Estate Homes Listings—Home Realty Group IA."

---

people use to find or search your site. You may be surprised. Watch for search terms you hadn't considered when you originally built the site (eRainmaker.com: Search, Internal).

TITLE TAG

The title tag should describe exactly what the document contains. It should contain keywords of terms you hope visitors will search, but avoid repeats. The words in your title appear in a searcher's web browser and in the blue title bar at the top of every page—hence the name *title*. The title tag should also make sense and be as readable as possible, because it is the first line prospects read when your site appears in a search result.

DESCRIPTION TAG

The description is a less than 250-character explanation of the page and its contents. The description should contain keywords and phrases, but it should also read like an introductory lead-in for your services and specialty. Using a call to action in the description tag helps maximize results. Again, Dick Mathes provides an excellent description example: "Mason City Iowa Real Estate listings brokerage, North Iowa's Online Homes, Clear Lake IA and North Iowa houses, commercial, relocation and homes realty listings needs. Agent Dick Mathes—Realtor." *Mistake to avoid:* If a user comes to your site and the title and description don't accurately match the content you have published, the visitor is not likely to stick around long.

---

eRainmaker Tip

Be Specific: Your title and description together should be compelling enough to generate a click-through from a search result. Remember, the visitor is looking for something very specific. The description you provide for your page must convince prospects that you provide exactly what they are looking for.

KEYWORD TAG

Keyword tags can be less than 250 characters including spaces but may be longer, using important keywords and phrases consistent with the content and title description. Be specific and accurate when choosing keywords. For an example, visit Dick Mathes' RelocationIowa.com site, drop down the "View" menu and click "Source" (the keywords are too long to repeat here, complete with consumers' common misspellings).

Be sure to include all forms of words that describe your core business: real estate, city/county/regional location, home buying,

---

eRainmaker Tip

A Rose by Any Other Name Would Search as Sweet: How is your site tagged? To find out, take a look at your HTML coding by opening your home page and selecting "View" from your toolbar. Click "Source." Near the top of the coding, you'll see something akin to:

< HTML >

< HEAD >

< TITLE > (your site's title) < TITLE >

< META NAME="description" CONTENT="(your site's description)" >

< META NAME="keywords" CONTENT="(your site's keywords)" >

---

home selling, homeownership, home showings, relocation, property management, and so on. But don't stop there—think creatively. What related information and services do you offer? You might want to include keywords relating to: mortgage loans, city/county/private schools, recreation (golf, parks, etc.), professional sports, cost of living index, employment opportunities, calculator tools, places of worship, other professionals (home inspectors, settlement agents, real estate attorneys), and so on. Include these keywords in the HTML keywords coding. Have your virtual tech consultant work on this. *Mistakes to avoid:* Avoid generic terms that bury your site in huge results lists. Use the same keywords your prospects use as noted by your traffic log.

eRainmaker Strategy #4: Find the Best Keywords

There are two ways to find the best keywords, both requiring keyword analysis software (eRainmaker.com: Keywords), which you can rent for a day or longer period to search the Internet for popular keywords. First, determine what words prospects type into search fields most often. This is called a *root keyword* or *top level keyword*, and it is found doing a vertical search. Second, determine what words competitor sites use most often—or don't use—in their keyword metatags. These secondary keywords are called *related keywords* and they are determined using a lateral search (eRainmaker Tip and Table 7.2).

eRainmaker Strategy #5: Create an Easy Road Map with Navigation

Clean link navigation on your website is critical for search engine optimization. Most important, it creates a site that's easy for prospects to use. It also increases the likelihood search engines will index larger parts of your website. Think of good navigation for your website as similar to good street directions and signage for an open house. The easier and more convenient directions are, the more traffic visits the open house—and you deliver more prospects for your home sellers.

Search engines use the navigation links within your website to crawl and index the pages that are connected to the links. A search engine starts at your home page and, ideally, crawls through your

---

eRainmaker Tip

Finding Best Keywords: To illustrate the process, we searched four common industry keywords—real estate, homes, realty, house for sale—to learn what words prospects are typing to find real estate websites. What we found was you can't assume the list generated by one keyword search will be the same list for another closely related keyword.

Each of our four-keyword searches turned up several unique top-level keywords that didn't show up on the lists generated by the other keyword searches. These unique keywords are less popular than keywords that appear multiple times in the results listing, yet should be included to maximize your results. When you find *underutilized* word(s) not being used by competitors (lateral search) but that do appear on the consumer list (vertical search), you've hit pay dirt. Beat the competition by inserting those underutilized keywords in your website keyword list and in the content of your pages.

In Table 7.2, unique underutilized keywords are not shaded. Even though plural and singular are two different words from a search engine's viewpoint, for illustration plural and singular are shaded in the table as if they truly were identical. (Example: "House" and "Houses" are not a true match, but to simplify our illustration they are shaded as a match in the table.)

---

entire website using the links as a road map. Search engines can crawl several types of links:

- ☑ *Standard text links,* ideally containing keywords;
- ☑ *Site-map pages* with links to major sections on the site (keep it simple);
- ☑ *Image maps* where regions within a large graphic contain different links;
- ☑ *Hotspots* where the entire graphic image is a link.

The more of your website the search engine sees, the more times you will appear in a search result for a certain topic. *Mistake to avoid:*

Table 7.2
Popular and Underutilized Real Estate Keywords

Columns: Commonly searched keywords by rank (repeated words are shaded).
Non-shaded words indicate popular keywords searched by prospects but not used
by competitor sites.

Keyword Rank	Real Estate	Homes	Realty	House for Sale
1	Real estate	Homes	Realty	House for sale
2	Home	Real estate	Real estate	Real estate
3	Real estate listings	Home	Property	House
4	Home for sale	Houses	Homes	Property
5	Homes for sale	Construction	Realtor	For sale
6	House for sale	Mortgage	Commercial	Sale
7	Homes	Relocation	Land	Houses
8	Houses for sale	Builder	Residential	For sale by owner
9	Realty	Property	House	Home
10	Florida real estate	House	Relocation	Property for sale

Source: Gooder Group search in WordTracker by MarketLeap.com, January 8, 2003.

Search engines have problems crawling links contained in dynamic HTML, Javascript, and Flash based pages. These technologies use languages and commands that a search engine crawler or "spider" can't easily travel. When a search engine sees one of these dynamic elements, it may stop crawling any deeper. Thus, much of the valuable content contained inside will never appear in a search result.

eRainmaker Strategy #6: Promote Your Most Popular Pages

Interior pages, not your home page, often attract very targeted buyer or seller prospects. That's because the prospects are looking for very

---

eRainmaker Tip

Free Search Engine Submissions: Many search engines and directories provide a free submissions page where you can submit your website and a few pages to be included in their results. Be sure to read the search engine's submission guidelines and avoid submitting your site unnecessarily or excessively. Using free submission pages doesn't guarantee your site will be included, but if you don't first succeed keep trying and resubmit in 8 to 10 weeks to get your page listed. (eRainmaker.com: Search, Free Placement)

---

specific information, such as listings in a specific community or relocating with teenagers or first-time home buying or changing out-of-state driver's licenses or certain communities or school districts. That also means these motivated prospects are more likely to request a related service or submit a response form on a targeted content page.

Innovative eRainmakers have learned that search engines create multiple entry points into your website. While your home page may be the page people find most often, especially through direct navigation, websites that have multiple pages indexed with multiple search engines pull more targeted prospect traffic to these specific pages located deep within the website. The secret is to use a traffic log analysis service to monitor traffic to your site and find out what are the most popular entry pages. Once you know what leads visitors to your site, promote those interior pages and content online and offline. (eRainmaker.com: Statistics)

An Easier Way to Earn the Big Bucks

Almost every eRainmaker I have met says they have better things to do with their time than become expert in a specialized field that doesn't make them as much money as listing and selling property. Remember, you are the engine that drives your business. Without a system and staff to run your business, your practice will only run as fast as you can peddle. Take a moment to calculate your hourly rate (divide your gross commission income for last year by 2,000 hours, e.g., $100,000 by 2,000 = $50/hour). Then ask yourself if you can delegate a task to someone who earns a lower hourly rate. If you can, do it. You'll be ahead of the game. Now you are working on your business, not at your business.

CHAPTER 8

Capturing E-Leads from Your Website

Online Marketing Is Not That Different . . . But It's Not the Same Either

Gathering information about your website's visitors is essential to developing relationships with them. But getting your visitors to divulge that information can be a challenge. After all, they don't know you— why should they trust you?

Study after study confirms that privacy and security issues are major concerns for many (perhaps even most) Internet users. For example, a study by AT&T (Research.ATT.com/projects/privacystudy) found Internet users are relatively comfortable providing e-mail addresses online, but are very uncomfortable about providing other contact information (phone numbers, street addresses); credit card and

113

social security numbers; and information about the names, ages, or addresses of their children.

The AT&T study also noted, "While respondents were concerned about the kind of information they provided to a website, how it would be used and whether it would identify them, the most important factor was whether it would be shared with others."

Another study, conducted by Georgia Tech, reported that 80% of respondents said they were "somewhat" or "very" concerned about security on the Internet. When conducting business online, 62% of respondents valued privacy over convenience.

Asked under what conditions they would provide demographic information to a website, 73.1% in the Georgia Tech study said they would do so if a statement was provided regarding how the information was going to be used; 31% said they would do so in exchange for some value-added service.

Allaying concerns about privacy and security is critical if you hope to secure the kind of information you need to establish relationships with your website visitors. The idea is to build trust, and there are a number of ways you can do that on your site.

1. *Put the customer first.* Above all, website visitors are searching for information and answers to their questions. Put the information they want first and highest on your site. Save the personal sales promotion for later.

2. *Show them you are real.* Prominently display your phone and toll-free numbers and street address. Make it easy for "ready" prospects to contact you in the method they're most comfortable using e-mail, phone, mail, fax, or office visit. Introduce yourself and your company deeper in your website, so visitors get a sense of who they're communicating with once they are interested. Add pictures of yourself, your team members, or your office building to show people you aren't a cyber-phantom.

3. *Get permission to follow-up.* Ask people to "opt in" for any subscription or information services you offer. Don't neglect to include a cancellation or opt-out mechanism, too. People just want to know they are in control.

4. *Use a confirmation autoresponder.* Put an e-mail autoresponder on your web forms so those who submit e-mail inquiries receive fast confirmation that their message was received and a more

detailed response will follow shortly. When you are away, set your e-mail program to send an "out-of-office" message. Respond as soon as possible, though. The first bird gets the worm.

5. *Publish a privacy policy.* Link to your privacy statement prominently on every page, especially on web forms. It can be as simple as a reassuring sentence: "E-mail addresses are kept private." Or "We respect your privacy and will keep your personal information completely confidential as stated in our Privacy Policy." Or "We never have and never will share your e-mail with anyone else." If you publish a complete policy (highly recommended), indicate how prospect's information would be used. Explain the security measures that are in place to ensure visitors' information remains private. Promise not to sell or trade the information to any other business or individual.

6. *Collect third-party endorsements.* Provide testimonials from other satisfied clients, including their names and city. Invite visitors to contact you for a list of people they can contact directly for recommendations, or post the comments and photos of happy customers on your site.

31 Hot Website Response Offers to Fill Your E-Prospect Pipeline

Ever wonder how top websites capture visitors? In a nutshell, the secret is to use as many of these proven effective direct-response offers as possible on your website. Every offer is designed to grab attention, compel a reply, and *always* asks prospects to complete their contact information:

1. *Free reports:* These include printed brochures, booklets, homes magazines, videos, virtual tours on diskette, newsletters, even books and relocation kits sent by regular mail. Not only do you capture accurate invaluable addresses, but also consumers receive proof of your responsiveness and consumer-oriented focus.

2. *E-reports:* An auto-responder sends e-mail with text links to electronic reports on specific topics. This works equally well with "ready" shoppers and "arm's length" information gatherers. Graphic HTML e-reports tend to get better reply response

than text-only reports. Be sure to include "call-to-action" links (such as Contact Us, Forward to Friend, Refer a Friend) and live links to your website. Include all your contact information on every e-report for visitors who print reports to keep or share with friends.

3. *Automated property updates:* Often labeled "Market Watch," "Home Finder," "Property Tracker," or "Dream Catcher," this service automatically sends notification, typically by e-mail but sometimes by fax or direct mail, of "new on market" properties or price reductions that match the buyer's dream home search profile. If your MLS does not provide the service, check popular providers listed at eRainmaker.com: Property Updates. Again, include complete signature and contact information.

4. *Find my dream home:* This powerful offer promises a one-time computerized sweep of all available homes for sale to produce a "Real Search," "Wish List," "Drive-Buy Home Tour," or "Personal Shopper" list of properties that match the features provided by the prospect. Prospects register their dream home features and provide complete contact information.

5. *Price estimate/market value:* Nothing attracts sellers better than finding out what their home is worth. Follow the lead of top eRainmakers who offer two types of service to qualify prospects upfront: Opinion of Value or Broker Price Opinion (delivered by phone within 24 hours), which provides an estimated price range; and a written CMA (promised in person 48 hours after first appointment to tour property), which includes recent comparables. For prospective sellers who ask, "What's my home worth?," several web-based property valuation services will provide a valuation to a consumer for a fee (eRainmaker.com: E-Valuations). Check out the instant online valuation service at MSN.com provided by Freddie Mac (MSN.com > House & Home > Selling Your Home > Estimate a Home's Value; requires sign-in to create a Microsoft .NET Passport account but otherwise is free). (See Figure 8.1.)

6. *Seller's package:* Designed to capture prospective sellers who are shopping for a real estate professional, this powerful offer includes information about the selling process. The response package is a prelisting kit, typically on paper but also on CD or via e-mail. The kit contains everything except a comprehensive

Figure 8.1
Specialty URL Links to CMA Offer at EmailHomeValue.net

Source: Courtesy of Prudential Northwest Properties (PruNW.com), Portland, Oregon.

market analysis for the seller's property. This two-step approach generates the lead. Follow-up closes an appointment to visit the property to review its marketability and make a listing presentation.

7. *Open anytime:* A powerful offer that turns classified ads for other brokers' open houses into prospects for you is sometimes called "Always Open" or "Open Yesterday." Prospects who couldn't get to other brokers' advertised open houses can

---

eRainmaker Tip

#5 Navigation Labels: Free Home Evaluation, What's My Home Worth?, Top Dollar Analysis, Request CMA, Seller Price Estimate, Right Price Analysis, What's It Worth?, Instant Real Estate Valuation.

---

eRainmaker Tip

#6 Navigation Labels: Sell A Home, Tips for Sellers, Seller's Package, Selling Your Home, Road Map for Sellers, Getting Top Dollar, Seller Marketing System.

---

submit several addresses to you during the week after the open houses, and receive one-stop property information by e-mail. Drive active shopper traffic to your "Open Anytime" website offer with a classified ad in the "Open Today" section ("Don't Lose This Page" or "Call Us in the Morning" are effective headlines), as well as handouts at your open houses.

8. *Schedule a showing:* The key to this offer is telling prospects you have it. Simply put, add a response form to your site where prospects list the properties they want to visit in person when they are ready. Often, eRainmakers qualify prospects first, either by requiring an in-office consultation, buyer's representation agreement or loan qualification by a lender. Next, prospects get a list of properties they can drive by. "When you see one you want to buy," the eRainmaker says, "just login, send us the addresses, and suggest a convenient time. We'll make the arrangements for a personal home tour." Brokerages and mega-agents with scores of listings have had outstanding success with the automated appointment-setting services that allow an hour-by-hour schedule to be maintained on unlimited properties (eRainmaker.com: Schedule Showings).

9. *Sweepstakes/giveaway contest:* Capture contact information by offering something of value related to home buying or selling, such as "Curb Appeal Makeover" or "Full House Power Wash." Everybody loves something free. *Caution:* All state and federal rules regarding sweepstakes may apply, especially because Internet prospects could live anywhere. Be sure to get legal advice on contest rules and disclosure.

10. *Survey:* Surveys work best when submission also enters prospects in a drawing or sweepstakes. Home-related prizes are the most effective, particularly interior furnishings, carpet/floor cleaning, maid service, window treatments, or winner's choice

because these interior items appeal to homeowners as well as renters.

11. *Relocation kit:* This proven offline standby to capture out-of-town buyers is still a solid performer online. A "Newcomer Package" meets the needs of the 21% of Internet inquiries that are moving into your market, according to Gooder Group's *Internet Prospect Study* of 4,500+ inquiries generated by our RAINMAKER E-CENTRAL® service in the first six months of 2003. You also get an accurate street address when you offer a Relocation Kit sent through regular mail.

12. *Outbound sellers:* A twist on the typical Relocation Kit, this technique offers assistance to local families considering a relocation to a distant area. Often these prospects need help gathering information to make an "accept/reject" job transfer decision. Information about the destination area as well as a referral to a top-quality real estate professional in that area is a compelling offer. The double bonus comes when you are the first in the door to help them list their old home, as well as generate a possible referral fee with a single long-distance phone call.

13. *Point-to-point relocation:* The Internet has made this lucrative niche explode for savvy eRainmakers. In Gooder Group's 2003 *Internet Prospect Study,* 22% of web leads are point-to-point prospects. These referral prospects live in another area yet discover your site and are interested in property in a third location. No matter if they saw your ads when passing through town or clicked through to your site from a search engine or directory or franchise site, the same referral services you offer local outbound prospects can capture leads from point-to-point prospects. Without the Internet, this target niche was barely a blip on the real estate radar screen. Navigation label: Moving Anywhere? *Caution:* Soliciting prospects that live outside your licensing jurisdiction, whether you intend to refer to others or work prospects directly, should be avoided. Check with legal counsel to understand the rules of "implied intent."

14. *In-file credit report:* Prospects can learn their credit score quickly and easily. Often done with a link to a lender's website or LIONs' Mortgage 101.com content plug-in. Credit report services also have affiliate programs that pay you for sales of credit reports generated from your site (eRainmaker.com: Credit Reports).

---

eRainmaker Tip

#14 Navigation Labels: Free Credit Report. Check Your Credit. Before you buy, know your credit. Free Credit Check. Get a FREE copy of your credit report. (*Remember:* Mortgage loan information originating on your site or framed in your site has special rules, such as RESPA, Reg. Z, and so on, that must be met. Talk to your legal advisor about compliance.)

---

15. *Interest-rate alert:* Ask clients to register their current interest rate, loan balance and monthly payment in return for periodic comparisons with current interest rates to determine when it's time to refinance. Promote the service upfront with your mortgage partner if you plan to lead-swap for this service. Regardless of rates being up or down, your e-mail can say either: "Good news. Your rate is as good as it gets." Or: "Good news. Let us help arrange to save you money by refinancing at today's lower rates."

16. *Calculators and other financial tools:* Offer access to online calculators for subjects such as Buying versus Renting, Moving Cost Estimates, Selling Cost Analysis, Budget to Buy (prequalification), Net Proceeds Analysis, and Trade-Up Down-Payment Analysis (seller's equity). Relocation calculators are popular, such as REALTOR.com's Relocation Wizard, Community Close-Ups, Salary Calculator, and Moving Cost Calculator (eRainmaker.com: Calculators).

17. *Market update:* Offer a service on your website to track home sale values by specific neighborhoods for prospective sellers. This on-going "Just Sold" relationship-builder service can be delivered by e-mail blast with automated e-mail programs (eRainmaker.com: Automated e-mail) or by sharing sold information where MLS rules allow (eRainmaker.com: CMA Updates).

18. *Contact us:* This most basic response can easily be turned to your advantage. Simply include some easily checked qualifying questions (Own or rent? When do you want to move? Selling, buying, relocating, investing?), or a check-off list for

free reports or a list of specific services the prospect can request (CMA, outbound referral, mortgage rates, new home builders, prequalification). Be sure to include your phone, street address, e-mail, fax, and perhaps the name(s) of team members (with job duties) prospects can ask for by name.

19. *Member registration:* Jay Burnham (NorthShoreHomePage .com), an Allen F. Hainge CYBERSTAR® and top producer with Coldwell Banker Residential Brokerage in Beverly, Massachusetts, has turned this technique into an art form. Burnham offers a collection of services as "Membership Benefits" including access to MLS, free reports, daily e-mail updates including property addresses—all for no cost. As Burnham's site says, "All I ask in return is that you will call me to show you any property that you are interested in. I call this a 'Fair Trade.' Will you agree to work with me this way?"

20. *Free agent-referral service:* Some top eRainmakers have made a business decision to accept only specific prospects that fit their business development plan, such as a certain price range, specific market area, exclusive buyers or sellers only. Prospects interested in real estate outside these parameters are referred. Offer a response form on your website to harvest these referral prospects that otherwise might leave your website and go somewhere else. Also, use the referral service as a way to attract other real estate sites to exchange a strategic link with your site.

21. *Prequalify now:* This form features the basic questions needed to prepare a prequalification analysis to estimate the prospect's monthly payment. Successful eRainmakers have learned to expand this lead generator with an offer of a personal consultation about the buying process or to arrange an appointment with a loan officer who could preapprove the prospect for a loan.

---

eRainmaker Tip

#16 Navigation Labels: Payment Calculator, How Much Can You Afford?, Estimate Payments, Free Pre-Qualification, Affordability Analysis, Get Pre-Approved.

22. *Subscribe to e-newsletter:* First get a monthly e-newsletter, either written by you or provided by a service for websites or an e-newsletter sent via e-mail link (eRainmaker.com: e-Newsletters). Next, offer a sign-up form for prospects to subscribe. Add a quick checklist of recent headlines, publication frequency, image of past issue or graphic icon to give sizzle to the offer.

23. *Gateway option:* Invite prospects to enter name and e-mail in return for access to sections of your site. The most effective position for a gateway form is sign-in access to "all the homes

---

Figure 8.2
Small Guest Book Captures Big Results

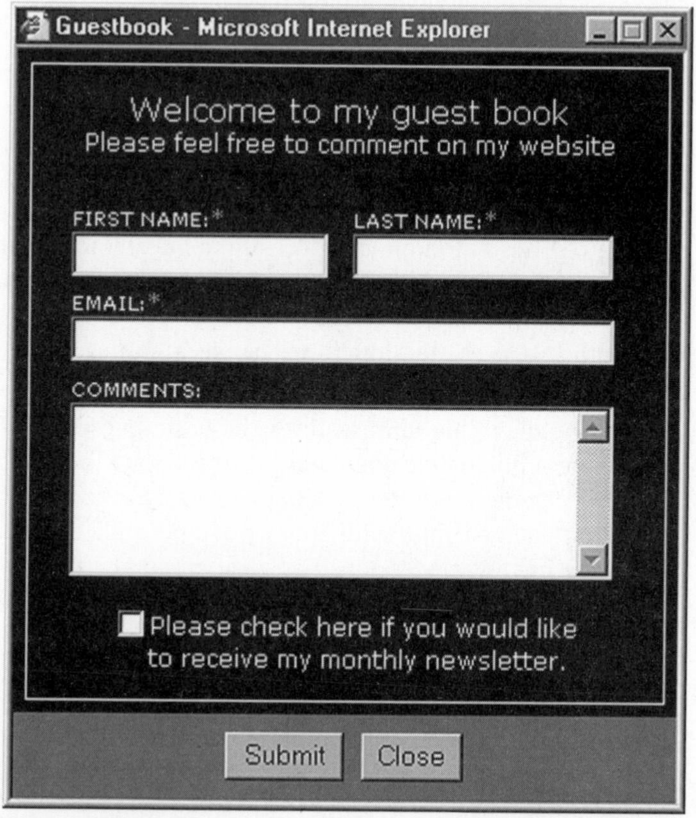

Source: Courtesy of Cindy Andrade (CindyAndrade.com), Realty World—South Bay Associates, San Jose, California.

for sale" in the market, using your MLS website through broker reciprocity Internet data exchange (IDX). Many eRainmakers make the form appear to be required for access but, in fact, registration is voluntary; clicking okay allows access without entry of data. Be sure to check your local MLS broker reciprocity and virtual office website (VOW) rules to see if any restrictions apply in your area regarding voluntary login to access MLS listings.

24. *Guest book:* A guest book is a response form that pops-up in a new window and invites visitors to sign-in (Figure 8.2). Completing the form typically is optional but can be required. Your web designer can program the guest book with a script to automatically send e-mail to you with the visitor's information. The script also can send the visitor a prewritten "Thank you" e-mail. Another popular approach is to use a "pop-under"

Figure 8.3
***"Thank You" Pop-Under Gives One More
Chance with Friendly Persuasion***

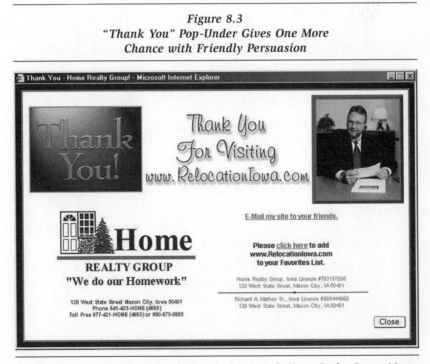

Source: Courtesy of Dick Mathes (RelocationIowa.com), Home Realty Group, Mason City, Iowa.

guest book form that appears when visitors close the website page (Figure 8.3). Often a special incentive gift (such as free software delivered by e-mail auto-responder for household inventory, pet vaccination record, essential phone numbers, or other service) increases the appeal to sign in.

25. *Free school reports:* Broker/owner Kathy Drewien (AtlantaRelo .com) in Atlanta, Georgia, provides invaluable school reports. Drewien offers printable PDF files of county-by-county, school-by-school "Report Cards" provided by the Georgia Department of Education. Prospects are asked to "just fill in this form and we'll direct you to the current list of public school rankings." Only an e-mail address is required, and prospects instantly get a school report menu to pages on Drewien's website. If you don't have local reports, school reports are also available for a fee or subscription (eRainmaker.com: School Reports).

26. *Forward to a friend:* This is a variation of the "e-mail this" form. It sends a page link to a recipient, and sends the name and e-mail address of the sender as well as the recipient's name and e-mail to you. The ultimate "word-of-mouse" technique, this approach is sometimes called *viral marketing,* where one customer generates another possible customer.

27. *Refer a friend:* Another word-of-mouse technique comes right out and asks for the referral. On every Gooder Group E-Report sent by our RAINMAKER E-CENTRAL automated e-mail program, for example, a margin button makes it easy for the contact to send you a direct referral. Here is the customer-focused text we found works best: "Referrals Are Our Business! Our business is thriving because our satisfied clients tell others about our exceptional service. Ultimately, our goal is to provide such outstanding service that all our clients tell all their friends and family. Let us show you how we do it."

28. *One-stop-shop info:* We call this service *e-Hotline* in our Gooder Group website content program, RAINMAKER E-CENTRAL. Prospects are encouraged to collect addresses of properties that interest them—regardless of which broker listed the property— whether they drive by, circle classified ads or homes magazine pictures, or surf the Internet. Prospects are invited to log into *e-Hotline,* enter as many addresses as they wish, and, instantly, the subscriber receives e-mail with full contact information for

easy follow up with MLS information. Some subscribers simply reply with the MLS numbers for the prospect to look up on the IDX portion of their website. Either way, you get the lead, and the prospect gets the information they need for easy one-stop shopping. Best of all you have turned other broker's ads, signs, and open houses into lead generators for you without spending a penny.

29. *Neighborhood sign watch:* This variation of one-stop shopping is oriented more to nearby homeowners. Simply provide a web form where locals can enter the address of a neighborhood house that has been just listed. You respond by phone or e-mail with the particulars about the home for sale—especially the price their neighbors are asking. Be sure to ask if the prospects are thinking of selling and want a current evaluation of their home's value.

30. *What did sellers get?* This is a slightly tongue-in-cheek version of the "Neighborhood Sign Watch" technique. Instead, this service offers to tell neighbors the exact sales price of a particular property that recently sold. Be sure to point out the ratio of listing price to sales price, and the elements of marketability that drive up a home's value in today's market. Also, be sure to ask if the homeowner would like to be put on a special list to receive "just sold" announcements by e-mail or direct mail in the future.

31. *For sale by owner:* This powerful technique can be as simple as an instant e-report, trifold brochure, or "Free FSBO Starter Kit" like the one offered by John F. Williams (MO-RE.com, HireMyTeam.com), a top producer with The MORE Company in St. Louis. From Williams' site prospects can order the downloadable e-book, *Selling Your Home Alone,* by Jim Edwards. The first chapter is free, and then consumer pays $39 for download. Williams earns 50% as reseller. Another approach is to subscribe to a FSBO search service that searches FSBO advertising nationwide and e-mails you daily lists of FSBOs who advertised for the first time in your area (eRainmaker.com: FSBO Leads). In the words of John F. Williams, "Producing a website is like oriental cooking. You have to do the preparation first. Once you have the vegetables chopped and the recipe in hand, the cooking is quick. The same with a website. With the

graphics in hand and the layout in mind, I've created a website from scratch in three hours."

Anatomy of a Response Form

Once your offer compels prospects to click through, you will need a response form (also called "web form") to be filled out and submitted. The form itself is almost as important as the promotion offer in the chain of response. The objective of a well-designed response form is to reinforce the benefits of your offer, as well as make it easy for the prospect to use. Achieving that goal is an art. Forms can be long or short—some require no more than a prospect's e-mail. Become a student of forms on successful eRainmaker sites and experiment with different styles on your site. To guide you, Figure 8.4 is a form with all the elements for illustration.

Six Simple Secrets to Maximize Website Lead Capture

Here are six promotional techniques for presenting your offers to website visitors. Think of them as signage in your Big Box website, directing and attracting traffic to your products and services. In a nutshell, the more ways you present your offers, the more leads you will capture. The best eRainmaker websites promote an offer or response form in as many helpful ways as possible, without being annoying. For example: six presentation techniques times 31 offers could create 186 efforts to capture visitors within one site—and that's only the *beginning* for creative e-marketers and website designers:

1. *Navigation menu:* Often these basic links appear in a top navigation bar or a left-side panel menu. Styles vary from buttons to tabs to straight text and submenus. Every offer should be exposed as a basic navigation option or high-level submenu.

2. *Hotspot images:* A hotspot is a space with a link behind it to another location. Typically, hotspots are graphics, icons, or photos, often with a headline such as "How much is your home worth?" or "Free Stuff" of "Free Reports Now Available," where the entire image is a linked area. Banner ads often are hotspots. Buttons such as "Submit" or "Enter" are hotspots.

Figure 8.4
Anatomy of a Response Form

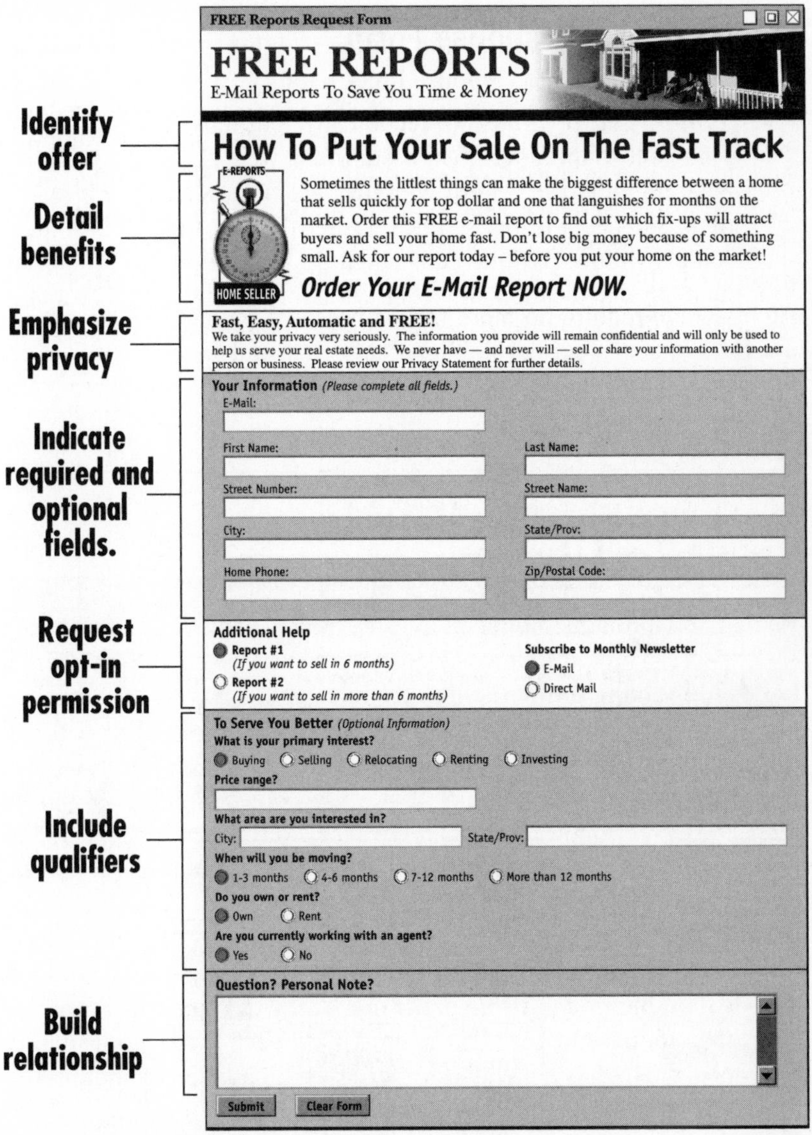

Identify offer

Detail benefits

Emphasize privacy

Indicate required and optional fields.

Request opt-in permission

Include qualifiers

Build relationship

FREE Reports Request Form	□ □ ⊠

FREE REPORTS
E-Mail Reports To Save You Time & Money

How To Put Your Sale On The Fast Track

E-REPORTS

HOME SELLER

Sometimes the littlest things can make the biggest difference between a home that sells quickly for top dollar and one that languishes for months on the market. Order this FREE e-mail report to find out which fix-ups will attract buyers and sell your home fast. Don't lose big money because of something small. Ask for our report today – before you put your home on the market!

Order Your E-Mail Report NOW.

Fast, Easy, Automatic and FREE!
We take your privacy very seriously. The information you provide will remain confidential and will only be used to help us serve your real estate needs. We never have — and never will — sell or share your information with another person or business. Please review our Privacy Statement for further details.

Your Information *(Please complete all fields.)*
E-Mail:

First Name: Last Name:

Street Number: Street Name:

City: State/Prov:

Home Phone: Zip/Postal Code:

Additional Help
● Report #1
(If you want to sell in 6 months)
○ Report #2
(If you want to sell in more than 6 months)

Subscribe to Monthly Newsletter
● E-Mail
○ Direct Mail

To Serve You Better *(Optional Information)*
What is your primary interest?
● Buying ○ Selling ○ Relocating ○ Renting ○ Investing
Price range?

What area are you interested in?
City: State/Prov:
When will you be moving?
● 1-3 months ○ 4-6 months ○ 7-12 months ○ More than 12 months
Do you own or rent?
● Own ○ Rent
Are you currently working with an agent?
● Yes ○ No

Question? Personal Note?

Submit   Clear Form

3. *Text hyperlinks:* Links may be individual word(s), phrases, or the entire sentence or headline where the viewable text can be turned into a hyperlink to a response-form page or window. The most powerful direct-response phrase in e-marketing is "Click here." Look for words and phrases within narrative text that can be turned into response links.

4. *Pop-ups and pop-unders:* Technically, pop-ups (on top of web page) and pop-unders (exposed when web page is closed) are separate windows. These windows are best opened by a visitor click, such as a response form, rather than an in-your-face automatic window. Within pops, include links to related material, such as a Relocation Kit form with further links to a "Moving with Kids" e-report or school information. Done sparingly and

---

Figure 8.5
Specialty Domains Make Great Navigation Links

Source: Courtesy of John F. Williams (MO-RE.com), The MORE Company, St. Louis, Missouri.

with relevance, these techniques can be very effective—and won't annoy visitors to your website.

5. *Specialty domains:* Every web page has a unique address called a Universal Resource Locator (URL). Your destination website URL typically points to your home page. Interior pages on your site also have URLs. Some top eRainmakers use these specialty domains (which read like a call-to-action offer or headline both in offline advertisements and direct mail) as internal navigation within their website (Figure 8.5).

6. *Banner ads:* Banner ads come in many different types and sizes, from "skyscrapers" (tall verticals) to "trucks" (wide horizontals). Use them creatively and mix your methods for maximum response. There are three basic types of banner ads:

   - *Static:* Billboard that doesn't move; entire image is hyperlink "hotspot;" most common sizes are 468 × 60 pixels (truck), 120 × 600 pixels (skyscraper), 300 × 300, 125 × 125 or 120 × 90 pixels (small) and 550 × 550 pixels (pop-under).

   - *Animated:* Motion created through animated graphics interchange format (GIF) images, scrolling text, streaming marquee text; banner ad itself may open and close ("window shade" effect).

   - *Rich media:* Uses interactive elements, such as multiple links or drop-down menus that allow visitor to select particular destination on advertiser's site.

9

Buyer Follow-Up: Converting Website Visits into Contracts

New Rules, New Opportunities

The primary technique for generating buyers has traditionally been to advertise listings. A listing creates its own buyer market of prospect calls through classified and homes magazine ads, yard signs, open houses, just-listed mailers, and the like. The marketing strategy is straightforward: Prospect to get sellers; advertise listings to get buyers. By dominating the listings in a market, top producers could dominate the market. "Control the listings and you control the market," and "If you list, you last," were the marketing maxims until now.

In the 1990s, along came buyer representation and the Internet. The pendulum shifted to a more balanced strategy of marketing to get *both* sellers and buyers. Many eRainmakers realized that, although buyers took more time and listings took more marketing expense, at the end of the year transactions of listings closed and sales closed tended to be 1:1—despite efforts to generate one more than the other. Once a buyer was under agreement (what some marketers call a "buyer listing"), real estate professionals had some protection against buyers naively or deliberately using another agent—and flushing all the time and work put into helping that buyer. Top agents discovered that, once under agreement, buyers could be given a list of homes for sale and turned loose into the marketplace (sometimes dubbed a "Drive Buy Tour"). "Call me when you see one you want to buy!" the agent would shout as the represented buyer drove off happily house hunting. In interviews for this book, more and more eRainmakers tell me most—if not almost all—their new business from new customers comes from their websites (past clients and referrals generated "old" business). Typical was mega-agent Steve Chader (ChaderTeam.com) with Keller Williams Integrity First Realty in Mesa, Arizona, who said more than 85% of his monthly leads now come from his website content—more than his homes magazine ads combined.

The Internet today adds a plethora of new opportunities—and new challenges. In theory, prospects can visit every listing on the MLS from their cyber-armchair, sift through the market and pinpoint the finalist properties that interest them. Once the tech-and-touch prospect chooses a short list of properties, the real estate professional steps in, shows the properties, presents the buyer's offer, negotiates the contract, and shepherds the transaction through to closing.

In practice, the Internet does not change the process, but changes the tools used by real estate professionals to manage the process. At the end of the day, the professional who adopts the best tools gains an edge over the competition. That edge translates into higher production, higher profits, and an ability to manage your offline and online marketing efforts smarter to deliver better service and grow your practice.

Exactly what tools top eRainmakers use to gain that competitive advantage to convert online buyer prospects into signed contracts is the focus of this chapter.

eRainmaker Strategy #1: Unlevel the Playing Field with Enhanced Electronic Advertising

A website without property advertising is like a candy store without chocolate. Both are fun to window shop but once inside, expectations are disappointed. The need to keep the real estate professional central to the transaction—and not be eaten alive by the "lion about to come over the hill" as 1993 NAR president Bill Chee said—was the motivation behind creating the first version of REALTOR.com shortly after Chee's call to arms.

By posting every REALTOR listing for free, including a photo if available, REALTOR.com created the most visited real estate site on the Internet. Every month the portal analyzes consumer behavior from more than 5 million unique visitors and offers a media-model Marketing System menu of property, personal and company online advertising. The unbundled suite is designed by Homestore to be a promotion tool to market listings in the style of an online classifieds that delivers results from REALTOR.com's huge traffic—rather than Homestore's previous strategy to be a one-stop shop for all technology. For two levels of enhanced listings and websites (standard or showcase), fees are paid annually or monthly (additional surcharge). Prices range from $10 to $50 per property. Fees are structured where those with more property ads and more traffic (larger practices in larger markets) pay more, and those with fewer property ads and less exposure pay less. One big plus of REALTOR.com is the added weight search engines give to your link popularity for referring links from the portal to your site, which you can add to your basic REALTOR.com web page.

Frame REALTOR.com

Perhaps the most common and easiest technique to put properties on a personal website is to display REALTOR.com in a *frame,* which allows multiple web pages to be displayed on a single screen. Framing REALTOR.com is permitted as long as the website sponsor is a NAR member that participates in an MLS (Multiple Listing System). Yet framing a portal website, which is a major gateway site large numbers of users visit to start their Internet search, can have its drawbacks. First, the listings are for the entire nation, not the local market which is what mostly interests local visitors. Second, many listings do not include even one photo; much less have multiple exterior and interior photos or virtual tours (12% of REALTOR.com properties were enhanced with additional photos in August 2003). Third, a portal site makes it easy for visitors to "Find a REALTOR" other than you with a few clicks. Fourth, property data cannot be easily rearranged to feature the eRainmaker's own listings or artfully presented with links and graphic lead-capture offers.

Listing Management Software

To fill this need, private vendors created software for websites that allows eRainmakers to add, change, or delete their own listings. Not only are the listings presented in a more pleasing display with thumbnail summaries opening to complete property information and printer friendly versions, but searches and selections are easier and the data can be enhanced with surrounding offers and links. In some markets where the MLS has not moved from proprietary software MLS to an Internet MLS or markets where broker participation in IDX (Internet data exchange) is minimal, listing management software for websites is still an effective tool to gain an advantage (eRainmaker.com: Listing Management).

Internet Data Exchange (IDX, Formerly Internet Data Display or IDD)

Also called *broker reciprocity,* IDX is a form of advertising. To advertise another broker's listings, a real estate professional needs the listing broker's permission. IDX is a means to offer blanket permission to advertise each other's listings. As of January 1, 2002, the National Association of REALTORS required local MLSs to offer IDX to their broker members. All brokerages that choose to "opt in" can display on their websites listings of all other area brokerages that also opt in to the program. Each listing contains the agent's name, brokerage, and contact information. Brokerages that opt out cannot display an opt-in participant's listings, nor are opt-out brokerages' listings included in the exchange. Thus, consumers have free access to all opt-in listings (which may be more or less of the total MLS depending on participation). Consumers are not required to identify themselves to get access. To add IDX listings to a website, all that is needed is an MLS authorized link (URL).

Virtual Office Website (VOW)

Virtual office websites are a form of brokerage, more than advertising. Effective January 1, 2004, the National Association of REALTORS requires the nation's approximately 900 MLSs to offer VOWs to their broker members. Although VOWs are an outgrowth of, and similar to, IDX sites, for listing data on VOWs the MLS can generally apply local rules similar to a property paper printout. VOWs enable individual broker-ages (participants) to display all the MLS listings on their website, including listings of opt-out IDX brokers. (The local MLS may prohibit including some listings, such as those that sellers forbid being elec-tronically displayed, or properties that are expired, withdrawn, or sold, as well as some confidential data fields.) Unlike an IDX site, visitors (registrants) are required to complete an agency disclosure (if required by local law) and "Terms of Use" forms, as well as provide contact in-formation in exchange for a password and access to MLS data. VOW advocates consider VOWs to be equivalent to bricks-and-mortar bro-kerages where registered customers are shown MLS profile sheets or faxed listing information.

To add a VOW link to your website—and the required disclosure forms, contact registration forms, and password system—requires somewhat more specialized programming than a simple IDX link.

Checklist to Add an IDX/VOW Link to Your Website

Although the procedure to add an IDX/VOW link is straightforward, real estate professionals need to be aware that IDX and VOW are governed by several local realities as well as local MLS rules. Keep in mind, answers to the following checklist vary MLS to MLS, and change regularly. In short, local MLSs set their own rules to imple-ment the NAR's VOW policy guidelines for a range of questions. Does broker opt-out allow blanket (all VOWs) or selective (specific VOWs) choices? Can agents operate VOWs? How are expired and sold listing data handled? If local practices are not well known, hiring a consul-tant who keeps tabs on what your MLS is doing may save you con-siderable time (eRainmaker.com: Virtual Consultants):

☑ *Is IDX/VOW available from your MLS?* MLSs that have not con-verted from proprietary software to browser-based Internet MLS may not offer IDX/VOW. Some MLSs use a "bridge" system that uses the Internet as a connection to replace the traditional dial-up access. Even though the MLS is viewable on the Internet, a bridge system may require proprietary MLS software be loaded on the member's computer to allow listing changes. Although NAR man-dated all MLSs provide IDX by January 1, 2002, not all MLSs who have an "internal" bridge system also have a "public" Internet MLS, and may not provide IDX and VOW. Be sure to check.

☑ *Does your MLS require a signed agreement and/or a fee to participate?* Practices vary; in some cases, not only is the broker required to sign an IDX/VOW user agreement, but MLS providers sometimes also require that your website designer sign an agreement. Ask.

☑ *Are there specific compliance rules for a website?* Any restrictions, rules, or regulations may also need to be provided to your web designer to adjust your website to comply. Again, practices vary, but to comply, your web designer must know what your MLS expects and allows. Don't assume your web designer knows local requirements, especially if the designer is not local.

☑ *What is the URL with your authorized link?* Once all is in place, you typically need to obtain a specific authorized link to IDX/VOW property listings and provide that link to your website designer.

☑ *Can the MLS data be manipulated?* Changing the display or sort features or enhancing the information with additional links, such as virtual tours or to schedule an appointment, requires specialized software. If the MLS vendor doesn't provide this function, your MLS should know of companies that do. Display of data is a specialized service because it requires downloading the data to a server, special programming to arrange the data as desired, then uploading the data to your website. If you want this service, be sure to ask who can provide it and at what price. Typically, the cost of hiring a programmer to do data display for just your practice is prohibitive. Participants are not allowed to change the property data itself.

eRainmaker Strategy #2: Showcase Virtual Tours to Sell Your Listings without You

Imagine a slide show running on a self-paced continuous loop, and then add voiceover and music background and transitions, and you can visualize a multimedia virtual tour. Top eRainmakers have learned to use this technology in numerous ways to promote everything from listings to themselves, their communities, and new neighbors. The power of these virtual walk-throughs comes from the rich information pro-vided by interior/exterior/room-by-room photos in a self-guided format (forward, back, replay, pause, etc.), as well as the flexibility of being able to deliver the information online (website or e-mail link) and by disk (CD or diskette). Another reason virtual tours have become stan-dard practice for successful eRainmakers is the ease of preparation and quick download (eRainmaker.com: Virtual Tours for a list of the leading vendors). The bottom line is: A virtual tour attracts buyers and im-presses sellers. Here's how it's done.

Panorama Technique

Wraparound panoramas are created by "stitching" together a series of still frames from regular 35mm photos or by using a special 360-degree "fish-eye" lens. The stitched technique provides a left-right motion that takes the visitor in a continuous circle. Photos are commonly taken with a digital camera, but you can also scan prints to create a digital image. Full circle, 360-degree images do the same, but also allow the visitor to pan up or down for a fuller view of the image, which is handy for cathedral ceilings and large entertainment rooms as well as tend to make tiny rooms appear larger. Using a tripod, you simply take two front-and-back photos or sometimes three photos in sequence to cap-ture the entire space with the 360-degree lens. Typically the software also provides the ability to zoom in and out on details. Photos are best saved as JPEG format to reduce file size. The overall effect for the prospect of either stitching or 360-degree is one of being in the center of the room, as if you are doing a home inspection tour in person.

Do-It-Yourself or Turnkey

Many high-production eRainmakers have invested in the digital cam-era, appropriate lens, tripod, and software to do virtual tours them-selves or delegate the task to staff or virtual assistant. Often the task is split between actually taking the photos, which requires physically visiting the property, and preparing the virtual tour itself, which re-quires having the software, digital images, and text information. In some markets, photographic services exist that will shoot images, prepare the tour, and post it to the Internet for a fee. Because of the expense, often in the range of $100 a property, the turnkey approach is not as popular as the do-it-yourself method. Another benefit of the do-it-yourself method is the ability to add additional images—in some cases up to 50 scenes are permitted.

Streaming Video

Another technique uses a video camera, but its shortcomings have kept this approach from wide use. Not only are streaming video files very large (requiring widespread use of high-speed Internet access to be practical), but viewers must rewind and fast forward to find a specific spot, such as the kitchen or master bath, which is annoying. Also, editing the video requires special skills and equipment.

Whatever type of virtual tours you develop, you'll be able to use them for so much more than showing listings on your website. Be sure to confirm the cost and ability to post your virtual tours on the Internet, where tours can be accessed easily by prospects through a hyperlink.

eRainmaker Strategy #3: Buyer Prospect Follow-Up Made Easy with Automated Listing Updates

The overwhelming success of online property information is what makes the second step of this strategy critical. More and more prospects turn to the Internet to do their initial information gathering and property browsing. For a host of reasons, from slow dial-up access and lack of market knowledge to not knowing the right URLs and listings with incomplete property information (no photos, no address, no price), once frustrated prospects find a few properties, they soon realize having a professional's help is the most thorough approach to a property search. Let somebody else do the work!

That's why one of the most powerful direct-response offers online is a home-search service. Links variously call this "Dream Home Finder," "Free Computerized Search," "Wish List," or "Property Sweep." In my company's website content product, RAINMAKER E-CENTRAL, we call it "e-Search." Over the years, the e-Search has been consistently the #2 lead-generation offer (33%) behind our "Free E-Reports" offer (44%), and combined these offers account for about 77% of the most recent 10,000 leads captured for our subscribers. Simply, the response form asks buyer prospects to complete the property features they want (or need) and e-mail the wish list to the real estate professional. In turn, the subscriber searches the MLS for matching listings and replies by e-mail with links to available properties.

Naturally, repeating the process as new properties come on the market (or are withdrawn, have a price change, or a contract pending), and trying to divine which listings the prospects like, can turn into a full-time job. This was exactly the case for an assistant to Gary Jacklin, a $4 million producer in Chicago, who helped David Huey buy a house in 1994. Huey realized the listing update process could be automated and started SOAR Automation (now SOARsolutions.net). Within three years, Jacklin had increased his volume 500% to $20 million annually using SOAR MLS, which sent updates by fax or mail. Today, SOAR Solutions has experience in 150 MLS markets nationwide and has upgraded to send the updates by e-mail.

With the NAR mandates for MLSs to provide IDX and VOW services to members, automated listing updates are now a commonplace MLS service. After all, once the MLS property data is available, software can be programmed to perform the search functions regularly, often daily, and send updates to buyer prospects. Many MLS vendors who supply Internet MLS include listing update functions as part of their service package. Top producer John Pinto (JVPinto.com) with Realty World John Pinto & Associates in San Jose, California, says, "I'd get callers who would say, 'I'd like to buy that property you e-mailed me.' What property? Who is calling? I may not know what they are talking about, but I don't tell them that." That is the power of automated property updates (eRainmaker.com: Property Updates).

Typically, with an IDX solution the real estate professional must enter the prospect into the update system. With a VOW solution, the prospect has already received disclosure (if required by law) and agreed to the terms of use, thus prospects can enter their own criteria to launch the search without requiring manual entry by a real estate professional. The updates received by the prospect end up being the same. In competitive markets, knowledgeable eRainmakers supplement their updates with virtual tours, informative additional e-mails on the purchase process, financing, moving pointers, and the ability to turn off the updates. Every e-mail should also include links back to different content sections of your website to convert the prospect into

Figure 9.1
Automated Follow-Up and Classic 1937 Pontiac for Showings

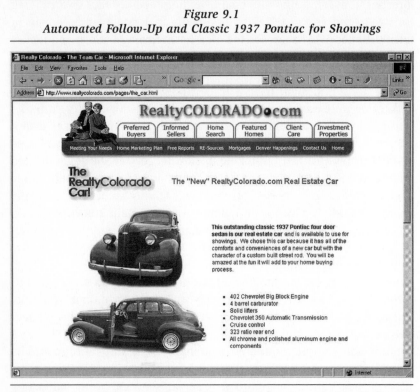

Source: Courtesy of Dave & Sally Herries (RealtyColorado.com), The Realty Colorado Team, Keller Williams Realty, Lone Tree, Colorado.

a shopper when they are "ready" to buy. You could also offer them a free car to visit properties (Figure 9.1).

eRainmaker Strategy #4: Be Available 24/7 to Close E-Prospects When They Are "Ready"

Once an automated buyer follow-up campaign is running, prospects need a method to set up an appointment. Capturing an e-prospect at the moment they turn from information gatherer to shopper is critical. One of the most effective techniques is the simplest. Create a special response form on your website that allows prospects to list the properties they want to visit and the time/day that is convenient. In short, the prospects create their own home tour, but need the real estate professional to assemble information and make arrangements. For an example, visit RAINMAKER E-CENTRAL from the Gooder Group and check out the e-Showing feature.

Promoting the scheduling service is a big key. If prospects are invited (early and often) to use the form, you will maximize your capture. A "Set-up Appointment" button is equally effective at capturing prospects in your system, as well as generating leads of new prospects direct from offline ads and direct mail. For example, print postcards that describe your free "Schedule a Showing" service. Include the URL to your home page or, better still, link directly to the form itself. This is a great way to drive preselected prospects to your website. Don't forget to put a prominent icon or button on your website in numerous places to make it easy for prospects to find the service.

Showing arrangements are a particularly burdensome task in markets where the listing agent must be present or keys to the property must be picked up at the listing broker's office (no lock boxes). That need has stimulated several commercial programs to help manage showing schedules. These services are especially helpful in automating the process for companies with hundreds (or thousands) of listings, and where showing requests need to be routed to listing agents, buyer's agents, or the brokerage lead-management desk.

The rapid growth of schedule showings programs indicates how useful the service is and how easy website plug-ins are to install (just add the link to your site and on listing pages). The results return multiples of the investment. Not only does an automated showing system maximize appointments that lead to sales, a system also generates listings from buyer prospects that must sell to buy as well as mortgage originations. Systems also provide management statistics to improve follow-up techniques. Some providers feature a live call-center solution to take calls and make appointments (eRainmaker.com: Schedule Showings).

eRainmaker Strategy #5: Use Open Houses to Drive Buyers through Your Website's Front Door

Once an open house is scheduled—for your listing or another property for sale—the secret to attracting prospects (both active buyers and future sellers) is to promote the opens. Your website is the ideal place to hold an "open house" opportunity to capture prospects.

The first step is to have your web designer add a function to your site where you can list open houses. Keep in mind, you will also want to include "Recent Opens" for prospects that missed the open house and are interested in properties still on the market. Separate the search results between "Scheduled Opens" and "Recent Opens" with future dates at the top chronologically descending through past dates.

For an outstanding example of Open Houses, go to LongandFoster.com, the superb company site of Long & Foster Real Estate, Inc. in the mid-Atlantic region. Not only can prospects search by county and ZIP plus price range, they can also search for opens by date (next 7 days,

---

Figure 9.2
Long & Foster Full-Page "Open House" Ad

Source: Courtesy of Long & Foster Real Estate (LongandFoster.com), Fairfax, Virginia.

next 14 days, next 21 days, all scheduled opens). Long & Foster also does a great job promoting this handy open-house service offline by featuring the service in full-page ads in the *Washington Post, Baltimore Sun, Richmond Times Dispatch,* and other major market newspapers (Figure 9.2). Vice President of Marketing Ed Sears said, "When these ads run on Sunday, we experience a substantial spike in website traffic over the next several days. Advertising offline to drive traffic to our on-line site is an extraordinarily efficient use of our marketing dollars."

10

Seller Follow-Up: Turning Online Leads into Listings

Attracting Sellers Is Key to Your Profitability— Online and Offline

Every real estate agent needs buyers *and* sellers. Yet, agents with a basic understanding of the Internet primarily use it to generate only buyers. For these agents, and for all of their peers who have yet to harness the engine of the Internet, there remains a largely untapped opportunity to generate the most lucrative prospects of all: home sellers. To take full advantage of the Internet in locating and landing listings, real estate professionals need to know which e-marketing strategies work—and which don't.

The preference for listings is no secret. Sellers are the most profitable clients. Although listings require more investment in marketing dollars to sell (compared to spending on buyers), listings are lucrative because they require less personal attention, and a busy eRainmaker can manage more listings at once than buyers. Also, through the MLS, every real estate agent in the market is trying to sell the property to a buyer.

We also know 69% of prospective home sellers list with the first agent they contact (67% of buyers work with the first agent they contact), according to the National Association of REALTORS *2003 Profile of Home Buyers and Sellers.* That means if you get a call from a potential seller who is ready to list, two out of three times you get the listing just by showing up! The challenge comes when we realize prospective sellers begin their process sometimes more than a year before they are ready to sell, and most begin to shop for a home to buy *before* they think about selling. That's plenty of time to forget you.

What's the best strategy to capture more sellers from the Internet? In a nutshell, grab 'em early and never turn 'em loose. But how do you work a large number of prospects all at once that may be ready tomorrow—or may not be ready until next year—without letting them slip through the cracks along the way? Two of the best ways are to use the Internet's web-centric marketing model:

1. Add features to your website designed to capture seller prospects, and

2. Cultivate prospects with drip-marketing follow-up using automated e-mail designed to bring sellers back to your website. (More on e-mail strategies in Part Three.)

Although most Internet prospects are homeowners (67%), two-thirds (65%) turn to the Internet first as interested buyers. Thus, one way to capture sellers is to market to them as buyers ("Homeowners, have you seen what your money can buy in today's market?"). For six years, the Gooder Group's *Internet Prospect Study* has analyzed online questionnaires from Internet prospects sent to subscribers of Gooder Group's RAINMAKER E-CENTRAL® service. (The service provides plug-in website content designed to capture Internet leads.) In 2003, the study analyzed more than 4,200 prospect questionnaires between January 1, 2003 and June 30, 2003. Table 10.1 shows what we learned.

Table 10.1
Gooder Group Six-Year Internet Prospect Study

	1998 (%)	2001 (%)	2003 (%)
Prospects reported currently...			
Owning a home	49	55	67
Renting a home	1	45	33
Prospects primarily interested in...			
Buying	65	55	65
Selling	15	23	23
Relocating	14	19	10
Renting	6	3	3
Prospects currently...			
NOT working with agent	70	84	74
Working with agent	30	15	26
Prospects moving in...			
1–3 months	29	36	41
4–6 months	27	39	26
7–12 months	26	20	16
1 year or more	18	15	17
Prospects who are...			
Inside subscriber's area, moving within subscriber's area	63	44	50
Inside subscriber's area moving outside	1	5	3
Long distance prospects moving to subscriber's area	23	26	21
Long distance prospects moving outside subscriber's area (point-to-point)	11	21	22
International moving to subscriber's area	2	3	3
International moving outside subscriber's area	1	1	1
Prospects who were...			
NOT prequalified for a loan	69	71	62
Prequalified for a loan	23	29	38
Not known	8	0	0
Prospects wanting to purchase a...			
Single-family home	51	45	72
Condo	4	6	5
Town house	6	7	9
Apartment	2	2	1
Other	7	5	13

Note: Rounding may cause totals to vary from 100.

Source: Gooder Group Six-Year Internet Prospect Study, © 2003. All rights reserved.

When Do You Want to Move?

As they used to say on early television game shows: That's the $64,000 question. One of the most effective techniques to self-qualify a seller prospect is to determine *when* the prospect wants to move. A simple way to do this using website response forms is to offer two check-off boxes: One "if you are planning to move in less than six months," and a second box "if you want to move in more than six months." The decisions and timetable of the near-term move versus long-range move shape the follow-up information that is right for the prospect's situation. Whichever box they select, you are now able to tailor your response—and your automated follow-up—accordingly.

Standing behind Your Domain's Claim to Fame

To earn ERA's #1 agent worldwide in 1988, 1992, 1996, and be the top-selling agent since 1987 in the Pensacola, Florida, area, Alexis Bolin (AlexisSellsHomes.com) with ERA Old South Properties knows how to deliver her domain's claim to fame using e-mail. One of Bolin's most successful techniques is an electronic highlight flier. "It's a great listing tool that makes me stand out from the competition," said Bolin. "We show the seller how—if they list with us—we will take digital photos of their home and e-mail a highlight sheet to 50 top agents who might be working with a buyer in their price range. Then we also e-mail the highlight sheet to all of our prospective-buyer list, as well as to our list of past customers who might know of a buyer for their home," Bolin said. Having IDX property listings on her website is another very effective tool Bolin uses both for buyers and sellers.

Nine eRainmaker Techniques to Capture More Sellers Online

1. *Sweet double deals:* First, concentrate on capturing the best of both worlds: the seller who contacts you first as a buyer. Remember 41% of home sellers used the same agent for both the selling and buying sides, according to NAR's *2003 Profile of Home Buyers and Sellers.*

Many of the most successful eRainmakers make it their first rule of
qualification to ask if a buyer has a home to sell. Because move-up
prospects are almost 60% of the market nationally—and even higher in
trade-up markets that have few first-time buyers—you'll want to be
sure on every website response form to ask prospects, "Do you have a
home to sell? If yes, do you have to sell before you buy?" or put another
way, "Do you own or rent?" Often in fast-moving, fast-appreciating
markets, sellers are worried more about finding a home they can *buy*
—because they know prices are high and inventory is low—than they
are worried about *selling* their home. Thus, growth-minded eRainmakers have learned to generate *sellers* by first marketing to homeowners
as if they are *buyers* (which leads naturally to a conversation about
selling). Focus on benefits to your target consumer (Figure 10.1).

2. *What's It Worth?* Competitive Market Analysis has experienced a
rebirth online. Various website buttons feature this offer: "Top Dollar

---

Figure 10.1
Company Site Sells Consumer Benefits for Less

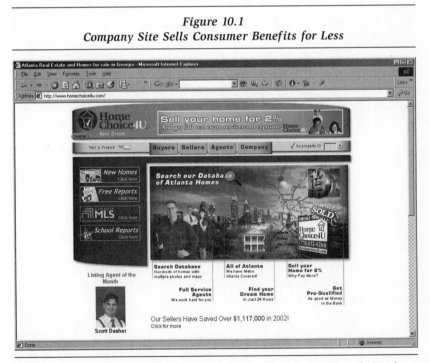

Source: Courtesy of Home Choice 4 U Real Estate (HomeChoice4U.com), Peachtree
City, Georgia.

Analysis," "What's A Home Worth?," "Price Your Home Online," "Over-the-Net Home Evaluation," "Right Price Analysis," "Market Price Estimate." Basically, the offers of "Free, no-obligation, service" are delivered in one of two ways: arm's length or personal visit. Consider both approaches. Some prospects prefer the "you will not have to meet with an agent" offer that sends a price range via regular mail or e-mail based on the information they provide on the response form. Other prospects will be ready for a "prelisting home inspection visit" or "marketability evaluation" to evaluate the marketable condition of their property. Use both. Still other eRainmakers require the seller to hire them before performing a full-featured CMA. (More secrets to maximize results from CMAs in Chapter 13.)

3. *Ask for the listing:* Don't forget the obvious. Simply create a web form with the headline "I want to Sell My Home!" This straightforward approach is used very effectively on the website created by web designer Gary Shade (ShadesLanding.com) for Allen F. Hainge CYBERSTAR® and top producer Don King (DonKingHomes.com) with RE/MAX of Rancho Bernardo in San Diego, California. Another technique is used by website provider Best Image Marketing (BestImage.com) on their sites, such as the outstanding site they produced for Peter With (PeterWith.com), a leading salesperson with RE/MAX Realty Enterprises in Mississauga, Ontario. The headline features a "Free In-Home Presentation," which promises a listing presentation with a CMA and marketing plan. If you use this type of form, link to it from numerous places in your website as well as offline promotions.

4. *Getting out of Dodge:* This special offer for relocating home sellers often generates leads that are deciding—or just decided—to move out of town. Although the lead-generation hook is information about a destination area (and a referral to a top agent in that market), follow-up and service is the key to landing the local listing. One particularly effective technique is to send seller prospects new-on-the-market listing updates via e-mail. With a special CMA function, you can register a prospective seller's property in the system, and the server sends an updated CMA regularly using the latest comparable homes data. The updated CMA function also works to make price reductions easier for sellers under listing agreement (eRainmaker.com: Property Updates). *Tip:* Check with your MLS first to see if using MLS sold data is permitted in your area.

5. *Nosy neighbors campaign:* Create a response form on your website that offers a service where neighbors can "Find out what the house down the street sold for" or learn "What they got!" All the homeowner has to do is complete the form. Feature this tool in your neighborhood direct-mail farming newsletters and "Just Sold" postcards. Simply include the button icon and URL (for example, WhatItSoldFor.info or RecentSalePrices.com, actual domain names available at press time) in the direct-mail piece and drive prospective sellers to your website. Once you've captured their contact information, a property update program can send a quarterly CMA update for all area sales. Interested neighbors will be delighted, and you will become a household domain name. The technique works great with past clients, too.

6. *FSBOs:* As we discussed in Chapter 8, generating a FSBO prospect is one thing. Converting the prospect with follow-up requires a ready plan. Have a system that is automated and that lasts a minimum of five weeks. A minimum of 10 contacts per prospect is recommended including five e-mails and five calls or five letters and five e-mails. Headline your e-mail letters with market updates, your guarantees, your commission rate(s), your listing services, and so on. Rather than browbeat FSBOs with "stop being so stupid and list with us" notices, offering genuine assistance to these do-it-yourselfers is the most effective follow-up technique. Helpful advice on pricing, marketability, property promotion, showing, terms, contracts, even local service providers are not only opportunities for continuous contact, but also capture "I give up!" listings more often. Offer to swap advice for extra buyer prospects who don't buy the FSBO property.

7. *Expireds:* Converting expireds to listings requires a two-step integrated offline and online marketing strategy to generate e-mail addresses and automate follow-up. The first step: Establish a web form on your site specifically for expireds and prominently label the navigation button ("Expired Listing" or "Sold This Time" or "House Didn't Sell?"). No matter why their listing didn't sell, from too few showings or too many days on market to no purchase offers, you can provide a free report that explains "How to Sell a Home That Didn't Sell" (buy preprinted reports or create your own). Emphasize that the report details how to price to sell, how condition can kill offers, how to know which repairs to make (and which ones don't payoff), how to attract buyers with terms. The second step: Capture the expired's e-mail address by launching a direct-mail postcard or letter campaign designed

to drive frustrated sellers to your website and response form(s). In your direct mail, promote seller reports to be ordered online from your expired page. Some of the most effective Gooder Group e-report titles include: "Proven Tips to Turn an Offer into a Solid Contract Fast," "How to Put Your Sale on the Fast Track," "How to Package Your Home to Sell," "12 Contract Options That Entice Today's Buyers," "Pricing: Beat Your Competition to the Contract." Don't give up. Studies show the vast majority of expireds move within two years of not selling the first time.

8. *Divorce:* Sad but true: Divorce is good business for real estate. Not only do many divorcing couples sell the family home (and vacation home), but then they also each buy another place. It's very common within the following year for the suddenly singles to marry again—and start fresh by buying a new home (often selling the new couple's two old homes). Create a special page on your site for divorcing sellers. Label it simply "Divorce and Real Estate" or "Your Home and Divorce." Offer a special report that tells prospects what they need to know about how divorce affects their home, their mortgage, and their home-sale taxes. Follow up with both seller- and buyer-oriented e-mails containing links to helpful services and e-reports. Remember: One of the best sources of divorce prospects is family practice and divorce attorneys who refer clients to real estate professionals specializing in empathetic service. To maximize your campaign, include these lawyers in your B2B referral source database. Send them your automated e-newsletter and offline direct mail.

9. *Trade-in:* Sometimes called "Guaranteed Sale." Again, label your navigation clearly with links such as "Guarantee Your Home Sells" or "We Buy Houses" or "Guaranteed Offer." Todd Walters (ToddWalters.com), whose residential team ranked No. 7 in the United States for RE/MAX in 2002, does an exceptional job and practices what he calls "octopus marketing" (many different tentacles reaching many different target markets). In an interview with RE/MAX Mainstreet, Walters said, "Most of the people selling right now are move-ups, and they need to sell their properties before they'll be in a position to buy something new. I addressed that problem by buying their home, for their price, if it doesn't sell within a set amount of time. I advertise this everywhere—on signs, advertisements, web-based ads, and so on. It makes the phone ring like crazy." Some restrictions and conditions apply. One secret is to price the property to sell in the first place.

More Strategies to Capture More Listings

A commitment to exceeding each customer's need is the key to success for Adrian Willanger (AdrianPWillanger.com), a successful sales associate with Windermere Real Estate in Lake Forest Park, Washington. Willanger's single most successful approach to capture sellers from his website begins with a promise. "My personal commitment to customer service is translated into trying not only to meet, but to exceed each customer's need. For every e-mail response, I consider the inquiry to be as important as a phone call. I handle their inquiries immediately," said Willanger. "I used to predetermine sellers' motivations, and now I assume that each inquiry is urgent." Willanger backs up his commitment by keeping his database of prospects current. "Then I relentlessly drive prospective sellers back to the site for interesting newsletters and valuable updates on current real estate and external market facts."

The difference between what sellers need and what they want is at the center of Beth Tyler's e-strategy (HomesDataBase.com/BethTyler) as a leading agent with Long & Foster Real Estate in Annapolis, Maryland. "What sellers *need* is a website that attracts buyers to the website. Then, it is up to the REALTOR to make sure the seller's home is highlighted and presented in a pleasing format to attract buyers to look at the home and its information. What sellers *want* is to see their home in a virtual tour," said Tyler.

Tyler focuses on delivering a specific set of services to sellers:

- ☑ Unique website address for their home, advertised on brochures and flyers. ("That way buyers can go directly to the home without shuffling through other homes," Tyler said.)

- ☑ Multiple websites highlighting their home. ("No matter how much I do," Tyler said, "One website isn't enough, and you don't know where the buyer is looking.")

- ☑ One virtual tour, one "commercial," and multiple photos on three websites, as well as up to five more sites with multiple photos. ("Not everyone likes—or has the capacity—to view virtual tours, so I offer a choice," said Tyler.)

- ☑ Accurate information, using all of the website's potential *and* updated as often as needed.

Tyler's ideal website keeps sellers in mind and includes "information a seller can look up for themselves—a sort of reference library. My list of buyer and seller tips, school information and links, and lists of local repair people, utility companies, and so on are just some of the features."

Generating Listings Doesn't Have to Cost an Ad and a Leg

Promoting his website in print is no longer a big investment for Gary Marshall (GaryMarshall.com), a top agent/broker with Assist 2 Sell Buyer & Seller Realty Center in Newnan, Georgia. Marshall no longer promotes homes in newspaper classifieds—only on his websites. "Every day in the local paper," said Marshall, "I used to run a small classified ad in the real estate section that read: 'INTERNET—View Coweta County homes and 46,000 more at www.CowetaCountyHomes.com.' Every Saturday I run a classified ad: 'OPEN HOUSES—View weekend open house schedule at www.CowetaCountyHomes.com.' That Saturday open house ad is now all I run. I do not run individual open house ads on each house I have open each weekend. We just run that little ad on Saturday. It saves me a ton of money on advertising costs."

Marshall doesn't stop there. When visitors open his site, a pop-up window appears with the appealing headline: "We are having an open house this weekend and you are invited." When visitors click through, they see a list including all of Marshall's open houses. "On the website," Marshall added, "we provide a picture of the houses being held open, all the information on the houses, and directions to the houses. We can provide a lot more information about each house at our website than in a small open house ad in the paper. And, that's exactly how we explain it to the home seller."

To generate listings from his websites, one of the best techniques Marshall uses is a simple button labeled, "List My Home." Visitors land on a form to fill out that gets e-mailed to Marshall. "That amazing little button gets me 8 to 10 listings per year," Marshall reported. "My website averages over 3,200 hits per day and you'd better believe we make a point to tell our sellers that at the listing presentation."

Costly Website Mistakes to Avoid

Mistake #1: Capturing Too Few Inquiries from Too Much Traffic

You are promoting your site and getting lots of traffic (according to your traffic statistics), but you are not getting as many e-mail inquiries as you want.

SOLUTION

A busy website that gets no response is like a busy listing that gets no offers. Make three fundamental changes to your website: (1) Makeover the content of the website to focus on the customer, not on yourself; (2) Reorganize the navigation to make it easy for your "target" customer (buyer, seller, relocation, etc.) to find the information they seek; (3) Add lots of lead-capture opportunities everywhere to compel the visitor to request solutions (your offers) to their problems via e-mail (see Figure 10.2).

Mistake #2: Converting Too Few Prospects from a Flood of Inquiries

You get lots of e-mail inquiries, but you don't have many conversions to actual closed listings or sales from your website leads.

SOLUTION

Build an automated prospect follow-up program that gives you an unfair advantage over your competition by following proven e-marketing principles:

1. Respond fast using auto-responders.
2. Launch a drip-marketing follow-up e-mail campaign that sends (1) personalized e-mail with merged data fields for each prospect, that is (2) oriented to the specific needs of the prospect (buying, selling, relocating, financing, etc.), and that matches the (3) timetable of the prospect's move date. Proceed at the prospect's pace, not yours, being careful to build relationship rather than push the prospect to reply.

Figure 10.2
Turn Home Page into Powerful Direct Response Offer

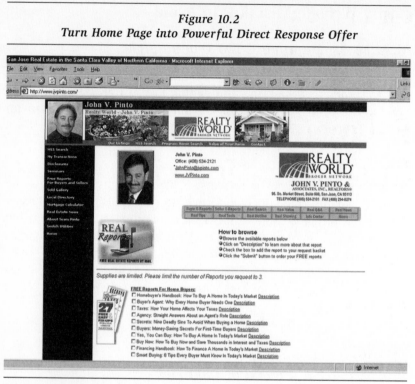

Source: Courtesy of John Pinto (JVPinto.com), Realty World John V. Pinto & Associates, San Jose, California.

3. "Touch" the prospect offline by phone and mail as well as online (e-mail).

4. Feature continuous direct-response offers designed to demonstrate your market knowledge and convert the prospect when the prospect is ready to meet with you face to face.

11

E-Loyalty: Keeping Customers for Life

OLD RULE

Market share is paramount.

NEW RULE

Lifetime share of customer
is even more valuable.

Honoring the 80/20 Rule of Referrals

Ultimately, what do loyal customers want? A real estate professional they can trust, someone who is friendly, offers reliable service, recognizes them, does favors for them, and builds a relationship. Vilfredo Pareto (1848–1923) was an Italian economist who observed that 20% of the population makes 80% of the income and he concluded that income distribution remains constant regardless of efforts to change it. Pareto's Law says that 80% of your business will come from 20% of your customers. So who are the 20%? Simply tracking your sources of business will tell you, especially if your records are good enough to note the names of referral sources. You may also find it enlightening to assign gross commission income (GCI) to put a value on working with individual customers. It's an eye opener.

Once you've identified your most valuable customers (MVCs), target the customers who individually represent at least 10% of your business profit (it is always a short list). Then focus on customers who contribute to the top 50% of sales and profit (still a short list). A third group of customers are marginally profitable, typically one-time transactions or lower priced properties (put them on your regular newsletter and stay in touch). By using a balanced attack of offline and online marketing, you can focus more attention on the high-potential customers in your Trophy Database and enjoy the dividends of valuing your prized customers.

Success Formula:
E-Marketing + E-Service = E-Loyalty

In real estate, we commonly target past clients for repeat and referral business. All eRainmakers know that a referral from a past client is virtually a slam-dunk. That's one reason referrals are the most profitable customers. It is also why referral sources are worth their weight in gold—"treat the referral source even better than the referral," says Gary Keller.

In the outside world of giant transnational global enterprises or large nationwide retail chains or small local real estate practices, building relationships with past customers to increase sales is called *customer relationship management* or *customer relationship marketing* (CRM). Here's how CRM works.

By identifying the most profitable customers, CRM experts say, and asking them what they value, then communicating with those customers in their terms individually (customers don't want to be treated equally, they want to be treated individually), the customer becomes the central focus, not you. Follow that strategy and an interesting thing happens. The *customers* have added value to the relationship by telling you something about themselves that the competition does not know. Now the loyal customer finds it is easier and less costly to do business with you—and send you referrals—than to start over somewhere else (what marketers call a "barrier to exit" or "cost of defection"). That's why CRM is about the customer, not about you; it's about the relationship, not the transaction; about on-going contact, not response promotions.

Experience shows you cannot buy customer loyalty. In the 1990s, loyalty programs offering points and reward miles and affinity rebates

---

GeekSpeak

Customer relationship management (CRM) is the art and science of building relationships with customers. Typically, a customer database and website are core requirements. Customer data enables all members of the team to improve sales by identifying most profitable customers (high return on investment or ROI), providing them the highest level of service and ideally forming individualized relationships (what marketers call "1-to-1," or "One2One"). Repeat and referral business are prime objectives of CRM and the cheapest business you can keep.

---

became a bandwagon that picked up speed so fast everybody got on it. Some promotions created sales, but few built loyalty, according to CRM experts. Soon, loyalty rewards weren't special—they were normal. Customers took the points and miles and still switched. The costly lesson was that it wasn't the miles; it was the benefits that counted. Customer loyalty was based on the service they truly valued.

Here are some examples of listening and delivering true value:

☑ Rental car customers don't like standing in line at airport terminal counters. Hertz, Avis, National, and others built covered facilities where your car and keys are waiting ready to drive away.

☑ Video renters walk out of stores dissatisfied if the movie they want is out of stock. Blockbuster uses predictive model software called Center Stage that allows the chain to anticipate demand and guarantee the availability of new releases in most markets.

☑ Cable TV subscribers have so many channels they can't find what they want. One cable company asked customers for their preferences and now delivers personalized monthly television guides along with a bag of microwave popcorn.

☑ Luxury car owners dread leaving their expensive vehicles in unattended airport lots. Porsche of Germany offered a "Park & Wash" benefit where owners can leave their Porsche at Avis' secure lot for free (saving parking fees) and pick up their car cleaned inside and out.

☑ Shippers were concerned they didn't know when a package would arrive if sent through the U.S. Postal Service. Federal

Express "absolutely positively guaranteed" overnight delivery by a fixed time the next day.

Clearly, you can foster loyalty by listening to what a customer values and providing service or information that strengthens the bond between the customer and the company. In a nutshell, a customer wants the service, not just the stuff. Use the knowledge you gain about a customer's interests to deliver benefits the customer wants. Put another way: Concentrate on customer benefits and values rather than on what you want to sell them. Your Trophy E-Mail Database and direct marketing are fundamental stepping-stones to developing customers for life, but don't stop with the data only. Use the information to keep customers for life. Use your website to build relationships, rather than just sell, sell, sell.

Remember, direct marketing is *transaction* driven; you want to compel a customer to respond, take an action, and make your e-mail inbox pop. Long-term contact is *relationship* driven; you want loyalty, repeat business, and a stream of referrals. From a marketers view, an effective CRM strategy is more concerned with share of customer (lifetime value) than share of market, more focused on retention than response, more defined by percentage of referral transactions than total units closed. The secret to a successful customer-for-life strategy is identifying what creates added value for the customer and then providing it. This means eRainmakers must be continuously trying to find out what customers are doing and thinking and what external factors affect their real estate decisions.

Many real estate professionals think a satisfied customer today will be a loyal customer tomorrow. Not necessarily. CRM experts have discovered that past satisfaction doesn't translate automatically into perpetual satisfaction over time. Most customers assume you have mastered the basics (if not, they aren't satisfied to start with!) and many assume you will offer some things that don't interest them or that irritate them. To retain their loyalty what they really *expect* is, however, that you go beyond the basics and provide them value. Here is where it becomes important to listen regularly to their situation as their homeowning life cycle progresses. Generally, customers want more and more value for their time and money, and that value must be focused like a laser beam on their needs and wants.

To maximize a lifetime customer strategy, savvy eRainmakers use an integrated marketing package that combines every marketing medium:

direct mail, advertising, publicity, telemarketing, e-mail, and website, as well as good old face-to-face visits.

Online techniques offer many advantages. One example is a key date reminder e-mail series. Use an automated e-mail program with a scheduler to send an e-mail reminder two days before key dates, such as birthdays (especially a spouse's birthday), anniversaries (wedding, home purchase), daylight savings change, smoke-alarm battery swap, scheduled home maintenance, holidays (mother's day, father's day), and so on. Ideally, you will know the customer's personal dates to get maximum benefit from this strategy. (*Tip:* At your first meeting, have clients complete a client profile survey with all their personal information.)

One-to-one surveys provide invaluable insights. Even a simple check-the-box e-mail question is effective such as, "What aspect of real estate interests you most right now? Buying? Selling? Relocating? Financing? Renting? Homeowning? Investing? Second Home? New Home? For Seniors?" Another simple question with huge returns is to ask what frequency they want to hear from you such as, "Daily? Weekly? Biweekly? Monthly? Bimonthly? Quarterly? Semi-annually? Annually? As needed? None of the above?"

With answers to these two questions, you can be assured every communication will be positive, and not annoying, from the customer's point of view. Tailoring e-mail to customer interests in even basic ways makes the customer feel unique because the touch is based on previous dialog. Remember: Record individual responses, not group averages. Indicate clearly the survey is not anonymous and is designed to "serve you better."

"Drip-drip" is the sound of money in the bank for Mollie Wasserman (MollieW.com, MyREConsultants.com), who leads a team with Keller Williams Realty in Framingham, Massachusetts, and is an Allen F. Hainge CYBERSTAR®. "In the olden days," Wasserman said, "people would refer you by saying 'Call my agent. Here's her number.' Now, I find my sphere is saying, 'Go to her website.' Which is good and bad. Good that many more people are likely to visit a website than call an agent—even if she's referred. (Fortunately, I have a site with a lot of content so they tend to stay.) But, it's bad unless you train yourself to ask them how they came to your site. I often don't know they're a referral until well into the transaction."

"I find it very effective to intersperse online and offline methods," Wasserman said. "Bright, colorful postcards in a mailbox are great tools to bring them to our sites. Since I've developed fee alternatives to commissions, postcard mailing campaigns to FSBOs are a great way to bring them to my consulting site, MyREConsultants.com, where they can get a lot more info on the consulting model and the unique fee options we offer."

"Nobody signs up for anything on our site without going onto some kind of action plan," said Wasserman, "which are all set up in my contact manager (Online Agent)." Wasserman intersperses both e-mail and offline mailings in her action plans to past clients. "My website, on the other hand, brings in slews of people that are not known to my team. The #1 source of sign-ups from our site (which should come as no surprise) is our property search and daily e-mail alert service. What I do, which is rather unique, is I have three different action plans preset depending on the sign-up: (1) local, (2) out of state, (3) e-mail only (without postal)," Wasserman explained.

Make a Home for Lifelong Customers on Your Home Page

Create a home for your clients on your website by giving every customer or transaction a private "Client Only" page. There are two effective approaches:

1. Design a separate page by adding a subfolder extension to your website domain (MySite.com/FolderName) where the folder is your client's name or property address (no spaces). Only those who know the address have access to the page(s). You can have unlimited folders.

2. Another approach is to create a password-protected private page for each client or transaction. Typically, clients click a "Member Login" or "Clients Only" or "Customer Care Center" button that displays an access page where they must enter a Client ID and Password. To manage password-protected pages, many innovative eRainmakers use full-featured transaction management software with success, or provide a private page using a special program from their web designer (eRainmaker.com: Transaction Management).

Once inside their own page in a transaction management program, clients experience the page as "prospects" from contact to contract, then as "customers" during the transaction from contract to closing, and finally as "past clients" in the after-sale sections for long-term contact. In the best programs, you can personalize each private page to communicate directly with the customer—and train customers to return regularly to your website—by posting information they need during that stage of their cycle. Periodically, send all clients—active or past—e-mail with a link to the private page or login to encourage them to make a habit of returning to your site.

Here are some content ideas to post:

☑ *Prospects:* Include virtual tours to featured properties. For prelisting prospects, post links to new listings and recent sales (if permitted by your MLS). Add links personally selected for the prospect to useful community and job sites, relocation hints, maps, public or private schools that match prospect's needs for grade level. Post answers to client's particular questions organized by date. List useful phone numbers. Make the page your virtual message center (Figure 11.1).

☑ *Transaction manager:* Post regular status reports for marketing activity, showing feedback, follow-up results, scheduled appointments, and inspections. Include "Do Lists" for the client and yourself to be ready for an open house, inspection, or closing. Prioritize the outstanding items by descending date with the shortest deadlines at the top, the longest timetable at the bottom. As closing approaches, include document deadlines and critical milestones with messages from you and your staff. Moving tips and checklists are very useful, especially calculated backward from expected move date. (Examples: LongandFoster.com > Relocation > Move Planner supplied by RelocationEssentials.com; or MonsterMoving.com > Move Planner which requires a free account registration.)

☑ *After-sale client:* For the past client, plus friends and family, post photos of the property and virtual tours, closing pictures, directions to the home with map link, suggested house-warming gifts—have fun. Add links for useful information on settling into the community, decorating a new home, helping children adjust, utility hookups, useful phone numbers, and community calendar. Consider links to home service providers who can help with improvements and repairs (ideal for strategic link partners). Include checklists of first-year maintenance dates. Many of these

Figure 11.1
Client Services Build Seller Satisfaction and e-Loyalty

Source: Courtesy of Roger Lautt (ISellChicago.com/dev), RE/MAX Exclusive Properties, Chicago, Illinois.

after-sale homeowner items are reusable for other clients, too. Be sure to post "Thank-you" notes for referrals or notifying you of changed e-mail or phone. Post your client's house-warming party invitation here, and announce your client appreciation event. Add a special RSVP e-mail account addressed to "Priority Attention" that is delivered direct to your inbox.

eRainmaker Techniques to Maximize Client E-Loyalty

Some of these eRainmaker CRM strategies are as fundamental as good service and good website design principles, others go right to the heart of building relationships with your best customers:

1. *Build value and trust:* The purpose of all websites is to build trust and deliver something of value. Content enhances value by providing in-depth information, not superficial lip service. Encourage trust with straight-forward privacy statements, such as "IMPORTANT: We will *never* sell, give, or rent your name or e-mail to anyone else—EVER!"

2. *Cater to most valuable customers (MVCs):* Include features that make your "relationship" MVCs (also, VIPs or VICs—very important clients) feel privileged. These are not your average "transactional" customers. Use a voice that addresses your MVCs directly (as in, "You may want to consider . . .") and organize the pages focused on what MVCs want most. Create MVC exclusives such as special services, rate alerts (periodic refinancing comparison of their interest rate with current rates), recent sale updates, and client party invitations. Leading real estate speaker Walter Sanford (WalterSanford.com) has created a special program for his real estate clients that accumulates discounts off the next transaction for specific responses, such as changed e-mail notification, referrals, testimonials, and so on.

3. *Practice two-click rule:* Employ the "two-click" rule to make it easy to locate information whenever possible in no more than two clicks: One click on subject, one click on topic/article to display information. Be sure your site navigation and customer-centered organization primarily solves customers' problems, not promotes you personally.

4. *Respond fast, in person:* Post your phone number and contact information prominently because many prospects prefer high-touch over high-tech responses, when they are ready for service. ("Our Customer Care Team is standing by to help. Call. E-mail. Mail. Or drop in.") Use auto-responders after hours and "out-of-office" messages when you are away. Consider a live operator service for after business hours and weekends, or a service that allows visitors to place a call from your website, or page you or exchange live chat (eRainmaker.com: Interactivity).

5. *Use multiplier marketing:* Make it easy to remember your site with buttons to "Bookmark This Page" or "Add to Favorites" and download your vCard (Microsoft Outlook contact record). Encourage visitors to recommend your site ("viral marketing") with "e-mail a Friend" or "Forward to Friend" forms. Customers

will use these buttons if they find the content valuable and you reward them for their referrals.

6. *Blow your horn:* Translate the offline Just Listed and Just Sold postcards and "SOLD" sign riders to your website. Letting folks know you really can sell houses is a powerful marketing tool. Take photos of happy clients: buyers in front of their new homes, or sellers with a check (maybe a BIG check, like the lottery hands out; use reusable white-board material and hand-write seller's name (payee) and sales price (amount) with washable marker for each photo). The digital photos will let website visitors know you have a track record they can trust. After all, smiles are contagious!

7. *Encourage community interaction:* If you've done everything to promote your site, the next step is to get somebody else to promote you. Install features, such as local service links pages (concierge services), community bulletin boards, even moderated forums (or links to others forums) and surveys that encourage dialogue in the future. Respond to inquiries quickly, and reinforce responses with rewards, such as printable coupons to local shops. See "Summit County Coupons" on the outstanding site of Ken and Mary Deshaies (SnowHome.com), Allen F. Hainge CYBERSTARS and top practitioners with RE/MAX Properties of the Summit in Dillon, Colorado (eRainmaker.com: Coupons). Use e-mail to boost participation in community features. For an excellent example of a recommended services directory of local providers, check out the site of Gary and Laury Woods (SantaBarbaraProperties.com). The Woods have listed scores of area businesses from accountants to bee removal and wine shops to wood finishing, generally only recommending one provider in a category and always using appealing descriptions—"If you've got kids, and they've got teeth, you need to see Keith (children's dentist)."

Costly Customer Relationship Mistake to Avoid

Mistake: Turning Satisfied Customers into Prospects for Your Competition

Nothing can turn off prospects and customers as fast as abusing the permission you've earned to send e-mail to your satisfied customers.

Sending an increasing number of hard-sell solicitations ("Buy Now! Sell Now!") that are too frequent, too loud, too long, or too insistent is a mistake. Using e-mail subject lines and messages that are misleading (even fraudulent), that exaggerate urgency, that assert performance claims or too-good-to-be-true guarantees, will backfire. Worst of all is the true client killer: providing a client's personal information to another party without the client's express consent beforehand. If these mistakes sound suspiciously like the definition of spam, you're right.

SOLUTION

Remember a permission-based customer list is a delicate privilege. You should take every opportunity to repeat for your clients the benefits of your relationship . . . but stop short before it becomes annoying promotion of greater interest to you than them. Give them reasons to want to continue receiving your messages (being their neighborhood expert is a great start!). Know your primary goal: Send e-mail and website services that inform and educate. After all, like any marketing campaign (online or offline), it takes multiple messages to achieve a desired response. Don't turn your customers off early. Over time, your one-time customers will develop into loyal clients if you consistently identify what they want and show them how you will meet their needs.

In the words of Richard Hiers (RealEstateHelpDesk.net), an online marketing pioneer and top producer with First Team Real Estate in Seal Beach, California, "While Internet marketing is an efficient and cost-effective means of keeping my pipeline full of good-quality prospects, it is gradually becoming my second-best source of new business. I believe my best source of new business will soon become referrals. I'll finish 2003 with 50% of my business coming from the Internet and 37% coming from referrals. In 2004 I expect these numbers to reverse themselves, and by 2005–2006, I think 75% of my new business will come from referrals."

Hiers concludes, "Relationships are begun with technology, but they are deepened with intentional high-touch over the years. Self promotion is out and benefit to the consumer is in."

PART

THREE

E-MAIL
MARKETING TO
CAPTURE AND
KEEP CUSTOMERS

CHAPTER

12

Planning Your E-Mail Marketing Strategy

OLD RULE

The Internet works best as a direct marketing medium.

NEW RULE

The Internet helps you generate transactions *and* build relationships.

E-Mail Is Still the Internet's Killer Application

When seminar attendees and customers ask me: "What are the essential eRainmaker strategies?" my short answer is:

1. Create a branded, customer-focused, destination website and promote it.
2. Build a permission-based, e-mail enhanced Trophy Database and automate the system.
3. Delegate technology tasks to virtual assistant(s) or staff so you rarely touch a keyboard (except for e-mail).

From the beginning of the Internet, e-mail was the "killer application" used first by customers and leading eRainmakers. In the

171

1990s, the graphic-enhanced World Wide Web superseded the early, first-wave text-only Internet. This second wave Internet exploded with the adoption of *browser* software (Mosaic, Netscape, Internet Explorer, Mozilla, Safari, and the like) to display and navigate web pages. In the 2000s, as high-speed access inched closer to penetrating a majority of households, nonbrowser Internet applications became a pleasure (games, movies, music, Internet telephone, messaging), all accessed outside the browser. Most important to e-marketers, these nonbrowser uses created a growing competition for website use.

How to Hit a Moving Target for Maximum Results

It's no secret that e-mail marketing is hot—really hot. Just open your inbox. Industry analysts say the volume of e-mail marketing is doubling annually. One Internet market research company, Forrester Research, predicts the commercial e-mail industry will be worth $6 billion a year by 2005.

Cost Savings

Compare the expense and speed of e-mail with direct mail, and you understand why everyone wants in on the action. For example, a simple direct-mail postcard costs about 50 cents to print and mail. More-sophisticated, envelope-clad marketing materials cost 70 cents to $1 per piece to produce and deliver. Transmitting a typical e-mail message, on the other hand, costs somewhere between 0.1 cent and 5 cents, depending on volume. These delivery savings, however, are offset somewhat by the cost of e-mail address acquisition and constant list maintenance.

Impressive Results

E-mail has another advantage over direct-mail marketing in that it is easier to measure results—and the results are impressive. Average response rates (the number of people clicking through from an e-mail to the advertiser's website) are 3% to 15% industrywide, compared with just 0.5% for banner ads and an estimated 1% to 2% for direct mail.

Combining direct mail with e-mail is the optimal choice, producing responses in the 18% to 20% range, according to Adam Komack, vice president of Gray Direct, a direct-mail service.

DoubleClick, a New York-based e-mail software vendor, reported in May 2003 in its *Q1 2003 E-mail Trend Report*, copyright DoubleClick, Inc., some very positive data gathered from analysis of its DARTmail e-mail delivery technology, involving over two billion e-mails from hundreds of its clients. The study revealed an overall average click-through rate of 8.9%, with consumer publishers the leading category at 11.5%. In other words, e-mail marketing works.

Content Is Key

Being able to deliver e-mail quickly and inexpensively is one thing, but the crucial factor is still e-mail content. Without the right approach, your e-mail campaign can fall on its face. Having a body of content to draw upon that is ready to be launched from an automated drip-marketing system can mean the difference between staying ahead of the competition—or being passed by while you reinvent the wheel.

Targeted Messages

The beauty of e-mail marketing is that each communication can be tailored to the recipient's preferences and needs. Put tracking software on your e-mail and website and you can pinpoint visitor interests, and produce response e-mail information that is particularly valuable to individual prospects. As your library of e-mail grows, you can slice and dice the information into rifle shots directly to a specific topic of interest.

An Opportunity and Challenge in Paradise

E-mail marketing is an essential marketing tool. Unfortunately, because e-mail is cheaper than direct mail, many practitioners have tried the shotgun strategy of "throw it out there and see if it works." It doesn't. Not only will your e-mail become less and less effective, it will also annoy your customer base. "As the (e-mail) readers separate the wheat from the chaff, it is imperative to craft the message so as to not be deleted before being read or swept into the dungeon of a bulk folder, never to be seen again," wrote Bruce McCracken in an excellent three-part series entitled "Targeted E-Mail: From Spam to Choice," for Jupitermedia Corporation's eCRM Guide (eCRMguide.com) in January 2003. "When hunting for the sale, do so as a sharp shooter, not Elmer Fudd with a shotgun," McCracken concludes.

Getting a response to your message has been an age-old objective for all direct marketers. E-mail is no different. Yet today, e-marketers face a great opportunity as well as a difficult challenge with e-mail. The huge opportunity for permission-based e-mail was created in October 2003, when the National Do-Not Call Registry that limits telemarketing went into effect. The big challenge for e-mail marketing comes from the deluge of spam.

National Do-Not Call Registry

The message the public sent about telemarketing is clear: Telemarketing is annoyingly intrusive. That point was reinforced when more than 52 million numbers were registered within a few months—almost one-third of the 166 million total numbers in the United States—after the Federal Trade Commission (FTC), the nation's consumer protection agency, opened it's National Do-Not Call Registry in June 2003. Almost 85% of the numbers were registered online at DoNotCall.gov.

While constitutionality and enforcement play out in the courts, real estate prospecting calls are affected, regardless if the rules change, such as for calls made within a state under the jurisdiction of the Federal Communications Commission (FCC), which will enforce the registry restrictions, or if the "prior business relationship" periods when it's okay to call are extended from 18-months after purchases or three-months after inquiries. (To avoid the risk of $11,000-per-violation penalties, real estate professionals must crosscheck their call lists against the registry every quarter by purchasing the list or using a service provider. More than 5,000 telemarketers bought the registry list by October 2003.)

If agents need another excuse not to cold call—and if brokers need the fear of another lawsuit to turn off the outbound phones—the National Do-Not Call List fills the need. The loss of "sell phones" creates a powerful opportunity. Many top-performing eRainmakers are shifting to permission-based e-mail that is less intrusive—and returning to unrestricted direct mail—to deliver valuable consumer information in a long-term customer-for-life relationship.

That Damn Spam

Increased e-mail: The average respondent got 254 e-mails weekly in Third Quarter 2002, up from 159 in 2001, according to a *Q3 2002 E-mail Trend Study*, copyright DoubleClick, Inc.

Use of bulk mail filters and delete key: Half of the respondents in the DoubleClick Third Quarter 2002 study use a filtering feature in their e-mail program that sorts e-mail into a bulk folder. Of that group, 76% report rarely or never reading e-mail in the bulk folder. The study also stated that 60% of that group is opting to delete unsolicited e-mails without reading them, up from 45% in 2001.

Challenge of Spam

E-mail is an easy, inexpensive, fast way to communicate. Unfortunately, the same qualities that make e-mail a great business tool also make it a potential annoyance. Spamming is the practice of sending unsolicited e-mails to recipients who haven't opted to receive your e-mail and are not interested in the information. Mass spammers are poisoning the well for legitimate e-mail. Inbox clutter ("spam jam") and annoyed prospects have made spam-sifting software one of the fastest growing technology segments. Blocked legitimate messages and unanswered business e-mail make e-marketers wring their hands in frustration.

GeekSpeak

Permission-Based E-Marketing: E-mail containing information or promotional messages recipients explicitly request to receive and that interests them. Sometimes, opt-in e-mail includes a statement that the recipient has previously agreed to receive such messages.

Two Proven Strategies to Fuel Your E-Marketing Engine

Strategy #1: Beat Spam with One-to-One E-Mail

What's the secret to beating spam? Focus on your customer. Include relevant content. Use merge fields to personalize the salutation with your customer's correct name (something almost no spam does successfully). Identify yourself clearly and upfront. Allow prospects to request preferences for content, frequency, and other choices. Use proven, customer-centered direct-response techniques that include calls to action. Build a business relationship with an integrated campaign of contacts by e-mail, mail, phone, and in person all focused on people who know you.

At the end of the day when spam is outlawed, priced out of business, or blocked and telemarketing remains risky, your legitimate permission-based e-mail marketing will survive. The successful techniques you learn along the way and the Trophy E-Mail Database you build will be invaluable to the buyer of your practice. When you consider the investment you have made to know what you know, the value of your experience will be priceless. Don't let telemarketing limits or spam put you off from using e-mail to stay in touch with current and past clients. Exactly how to use e-mails effectively—and not become a pest—are the keys to your success.

Strategy #2: Multiply Results with Integrated E-Strategy

Why hasn't e-mail made direct mail entirely disappear? After all, e-mail saves or eliminates costs of design, printing, and postage, plus the execution time and response time is so much faster than with direct mail. The reason both e-mail and direct mail survive is they both deliver results. In a nutshell, what works best is an integrated e-strategy that combines e-mail and website tools with offline marketing such as direct mail, print advertising, signage, and broadcast. Today, e-mail has joined the mix in your marketing toolkit, but like the hybrid "tech-and-touch" customers themselves, your toolkit has more tools now not less (what marketers call "channel enhancement").

In the postdot-com era, simply sending e-mail is not enough to break through "inbox clutter" and get results. As you develop your e-marketing strategy, remember the cardinal rule: Customer-focused marketing works best when it answers the prospect's first question, "What's in it for me?"

☑ "Buy for less"; "Sell for top dollar" (make them richer).

☑ "Buyer's representation is free"; "Close your sale in shortest time" (save them money or time).

☑ "Avoid the costly mistake of a double mortgage or money-pit property" (protect them from bad things).

☑ "Leave the selling to us"; "Stress-free move" (improve their lives).

☑ "New neighbors, community connections" (help them have good relationships).

☑ "Find your dream home" (help them be more successful).

☑ "Getaway vacation home"; "Rental property for retirement" (lead to better health, a longer life).

Experienced eRainmakers know—above all else—successful marketing must provide solutions to prospect's problems. Combining e-mail and offline marketing that targets customer needs is one of the best ways to fuel your e-marketing engine.

Checklist of Effective E-Mail Principles

☑ *Don't fish with dynamite:* Beyond lead generation, e-mail also works for prospect follow-up and long-term contact to retain customers. At its most effective, e-mail is a personal communication channel. Learn how to avoid blasting out one-size-fits-all messages that don't target the specific interests of your audience. With more customers using e-mail filters, generalized nontargeted messages too often are zapped to the bulk folder.

☑ *Customer contact is forever:* Avoid the tendency to treat e-mail as a standalone marketing effort. Remember, all your marketing is a myriad of "touches" with every customer that accumulates over time and has no defined starting or ending point. Strive to make every e-mail effort worth reading and build a mutually beneficial customer relationship. Practice "one-to-one" marketing.

☑ *Build a Trophy E-Mail Database:* Your own customer and prospect lists are the most valuable assets you will cultivate. Because this invaluable goldmine is built one contact at a time over years, your Trophy E-Mail Database is the principal asset a buyer of your practice will pay for in cash. A case in point: Typically, you will receive more than twice as many responses to an in-house list than a purchased list of strangers, according to the AMR Research report "Turning E-Mail Campaigns From Trash to Cash" (2001).

☑ *Offer clear privacy policy:* Having a simply written privacy policy with an easily accessible link is comforting and not only increases effectiveness, but also builds customer loyalty and trust. Add a strictly enforced privacy policy and you will discover your opt-out rates will decline as loyalty increases.

☑ *Make opt-out a preference not a yes/no question:* Opt-out is best presented as a link to a response form, not a direct reply (e.g., Don't use: "Reply to message with 'Remove' in subject line"). You must give customers a chance to indicate their preferences. A good example is a listing prospect that also wants to buy a home. The prospect wants to opt out of selling information, but is eager for buying information. Another example is a customer who simply wants to contact you, and the preferences form is handy. Creating a form that allows prospects to register their preferences—even as those preferences change—is critical. (For an example form, see eRainmaker.com: Preferences Form.)

Tracking Your E-Mail Response Rates Is Critical

Just as tracking your website results is important (unique visitors, referrer links, page views, exit pages, and so on), tracking your e-mail results can take your e-mail marketing to the next level. E-mail open-rates, click-throughs, bounce-backs, opt-outs, and viral marketing are all critical benchmarks that require keeping records. Once the technical ability to keep track is in place, then you can set objectives to improve the results (more opens, more click-throughs, fewer bounce-backs, fewer opt-outs) in the months ahead. Ultimately, your track record of enhancements steadily will increase response and add greater profits from efficiency and productivity.

Checklist of E-Mail Marketing Statistics

Here are the five key e-mail statistics you should be tracking:

1. *Open rate:* Recipient opens e-mail from inbox, expressed as a quantity and as a percentage. Averages widely vary, some e-marketers report 35% to 50% open rates for their best opt-in client lists, although those rates are the exception. Remember, an open rate is equivalent to opening a direct-mail envelope—it is not equivalent to an order or an appointment. (For comparison, analogous website advertising terms are "impression," "ad view," or "page view." Web page impression rates, however, do not indicate as interested a prospect as an e-mail open rate.)

2. *Click-through rate:* Recipient opens e-mail *and* clicks a hyperlink within e-mail message, as tracked by number and percent of e-mails sent. Figures widely vary. DoubleClick reports indicate 6.6% to 11.5% historically. Some providers report 12% to 15% click-through rates for in-house lists, up to 4% for rented lists. An e-mail click-through rate is equivalent to sending in a reply card for more information—it is not equivalent to an order or an appointment (see Figure 12.1). In contrast, click-through rates for high-repeat, website ads vary from 0.15% to 1%. Banner ads with provocative, mysterious, or other compelling content can induce web ad click-through rates ranging from 1% to 5% and sometimes higher. The click-through rate for a given ad tends to diminish with repeated exposure.

3. *Bad e-mail/bounce-back rate:* Number and percent of e-mails sent that are returned undeliverable due to temporary or permanent problems. Bounce-back rates averaged 12.5% of all marketing e-mail, according to first quarter 2003 figures by DoubleClick (DoubleClick.net). Of all bounce-backs, about half (53%) are soft bounces due to full in-boxes or temporary server outages and about half (47%) are hard bounces (incorrect, nonworking, abandoned, or false/nonexistent addresses).

Figure 12.1
E-Mail Results Holding Up against "Spam Jam"

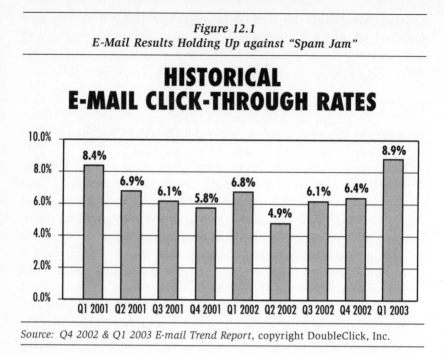

HISTORICAL E-MAIL CLICK-THROUGH RATES

Source: Q4 2002 & Q1 2003 E-mail Trend Report, copyright DoubleClick, Inc.

Annually, the percentage of addresses on an e-mail list that go bad ("churn") averages 20% to 40%.

4. *Opt-out/unsubscribe rate:* Recipient chooses to receive no further e-mail as a number and percent of e-mails sent. Averages widely vary; 7% to 10% typical, up to 25% opt-out rates reported in worst cases.

5. *Forward rate/viral marketing:* Recipient forwards e-mail to another party (what marketers call "member-get-a-member" or "tell-a-friend" technique), tracked as a quantity and percent of e-mails sent. Highest rates are from past-customer "advocates" segment. Averages widely vary; 1% to 2% referral rates reported. Include a place for text in your forwarded e-mail for a personal note from the forwarder to validate the message.

Costly Mistakes to Avoid When Sending E-Mail to AOL Prospects

Mistake #1: Sending Dead Hyperlinks

AOL does not use standard web conventions for website links and e-mail addresses. When an AOL member clicks on what other browsers see as an active link, nothing happens. This is especially aggravating because there are so many AOL users.

SOLUTION

To make your links active (URL or e-mail address) in e-mails to AOL users, you need to surround your link with some HTML code, which will make the text display as an active hyperlink (ask your tech staff for help if needed):

- ☑ Use quotes and no spaces to add a "prefix" of: < a href=" before your active link.
- ☑ Follow the link with a "postscript" of: " > www.MySite.com after your active link, repeating the text or link which is to be displayed to AOL user.
- ☑ The AOL link looks like this: www.MySite.com when you are all done.
- ☑ *Note:* Any text between the < . . . > brackets displays as a hyperlink, but it is usually best to simply use your URL or e-mail address. You can make an e-mail hyperlink by replacing your web address in the previous example with your e-mail address in both places with mailto:MyName@MySite.com.
- ☑ Add these AOL-friendly links to your signature on all e-mail after the text: "For AOL users." Put the AOL link in a standalone line to make it easier to copy and paste.

Mistake #2: Sending Attachments That Get Corrupted

Often, e-mail attachments sent to AOL customers get corrupted or simply do not appear at all. Not only is it a nuisance to resend, but you also look unprofessional, as if you forgot to include the attachment you referenced.

SOLUTION

This can also happen when one party is using a Mac and the other is using a PC that is not compatible. One simple solution for current clients is to use a web-based service as a holding center for large files and file sharing. Create an account, and then establish a "safe deposit box" on the site where you can upload any file using your browser. It works very much like inserting an e-mail attachment. The service sends e-mail to your recipient notifying them the file is available at the following link address. The recipient opens the link and retrieves the file through their browser (eRainmaker.com: Large Files).

13

Creating E-Mail That Gets Response

OLD RULE

Spam will be the death of e-mail.

NEW RULE

Permission marketing will survive
after spam is outlawed.

How to Write No-Fail E-Mail

The great power of e-mail comes from being one of the two interactive media (the other is the telephone) that inherently gives the prospect the ability to respond immediately and you the ability to communicate one-to-one. As an e-mail recipient yourself, you know that results depend on an instant positive reaction and action—or zap, the message is toast.

E-mail's unique combination of one-to-one personalization, timeliness, and requiring far less time to produce than other promotions make e-mail the perfect follow-up and client-retention medium. Except for driving traffic to a website with the most powerful two words in e-marketing—"Click here," cold-call lead generation is often better left to mass media such as direct mail, print, broadcast advertising, and signage. Yet, for nonintrusive conversion of prospects, e-mail is king. The place to begin for successful e-mail is at the top. That's why the sender From address and every Subject line is crucial.

Putting Your Best Foot Forward

Top eRainmakers know you only get one chance to make a good first impression. The same is true with e-mail. "The connection between the consumer and the marketer is paramount: the 'From' line is the most important factor motivating consumers to open e-mails; 60% of respondents cited the from line, while 35% cited the subject line," according to the *2002 Consumer E-mail Study*, copyright DoubleClick, Inc. that surveyed 1,000 consumers in September 2002.

Why are the From address and the Subject line critical? Based on a cursory glance at these two items, recipients decide to open or delete your e-mail in an instant. The process is analogous—but absolutely different in a critical little-known way—from a person scanning their regular mail to decide to open the envelope or toss it. If you don't get the recipient to open your e-mail, you've lost your chance to convert them into a customer.

Here are some inside tips on successful *From* addresses:

☑ *Leverage your brand:* People want to work with people they trust. If your brand or company name is well known, send the e-mail from that company name, so that "The Real Estate Team" appears in the From address.

☑ *Use your name and title:* If you use your name in the From address, the best response comes from using a name with a title (such as, Dan Gooder Richard, President), not just the name alone.

More tips to get your e-mail opened with great *Subject* lines:

☑ *Put something newsworthy in subject line.* E-mail recipients indicate that compelling information, news, trends, and discounts are what grab them most in a subject line. "Low Rates Mean Buying More for Less" or "Update: Home Vacant, Owners Anxious to Sell"

☑ *Tighten up your subject line:* Resist the temptation to go over 45 characters (five to seven words). Focus on your key benefit. Boil the words down to the real information the reader cares about. Stick with the facts. Use simple, descriptive words: "Sell For Top Dollar with Northside Expert"

☑ *Make the subject relevant:* Write a subject that is benefit-oriented and relevant to the recipient (such as, "Responding to your inquiry;" "You can buy more home than you think"). To begin rapport building in your subject line (rather than suspicion), use a "How to . . ." sentence or an active power verb (Visit, Hurry, Jump, Run, and so on). Just be aware that some aggressive spam filters consider some imperative verbs too aggressive and may route your e-mail to Filterland for using Get, Open, Download, Buy, Save, Make, Take, Respond, and so on.

☑ *Personalize your subject line:* Merge recipient's name or town or street into the subject line if your technology permits. Use a single noun that puts the right hat on the prospect (Home Buyer, Home Seller, Investor, etc.), or a question ("Want to pay less in taxes?").

☑ *Avoid spam filter triggers:* The challenge of spam filters will be an evolving problem for genuine e-mail. Stay away from commonly identified spam words, such as "free" (try "no charge," "complimentary," "gift"). Avoid disguising words by replacing letters with punctuation ("F**E"). Refrain from filter triggers such as all upper-case words, exclamation points, miscellaneous characters. Even personal pronouns as the first word in the subject line ("You," "Your," "I," and "Me") and even some colors, such as red, can block delivery. Using the abbreviation ADV implies your message is not permission based.

☑ *Critical little-known secret:* Remember, direct-mail teaser copy techniques used on envelopes do not translate into effective e-mail subject lines. Today, using direct mail teaser text is one of the surest ways to send your e-mail to the recycle bin in a click. Use this little-known secret to make your e-mail more effective.

Top Tips to Grab Maximum Response with Hooks, Lines, and Buzz Words That Work

Writing effective e-mail requires you get to the point quickly, in short, pertinent sentences or bullets, "above the fold" before the reader has to scroll downward. Remember, specifics are always more effective than generalities. Matching your message to the prospect's interests is easier with e-mail and critical to maximize your success:

1. *Sharpen your hook:* Turbo charge the first few sentences to grab the reader with your central message. Many prospects preview the top text before opening. Focus on what they'll get (benefits), not the features you offer. Make sure your offer, call to action, and key links are up top. "Search for properties on-line, real time, anytime. Click here."

2. *Use the "five-second rule:"* To decide to open your e-mail, your reader must understand the purpose of your e-mail in seconds, just like a highway billboard. Use the first two inches of your text to make your intentions known. Burying your offer deep in the text ensures your e-mail will get dropped into the recycle bin before the reader gets your point.

3. *Less is more:* Test short and long copy. You may be surprised what works best. If in doubt, go short. Focus. Short, concise sentences. Short paragraphs of 3 to 4 lines. Less than 250 words in total. Emphasize key points with bullets or stars. Write for both the scan reader and the careful reader gathering information. Concentrate on one offer; sell one item, one concept, include one call to action. Avoid the temptation to throw all your eggs into one basket.

4. *Use hotbutton words:* Direct marketing has proven certain words out-pull ordinary English. Insert them early and often in text, *not in the subject line:* you, free, save, now/at last, new, today, discover, introducing, announcing, guarantee, easy, limited offer or time, urgent, bargain, last chance, exclusive, improved, revolutionary. It is almost impossible to use them too much. Every time you write a "we" phrase ("We sell faster."), change it to a "you" phrase ("You sell faster.").

5. *Feature direct-response offers:* The key to getting response from your target prospect is to offer something of value that only an interested prospect would respond to get. A well-crafted offer that "adds value" or provides a solution (save money, save time, avoid mistakes, make them richer, provide essential information, and so on) maximizes e-mail response. Remember, the five great motivators to action are fear, exclusivity, greed, guilt, and need for approval.

6. *Tell them what to do:* Clearly state what you want them do: e-mail, call, or go to your website. Give them the information they need. Make it easy to respond. Don't expect them to go to your website to get your phone number. Repeat your call to action: Once above the fold (hook) and once in the postscript just above your e-mail signature.

7. *Toss in a freebie:* Consider giving something free, extra, or a bonus item of value as an instant reward in return for their action. Remember a deadline motivates people to get off the fence and act.

8. *Expand your reach:* Encourage forwarding your message. For maximum viral marketing give reasons and benefits to recipient that says why they should bother. "Help a friend find their dream house—before someone else buys it." Avoid an incentive (bribe) to the sender. Consider specifying a "distribution list" of who should see the message (friends, neighbors, coworkers, relatives).

9. *Close with a postscript (P.S.):* Unlike direct-mail letters, place your P.S. *above* your e-mail signature, because many people don't scroll past the signature. Restate your offer. Word the text to add urgency ("Request your free copy of my printed report while supplies last."). Make it easy to respond ("reply to this e-mail," "click on hyperlink for instant order form" or "call this phone number").

10. *Add artful link to your letter:* If you are a twenty-first century real estate professional, you already know what a powerful marketing tool e-mail can be. But many e-mails lack the hypertext link to a web page that makes the effort worthwhile. To make sure those who receive your message actually visit your site or look at the homes you are marketing, be sure to include several hyperlinks throughout your e-mail message, especially one connected to your response offer. If you write out the entire web address (beginning with http://) then your readers can simply click and go!

11. *Be interactive, not hyperactive:* Graphical HTML e-mail can be quick to scan, but not if it is busy, cluttered, or overly "designed." Using HTML messages, interactive links, and drop-down menus allows readers to find information easily that interests them. Avoid hyperactive multimedia e-mail, especially

slow loading Flash animation that annoys more than it impresses because it wastes your reader's precious time. Worst of all, hyper-media may require downloading a player to view or hear; avoid these options like the plague. See more on HTML e-mail later in this chapter.

12. *Protect your image:* Have someone else proofread your message. Put it aside overnight. Send it to yourself for a fresh read in an actual inbox environment. Check for errors, especially confirm every link is active and no URLs break in two lines which can cause difficulty. Remember, you are building an ongoing dialogue with customers and prospects.

13. *Seed your list:* When you are done, send e-mail to staff to prepare them to handle responses. You'll also be able to verify delivery.

14. *Cover the "black hole":* Plan ahead to retry soft bounces and decide how to communicate with opt outs and hard undeliverables that need an e-mail address change (call, write, or delete as last resort).

15. *Shop your competition:* Visit your competitors' websites and request information. Get on their e-mail list. Evaluate what they are doing well or poorly.

Maximize Results with Ever-Popular Market Analysis

When you find a winning offer that generates response year in and year out, there is the risk you will tire of it and think prospective home sellers have, too. Don't make that all-too-common mistake. One of the best examples is the competitive market analysis (CMA). One of the best ways to fill your inbox with prospects is offer to show prospective sellers what their home is worth (Figure 13.1). Because the market and prospect pool are always changing, the results of a CMA offer are always fresh.

Here are several ways to keep this all-time winner working for you:

1. *Register your own domain:* Create a specialty web domain that points to the CMA response form on your website. To find an available domain, experiment with different

Figure 13.1
"What Is Your Home Worth?" Postcard

Source: Courtesy of Russell Arkin (NorthernVAHomeInfo.com), RE/MAX Distinctive Real Estate, McLean, Virginia.

syntax, such as: (City)HomeValue.com, (County)HomeValues .com, PriceYour(City)Home.com, and so on. As of this writing, CompetitiveMarketAnalysis is available for all these domains: .ORG, .BIZ, .INFO, .US, .CC, .BZ, .TV. Throw in two hyphens, and .COM is available (Competitive-Market-Analysis.com).

2. *Give CMA a new name:* For decades, I have seen this classic offer given new legs by giving it a new name. Test replacing the competitive "C" word with Comparable, Confidential, Computerized, Complimentary, Comprehensive, Complete, Customized. You'll discover it gives the CMA an entirely new slant with fresh benefits for the homeowner. Then really pull out the stops, for example, with a CCMA: Confidential Computerized Market Analysis.

3. *Deliver CMA in a new way:* Another technique is to make the CMA appealingly easy for the prospect to request. Test headlines that offer your CMA as an "on-the-phone evaluation" or "over-the-net value" or "CMA by mail," which means the prospect can *request* the CMA via phone or e-mail or reply mail. How you *deliver* the CMA can be up to you and your prospect—by phone or e-mail or in person.

4. *Change your offer often:* In your e-mail and on your website, sprinkle the offer of a CMA or "CMA-lite" (see "Tiered CMA" below) throughout by presenting this proven lead-generator in different ways. Change the hyperlink display text. Change the button image. Change the subject line. Add it to or remove it from your e-mail signatures. A fresh approach will capture fresh leads.

5. *Create a tiered CMA offer:* Different prospects require different service. Some prospects are ready to sit down with you and get a full-blown, in-person listing presentation complete with CMA. Others want a simple broker price opinion or an approximate "drive-by" or "MLS" price range for planning purposes or refinancing. Consider offering a variety of services and give them different names, such as an Analysis, Evaluation, Estimate, Internet Range, Market Value, or Ballpark. Use the difference to qualify prospects by asking, "We have two pricing services, one for owners who want to sell and move soon, one for owners who want a planning figure. Which one fits your needs?" One CMA

could be called: "ValueOne," the other: "ValuePlus" to differentiate the services.

Creating High-Impact Graphic E-Mail That Looks like a Web Page

You have probably received advertising e-mail that is designed in
HTML (Hypertext Markup Language) to give it more impact than text-
only e-mail. Not only does a web page embedded into an e-mail message look great, it also can contain forms, pull-down menus, buttons,
and links that function within the e-mail message.

In the 1990s, eRainmakers had to be concerned that some e-mail
client software and AOL could not display HTML code. Today, the vast
majority of e-mail clients support graphic e-mail. There are, however,
older versions of e-mail applications still being used, such as AOL 4.0
and Lotus Notes 5.0, which do not display HTML properly. Many
eRainmakers use a variety of e-mail formats including HTML, text-
only, and multipart formats (blended HTML and text only). Avoid the
temptation to use framed web design, because frames don't always
display properly in e-mail. Check with your e-mail software provider
(such as Earthlink Web Mail, Lotus Notes 5.0, Yahoo!, Eudora 5.0,
Microsoft Hotmail, Outlook Express, and Outlook 2000, AOL 6.0 and
4.0) for tips on designing and embedding graphic e-mail.

---

eRainmaker Tip

Rich Multimedia: Strictly speaking "rich media" or "multimedia" e-mail includes graphics, interactive menus, and perhaps motion and sound. Including motion and sound is possible
but requires more plug-in software for the recipient to be able to
view or listen to the message. Hold off on multimedia e-mail unless you know the recipient can receive it properly—and quickly
(not downloading several programs). Be sure to keep your opt-
out "Preferences Center" form in text only or HTML links.

Not Just Your Father's Text Anymore

Text-only e-mail and graphical HTML e-mail both generate results. The secret for eRainmakers is that both types of e-mail work in different ways.

☑ *Text upside:* Text-only e-mail is better when you want to deliver a message. Text tends to add *urgency* because, done right, it looks like you just wrote it for the reader. Also text is simpler to create and easier to personalize. Text pulls best for an introductory letter or opt-in offer.

☑ *Text downside:* Text is words, and words need to be read— which comes close to being work if the words are not crafted carefully.

☑ *HTML upside:* HTML e-mail, on the other hand, tends to add *experience.* The visual impact of embedded links, images, and design (even sound and motion) conveys emotion—which is ideal for selling properties with virtual tours and panoramic photos. The graphics allow more information to be presented in a smaller layout than linear text.

☑ *HTML downside:* HTML is harder to create and it tends to look like advertising which can be a turn-off or turn-on, depending on whether the prospect is ready to be pitched.

Pick Your Shot

When you are ready to juice up the e-mails you send to your clients, use the HTML format rather than plain text. By using HTML, you will be able to select any font, color, or type style. Adding graphics and photos will really bring your correspondence to life (Figure 13.2). Be careful, however. Messages that are too large may frustrate rather than fascinate. Keep HTML files under 65K and no more than 675 pixels wide.

Generally speaking, HTML e-mail gets more response than a text-only e-mail, just like a display print ad has more impact than an all-text ad. Everything from color to layout to interactivity (links, drop-down menus) and animation (movement) gives HTML e-mail a greater response rate. Click-through rates can be as much as two to three times higher for HTML than traditional text e-mail, according to

Figure 13.2
HTML E-Mail Delivers Maximum Results

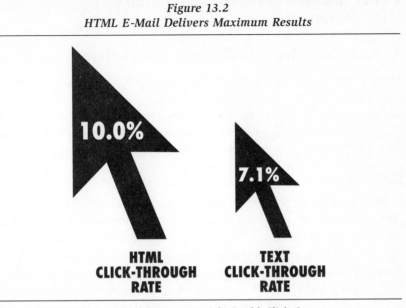

Source: *Q1 2003 E-mail Trend Report,* copyright DoubleClick, Inc.

DSTechSolutions (DSTechSolutions.com), a web services and e-mail marketing firm based in Pine Valley, California. In the *Q1 2003 E-mail Trend Report,* copyright DoubleClick, Inc., the firm reported HTML generated a higher overall click-through rate for their clients of 10.0% compared to 7.1% for plain text (down from fourth quarter 2002 where HTML drew 11.2% and text pulled 5.6%).

DoubleClick also reported in the fourth quarter 2002 that HTML e-mail made up 81% of promotional e-mail DoubleClick transmitted for clients, while text-only and multipart format (both HTML and text for AOL users) made up the rest. Most important, click-through rates for text e-mails continued to decline during 2002 (from 7.1% in the second quarter 2002 to 5.6% in the fourth quarter 2002), while HTML click-through rates fluctuated (from 10.0% in second quarter 2002 to 11.2% in fourth quarter 2002 to 10.0% in first quarter 2003), according to DoubleClick's *E-mail Trend Reports.*

The bottom line is: Test for yourself. Experiment and develop your own results for your trophy e-mail list and target customer groups.

Costly Mistake to Avoid When Preparing Your E-Mail

Mistake: Sending E-Mail on the Wrong Day

Many website analytics report that e-mail responses to real estate web-sites are the highest on Monday, as if prospects drove through neighborhoods over the weekend and decided to get serious on Monday. Given the growing e-mail volume people receive, sending prospecting e-mail that gets lost in the clutter is a mistake in any industry.

SOLUTION

Large e-mailers track their results and tend to send more e-mail on particular days of the week. The most popular days are mid-week, generally Tuesday through Thursday, according to DoubleClick, one of the top e-mail service providers with international headquarters in New York City. Every quarter, DoubleClick sends more than two billion permission-based e-mails for hundreds of clients. They have studied the favored mailing day and found almost a quarter of all e-mail was sent on Tuesdays in Q1 2003 (consistent with fourth quarter 2002), followed by Wednesdays, then Thursdays. By industry, 30% of retail and catalog e-mails were sent on Tuesday, while financial services sent the most (16%) on Tuesday.

What are the best months? The highest volume months for e-mail and postal mail confirm direct marketers practice the "Bookend Technique" outlined in Chapter 2 where direct mail and e-mail are sequenced in tandem for maximum results. The three highest volume months for postal mailers are September (14%), October (13%) and January (19%) which are followed by the busiest e-mail months: November (15%), December (13%) and March (13%), according to the first-ever Direct Marketing Association study, *State of Postal and E-Mail Marketing 2002,* that surveyed 2,000 voting members and got 386 responses by April 2002 (19.3% response rate).

14

Converting Prospects with E-Mail Follow-Up

Fast, First Response Can Spell Victory or Defeat with Internet Prospects

Fast response is critical. Yet many real estate professionals don't respond professionally—if at all. Scot Kenkel (TheEmailDoctor.com) is an e-mail marketing trainer and consultant based in Oak Ridge, Tennessee, who works with real estate brokerages nationwide to help agents improve their e-marketing skills. In summer 2002, Kenkel put the e-marketing savvy of nearly 1,000 agents in five different franchises in five different cities to the test in an independent survey.

First, Kenkel visited agent websites and discovered only 26% of the agents promoted their e-mail address on their website (in addition, he later discovered 16% of the published addresses bounced back as bad e-mail).

"Next I wanted to determine what percent would respond to a gimme, a golden nugget inquiry," Kenkel said. He sent an e-mail that stated he was moving to their area with his wife and family and he was looking for an agent to work with to buy a house priced at the market average. "If you are interested please respond by e-mail," he wrote (Kenkel did not include his phone or address). Only 42% responded. Kenkel subsequently has experienced response rates as low as 20% to his mystery shopping surveys.

"Of the respondents," Kenkel said, "44% asked me to call them back on the phone." What agents don't understand, Kenkel says, is that e-mail is the language of communication for this prospect and to ask for a return phone call is like asking the prospect to use a foreign tongue. Kenkel also discovered 55% of the respondents did not include their name or the company name in their e-mail, apparently assuming a "reply" was all the identification needed.

"Most agents and brokers who think their website doesn't work, think the problem is with their website. In fact, the problem is they don't know how to handle Internet leads," Kenkel said. "Most agents today don't understand the devastating impact a bad response has on an e-mail prospect."

Beyond the need to respond quickly, in many cases, the best "first response" e-mail to new prospects is a personally written message crafted to answer specific questions and circumstances of the prospect. This is particularly true if you want to match the prospect's needs with links to virtual tours or specific community information. Unfortunately, writing personal notes is tiresome and time consuming. Here are several options for rapid first response:

Auto-Responders

An auto-responder is a program that automatically sends a one-time e-mail reply message when a unique "trigger" e-mail address receives a message. In Microsoft Outlook 2000, a good example of an auto-responder is your "Out of Office Assistant" (Tools > Out of Office Assistant). If you use your regular e-mail address as the trigger, the software replies instantly with a prewritten message to every inbound e-mail you receive until you turn off the auto-responder.

Signatures

One of the simplest techniques is to use your signature files in your e-mail program to store a variety of "first-response" e-mails that you use over and over. Consider the signature as a complete e-mail with salutation, message, and a closing signature. Another solution is to save your e-mails as you go. Before long, categories will emerge to help you group the e-mails in subfolders for easy retrieval as templates. You can also use existing print letters you have saved as documents, copying and pasting them as replies. Group your e-mails in a Consumers folder with subfolders for Buyers, Expireds, FSBOs, Open House Visitors, Sellers, Transferees, Investors, and so on, or into a Business folder with subfolders for Agents, Attorneys, Brokers, Builders, Closing/Settlement, Inspectors, Lenders, Title, and so on.

When you (or your assistant) click reply to an inquiry, simply go to Signature Picker (Outlook 2000: Tools > Options > Mail Format > Signature Picker) to select the first-response message you want, and click. The entire text message appears in the body of your e-mail reply. To spot where to add the personal information specific to a customer, put those items in brackets and upper case: [FIRST NAME] or [PROPERTY ADDRESS] or [VIRTUAL TOUR LINK]. Add a name to your salutation (Hi [FIRST NAME]!) and perhaps dash off a quick first sentence or two. The message body can promise a more complete reply to come "shortly." This solution buys you time for a more tailored response later or an automated "drip" campaign. Remember: These signature templates can be used for any routine e-mail, such as your transaction checklist, not just your web inquiry first response. Be sure to include your complete contact information at the end.

Showing prospects how to use her website to search properties is one of the most successful uses of signatures for Margaret Rome (HomeRome.com), a CYBERSTAR® and top producer with Coldwell Banker Residential Brokerage in Baltimore, Maryland. Rome promotes the tagline "Locate every home for sale through my website" in her print ads. When prospects call, Rome says, she often sends the following e-mail response saved in her signature file while still on the phone with prospects:

☑ You can find properties listed by me by going to www.HomeRome .com and clicking "MY LISTINGS."

☑ You can find EVERY property listed on the MLS by going to www.HomeRome.com and clicking "ALL LISTINGS."

☑ If you put in your criteria, such as number of bedrooms, zip code, county, price, etc., you will be given all properties that are currently on the market.

☑ By putting in your e-mail address, you will be notified daily as new homes meeting your search criteria become available. You will be given price, photos, and even the address. Don't forget your e-mail address.

Rome also keeps another signature response ready with a list of lenders and their phone numbers.

Top agent and CYBERSTAR Linda Soesbe (ColoradoHomeSource .com) with McGinnis GMAC Real Estate in Colorado Springs, Colorado, sets aside a half hour at the end of each day to send follow-up e-mail from her office. "Using saved signatures it just takes a click and I send it," said Soesbe. "The e-mail is waiting for them in the morning." Soesbe has built a repertoire of scores of saved signatures as templates, as well as loading in most of Dave Beson's Letterwriter and eLetterwriter messages as signatures. Every e-mail asks the prospect how and when they would like to be contacted. At home? Work? On road? Phone? E-mail? "That leaves them in control, as they should be," Soesbe said.

Some signature examples:

☑ *Linda* (plain signature only)

☑ *Special interests* (anniversaries, birthdays, golf, Denver Broncos, and more)

☑ *First basic response* (Often sent from Motorola e-mail pager; "What would you like in your relocation packet?")

☑ *Second basic response* ("Haven't heard from you. Tell me your needs so I can personalize your relocation packet.")

☑ *Third basic response* ("Click this link to relocation information on my website. I'll personalize your packet after I hear from you.")

☑ *Fourth basic response* ("Haven't heard from you. Are you still interested?")

☑ *Buyer prospect* ("What features are you looking for?")

☑ *Seller prospect* ("When would you like to move?")

☑ *Closing invitation* ("You are cordially invited to the closing of [address] on [date/time] at [place]." Uses special signature e-stationery.)

☑ *After closing* (2 days after settlement, "How is move going? Anything you need?")

☑ *After sale coupon* (Within week after closing, printable coupon for restaurant, maid service, or handyman as PDF attachment, "Here's something for you.")

☑ *After sale documents* ("Here are some closing documents you will need." PDF attachments)

Soesbe used her e-mail first response system to close 50 transactions in 2002 for a production of nearly $9 million that made her #1 in her company. Soesbe projected she would close 60 deals in 2003 "all without an assistant."

E-Mail Templates

In addition to Signature files, you can also save e-mail templates in Microsoft Outlook 2000 (or higher). These handy, ready-to-go e-mails can be text-only or graphic HTML, and can include subject line, attachments, and Cc: and Bcc: addresses (such as your virtual assistant). To learn more, read an excellent three-part series written by Michael Russer (aka, Mr. Internet®) and published in *Realtor* magazine, October 2002, December 2002, and January 2003. It is available online (Russer.com > Articles), complete with animated tutorials, titled: "Business-Building E-Mail Templates on STEROIDS! (PART I & II)." Also, check the template and template organizer tutorials.

Avoid the Bed Bug Letter

Answering routine e-mail quickly and accurately is a challenge in any business. Here is a cautionary tale: In the travel industry, the "Bed Bug Letter" is legendary, according to Pete French, owner/manager of a popular skiing and tennis resort in Taos, New Mexico (QuailRidgeInn .com) and one of my oldest friends from our Peace Corps days in India. Apparently, a famous New York hotel received a query from a guest that asked, "It couldn't have been bed bugs, could it?" The manager fired off a quick letter reciting the glories of the hotel and extraordinary housekeeping measures routinely implemented, adding in a P.S. a plausible denial that *his* hotel could not possibly be the source of the *guest's* bed bugs. Dutifully the letter was saved—complete with the bed bug denial postscript. It wasn't until some time later that a new secretary used the letter in a follow-up "thank-you" campaign to *all* previous guests, but never changed the bed bug P.S. Soon the hotel was caught up in a PR whirlwind of back peddling and explaining and trying to reestablish the facility *never* had had a bed bug problem, *neither* caused by the hotel, *nor* caused by a guest. *Moral:* Proof every e-mail before you click send.

Automated Drip Marketing by E-Mail Comes of Age

Imagine an automated marketing system where you don't have to lift a finger because scheduled, personalized e-mails are sent as long as it takes to get the appointment.

Imagine an automated marketing system where your production and income are double what they are today because all you have to do is close presold customers who contact you when they are "ready" to buy or sell.

Imagine an automated marketing system where you can go on holiday *and* build a million-dollar practice because other eRainmakers realize how much your steady flow of transactions would be worth to them.

What you have imagined is an automated *drip-marketing* system for e-mail follow-up. Drip marketing has become one of the most essential tools inundated eRainmakers use to convert what can be an overwhelming flood of cyber-prospects into real-world customers.

The technology that makes drip marketing possible is a server-based software program controlled through your web browser rather than your desktop contact manager. These powerful programs are designed to be "set it and forget it" systems that send a personalized series of e-mails to a contact automatically. The best services provide prewritten messages (you can edit if desired or add your favorite letters) *and* send the e-mail automatically.

Ideal Systems

Look for a system that allows you to bulk-import batches of contacts or auto-populate contact records from response forms on your website as well as enter contacts manually. Once prospects are in the online database, you assign a series of e-mails to be sent to the individual contact as frequently as you wish. E-mails are scheduled counting from the date a series is assigned, which means one contact receives the series on a schedule completely independent of another contact.

In addition to an Action Plan (with a set number of e-mails), you can launch an ongoing Campaign that continuously e-mails an e-newsletter or series of savvy quotes on any automated schedule you select (weekly, biweekly, monthly, bimonthly, quarterly, etc.), depending on how often you want to "touch" a contact. Campaigns are particularly helpful with prospects that contact you early in their information-gathering stage, but need to be cultivated until they are ready to act, sometimes months even years later. A fast, easy, automated drip-marketing e-mail machine does most of the work for you.

B2B Network

Veteran eRainmakers often expand their network beyond consumer contacts. Business contacts (agents in your office, your company, area cobrokers, out-of-area referral contacts, franchise network contacts, agents you met at conferences or who are members of your designation, and more) are equally good targets. You can also include transaction-related professionals and home service providers. The possibilities are endless.

Creative Content

The leading systems also include comprehensive content in the form of prewritten e-mail messages and e-newsletters. Not only will you need content for a wide range of prospects about buying, selling, financing, and relocating, but you will also want to tweak system e-mails with your own edits—or copy and paste your favorite letters into the automated system.

The most effective content is well-written, in a conversational style that reads the way you talk, features response-oriented subjects, allows merge fields to maximize personalization for the recipient, generates further response with links to your services and special free reports, and includes a signature customized to the target market (consumer, business, personal). Ideally, content is a mix of text-only messages and graphic-rich HTML designer e-mail that always stays fresh and engages the contact.

A true preferences link that manages unsubscribers automatically is essential and allows the contacts to tell you why their preferences have changed without you doing anything, plus notifies you for possible follow-up (eRainmaker.com: Automated E-Mail).

"Able, Willing, and Ready" E-Technique Turns Old Adage on Its Head

As websites have matured, the focus has changed from being a marketing cost to being a revenue generator. Today's best sites are more than marketing tools. In addition to providing a wealth of information, the leading real estate websites prequalify leads, encourage cross-selling of related services (mortgage, property management, warranties, homeowners insurance, title, and settlement services), and delegate follow-up tasks to assistants and automated e-mail systems.

Peter McGarry is one of the leading real estate marketers in the country. As vice president of business development for Fonville-Morisey Realtors (FMRealty.com) in Raleigh, North Carolina, McGarry has helped build the company into the 56th largest brokerage in the

---

Figure 14.1
Fonville-Morisey "Able, Willing, and Ready" System

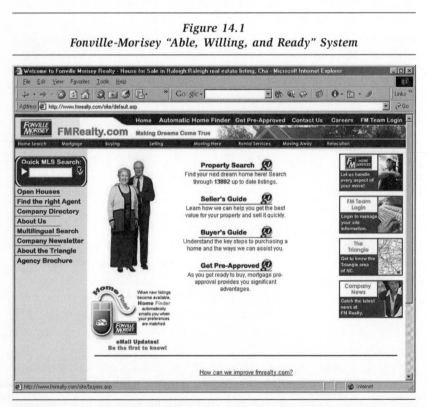

Source: Courtesy of Fonville-Morisey Realty (FMRealty.com), Raleigh, North Carolina.

nation with more than $1.7 billion in annual sales, according to the *Real Trends 500* report published in May 2003 (Figure 14.1).

McGarry has polished an innovative "Able, Willing, and Ready" prospect follow-up program where "able" prospects register on the company website and are "willing" to receive updates until they are "ready" to meet with an agent or loan officer. "People that hit a hook as they are swimming through the site are self-qualified," said McGarry. "The follow-up system is designed to be a loyalty building technique." The average time for a prospect to move through the Fonville-Morisey system from first registration to final settlement is four-and-a-half months. McGarry's system practices four powerfully profitable strategies of generate, incubate, scrub, and capture.

Generate

Prospects are generated by straight-forward e-mail inquiries and registrations for e-mail listing updates in the Home Finder system ("Be the first to know!") as well as a "Get Pre-Approved" offer on the company website. The company site averages 910 unique visitors a day and generates about five leads a day, on average three for real estate and two for loan preapproval requests. At any one time, the system averages 700 or more prospects registered for e-mail property updates. McGarry constantly monitors site statistics for "swimming patterns" to be sure prospects are driven to and through the website.

Incubate

The automated Home Finder service incubates "willing" prospects as if they were a "stock pond," said McGarry. Prospects working with an agent are always forwarded to that agent. "Ask for me, there's no fee," is company policy. McGarry's team is careful not to fish with dynamite in this prospect pool to avoid "spooking the herd."

Scrub

Most important of all, the full-time e-Services Coordinator launches an automated e-mail and phone follow-up with prospects, always asking for a response—what McGarry calls "e-Tennis." Using permission marketing, scheduled short e-mails are sent to the prospects often using a question hook (Are you preapproved? Do you want to visit properties? Are you ready to meet with an agent? Do you want to meet with a loan officer?). From experience, McGarry has learned a mortgage preapproval appointment with a loan officer is the ultimate loyalty multiplier. Few services increase the quality of prospects like having cash in their pocket.

Capture

"The most bone fide lead is an appointment—not an information request," said McGarry. "At the moment they ask for an appointment, they have gone from being a cyber-surfer to being a real-world customer." McGarry uses Home Finder to generate appointments, and web-based appointment scheduling software that features the available showing times for all inventory. Prospects are then referred through the Relocation Department to a group of qualified agents and loan officers who meet and close the customers.

Success is in the results. In 2002, 105 "working with" prospects were forwarded to their identified agents without a fee. Out of the 743 referrals placed, the agents closed 82 transactions (11% conversion rate which is expected to reach 25% in 2003 from carryover and new prospects). The bottom line was a total gross commission income for company and agents of more than $290,000 from website leads alone in 2002.

"Not only does it work for the consumer to jump into our net when they're ready," explained McGarry, "but our agents and loan officers have closed a boatload of business that could have slipped through our fingers—or worse—been swept up by our competition."

Win-Win Techniques to Capture Prospects When They Are Ready to Act

How to get prospects that are on the fence to leap to action (ideally, an appointment with you face-to-face) is an on-going challenge. One of the most effective techniques is what I call the "Last-Chance Trigger."

Last-Chance Trigger

Begin with a time-sensitive offer, that is, an offer that expires at a certain date. "Register now for our free 'How to Get Top Dollar' home-seller's seminar while seats are available. First come, first served. Reservations close Friday, February 28, 5 P.M." Advertise in print or broadcast and promote the seminar by mail. The expiration date (February 28) will trigger you to send a pair of "Last Chance" e-mails three days before and then one day before the expiration date. Only the just-in-time delivery ability of e-mail makes the Last-Chance Trigger possible.

Besides restating the "What's In It For Me" benefits to the prospect for responding to your offer and attending the seminar in the message body, put the power of response e-mail to work in three specific places:

1. *Subject line:* Repeat the deadline date in subject line. "Last Chance to Register."

2. *Billboard rule:* Give them your best shot in the first sentence or two. "Read this ASAP. Registration is closing February 28 for the last remaining seats in our popular 'How to Get Top Dollar' home-seller seminar. It's free. Click reply to register."

3. *Postscript:* After the benefit-oriented text, above your signature, include a call-to-action postscript. "P.S. Any real estate sale can be fraught with pitfalls if you don't know exactly what you're doing. When you're juggling the sale of one home and the purchase of another, the potential dangers multiply. You don't have to go through this obstacle course blind! Register now for our free seminar 'How to Get Top Dollar for Your Home in Today's Market.' Registration closes February 28. *Register Here* or reply to this e-mail or call [assistant's name] at [phone number]."

Selling His County One Yard at a Time

As "Wright County Minnesota's #1 Home Seller," Steve Tryggeseth (WrightCountyHome.com), a top producer with RE/MAX Professionals in Maple Grove, Minnesota, and Allen F. Hainge CYBERSTAR, the best listing and marketing strategy is the pursuit of expired and cancelled listings. "With a consistent and relentless follow-up campaign of *every* expired and cancelled listing, this segment now makes up almost 50% of my business," said Tryggeseth. "The key to my success is very simple. Identify the expired prospect, and systematically show them I am the most aggressive agent in the area. When they call, I have no competition. I *am* the expert. Currently, I mail out 13 pieces of follow-up in the first 30 days. After that, the prospect goes on a monthly follow-up postcard campaign." Tryggeseth said, "until they list with me, list with some other agent, call and ask to be removed from my database—or they die."

Every piece Tryggeseth mails features a call-to-action to visit his website or call him to learn how he markets other properties, uses virtual tours, and continuously captures buyer prospects. "When I go out there (on appointment)," says Tryggeseth, "they usually have checked me out thoroughly and they know my marketing and follow up is the best they can hire."

Costly Mistake to Avoid When Preparing Your E-Mail

Mistake #1: Wording Opt-Out Link without Thinking

I once chatted at a seminar with a real estate professional (who shall remain nameless) who experienced an opt-out rate of 25% of their list from their first bulk e-mailing. It was a disaster. To make it worse, they continued to e-mail to their customer list over the next few months and got as much as 7% of their customers opting-out every time they mailed. They were losing customers faster than they could bring them in! In the end, they lost huge chunks of their permission-based list. To make it worse, because of the way they worded their opt-out link, they weren't sure if they could send the opt-outs e-mail ever again!

SOLUTION

First impressions count. Be careful not to promise *never* to send them another e-mail or promotion of any type whatsoever ever again. Word your preferences link and response form carefully. Example: "To no longer receive automated e-mail, *contact us.*" Here are some more tips:

☑ It's worth repeating: Spam filter software sometimes is set to block phrases such as "Opt-out," "Unsubscribe," or "Remove." To avoid having your legitimate e-mail blocked and undelivered, use the phrase "Contact us" or "Preferences" as display text on the link to your preferences form.

☑ Add a message box in your preferences form to allow the customer to type a message. You'll be surprised how often they send you a nonopt-out message, such as; "I'll be out of town for the season. Start me up again in six months." Or, "We just bought a house, but keep in touch about investment property."

☑ Remember, customers have something they want to say to you. They often don't think which technology will receive their response or realize what they are saying is being delivered to a different recipient or department than the one sending the original e-mail. What matters is that you respond to their request, no matter if it is to opt out or something entirely different.

☑ Be sure to include your e-mail, name, company, address, phone, and fax on the preferences form.

15

Using E-Mail to Build After-Sale Referrals and Repeat Business

OLD RULE
The dot-com era was the peak
of the Internet.

NEW RULE
The Next Wave Internet boom
is here— and it's going to last.

Word-of-Mouse E-Marketing

Every eRainmaker knows referrals and repeat business are the most profitable source of business. Referred prospects and past clients already trust you, have proven loyalty, and have an affinity for your service (brand). Build a unique e-strategy to maintain communication with this *very* lucrative segment as they move up the "Eight-Level Scale" of customer lifetime value.

The Eight-Level Scale as outlined by famed direct-marketer Hershell Gordon Lewis in his landmark book, *Effective E-Mail Marketing*, includes:

☑ *First level:* Inquiry
☑ *Second level:* One click-through

☑ *Third level:* Second website visit

☑ *Fourth level:* Transaction

☑ *Fifth level:* Second transaction

☑ *Sixth level:* Multiple transactions

☑ *Seventh level:* Advocate

☑ *Eighth level:* Forwards your communication to others

Customer retention is so important to every business that an entire industry has grown up to serve this need. As mentioned earlier marketers call it Customer Relationship Management (CRM). eRainmakers have learned that cultivating these referral sources (also, "advocates," "disciples," "ambassadors," "bird dogs") is a gold mine. Leading real estate trainers have trademarked slogans to capture the CRM idea, such as Brian Buffini ("Working By Referral™") and Joe Stumpf ("By Referral Only™"). Here's how to build a word-of-mouse e-marketing strategy.

E-Techniques to Turn Clients into Slam-Dunk Referral Sources

For Dianne Sutton (DianneSutton.com), a mega-agent with RE/MAX Distinctive Real Estate in Fairfax, Virginia, and an Allen F. Hainge CY-BERSTAR®, generating referrals from past clients was almost an afterthought. "I have never been really great at continually asking for referrals from past clients, friends, et cetera, so I added a 'P.S.' on all of my communications with my past clients, sphere of influence, everybody I know," said Sutton. "The P.S. tells them that everybody who sends me a referral goes into a drawing for a romantic trip for two which will be given out at the annual Client Party."
Suttons' simple referral-generating postscript reads:

P.S. Don't Miss Out! For Every Referral to Dianne, you earn an entry in the drawing for a "Trip for Two to the Caribbean" award at the Annual Client Party.

Building on that success, Sutton tapped another not-so-close-to-home referral market. "My largest mistake was not to include my out-of-town sphere of influence in my communications. I receive referrals from all over the world, now that I have started mailing to all of my friends, especially since we are a military family and have lots of friends coming to the Washington area." Sutton added with typical good humor, "I don't know what I was thinking."

For Barbara Weismann (BergenCountyHomes.com), a CYBERSTAR and top producer with Weichert Realtors in Tenafly, New Jersey, generating referrals online came with a learning curve. "My biggest mistake was not to have a system for following up," explained Weismann. "Until I put in place a structured system, no matter how good my intentions, I never got the job done consistently and lost many opportunities. Initially my concern with my budget lost me much more than I would have gained had I not relied on my time management system exclusively."

Friends Don't Let Friends Keep Their New Home a Secret

Make it easy for your happy buyers to show their circle of family and friends pictures of their new home. One way is to create a virtual tour of their new property—even if you were not the listing agent. Make a virtual tour of the property with establishing photos of the neighborhood, front elevation, inside rooms, and backyard views, then post it on your website. Offer to send e-mail with a link to the tour to all your buyers' friends and family. Be sure to provide the buyers with the tour link in case they think of more people to show their new house.

Three different variations give you flexible choices to bring your clients' friends to your site:

1. Place the tour on your website and send an e-mail message containing the link.
2. Send the tour as an e-mail attachment and include links to your site in the tour and your signature.
3. Burn the tour onto a diskette or CD with active website links programmed into the file, and mail copies to your buyer's friends.

Some virtual tours are professionally photographed and prepared by fee-for-service companies, while other virtual-tour software is available to create a do-tour-yourself option (eRainmaker.com: Virtual Tours). For the do-it-yourself approach, you take your own photos (digital or scanned) of the new home and happy buyers, and insert them into the program with text and voiceover if desired. Every tour is branded with your contact information, so you get credit helping your buyers find their dream home. Create a ready-to-go "Welcome Home" template with generic slides (community, location maps, new address, referral request, and so on) that you use over and over for all area newcomers.

Be sure the do-it-yourself software includes a royalty-free viewer you can distribute at no cost that allows your buyers and their friends to view your tour. This gives you the handy option of copying the diskette for distribution. If you end up with two tours—such as one for the home and one for the neighborhood, or one for the home and one for the tour viewer software—remember some e-mail programs (such as AOL) don't handle multiple attachments gracefully. You may want to send each tour separately if sent as attachments.

Staying in Touch with Newsletters Keeps Referrals Coming

Provide an e-newsletter that customers devour cover-to-cover (or, at least, everybody finds something of interest in every edition). Balance online promotion with a printed newsletter for clients who don't have e-mail or haven't given you an e-mail address yet. Ron Street (WineCountryEstates.com), a top producer and CYBERSTAR with RE/MAX Central in Santa Rosa, California, is a believer in e-newsletters. What is Street's most successful technique for generating referrals from past clients, sphere of influence, and B2B contacts? "The e-Newsletter from the Real Estate Cyber Society with Cyber Tips," said Street. "It's different than most real estate newsletters. If I am even a day late in sending the monthly newsletter, I get phone calls. I can track two referrals from e-newsletter readers in 2002."

Checklist of Tips for Promoting Your E-Newsletter

☑ *Use an outsource provider:* Just like producing a quality printed newsletter, an e-newsletter takes time and resources that are better spent on your core business—listing and selling. Several excellent e-newsletters are available from providers (eRainmaker .com: E-Newsletters).

☑ *Concentrate on real estate:* Because you are the area real estate expert, most contacts expect an e-newsletter on what you know best: real estate. An effective alternative is a newsletter that focuses on homeownership (home improvement, repair, maintenance, decorating, landscaping). If your goal is client retention, a homeowner slant (rather than buying and selling) will match your objective and the interests of your client audience.

☑ *Practice viral marketing:* Have your web designer include a "send page to a friend" button and "ask your own question" form for ongoing feedback on the e-newsletter pages, as well as an "add to favorites" icon.

☑ *Promote the e-newsletter:* Feature the e-newsletter on your home page and with link icons throughout the site. Avoid the mistake of simply saying "Sign Up for e-Newsletter." Tell visitors the frequency, what type of content they can expect, and include a clear "will not share your e-mail" privacy statement. Insert a direct link to the "latest" e-newsletter in your standard e-mail signature (be sure the link to your e-newsletter never changes, even though the edition content changes). Add the link within the message text or "P.S." in saved e-mail template messages.

Self-Publishing Can Work for the Committed

If you are considering producing your own e-newsletter check out two outstanding examples. Kathy O'Rourke (RealEstateObserver.com), a top agent with Prudential Wilmot Whitney in Weston, Massachusetts, publishes a monthly overview of real estate trends in her Boston suburb.

Gary Ditto (GaryDitto.com), a leading producer with Long & Foster Real Estate in Bethesda, Maryland (Gateway Office), publishes another outstanding newsletter example on his website. Ditto's newsletter concentrates on local Kensington, Maryland, history and has won numerous

---

eRainmaker Tip

Handy Reference: Use links to specific articles in your e-newsletter as an instant answer to prospect's questions.

---

eRainmaker Tip

Befriend Anniversary-Challenged Spouses: Several sites on the Internet provide interesting information that's useful for client follow up and generating after-sale referrals. One fun site is Re-Date.com, which is a date calculator. Enter a date such as a wedding or purchase anniversary and the site returns a long list of calculations (length of time since . . . , days left to next anniversaries . . . , time trivia, and more). It's free. Compose an "Anniversary Alert" e-mail to clients and insert the link. Send a few days before their wedding anniversary. Clients will forget you not.

---

commendations, as well as being locally archived by the Kensington Historical Society. The heart of Ditto's website is his Sold Reports, which continuously update sales for 14 communities in an easy-to-read chart that lists address, house style, list price, settlement date, sales price, bedrooms, full baths, half baths. Ditto's web designer programmed the formats to be updated by Ditto's assistant using DreamWeaver software. Many of the reports can be printed as PDFs using Acrobat Reader right from Ditto's website. The impact of information on client loyalty since he began his career in 1977 has made Ditto the "King of Kensington" real estate.

Additional Cross-Selling Referral Opportunities

Popular speaker and superstar loan originator Greg Frost (GregFrost .com), owner of Frost Mortgage Banking Group in Albuquerque, New Mexico, has developed a powerful system to multiply his mortgage business by cross-selling 13 referral sources in every transaction. Frost's trademarked system, *ACTion! Marketing & Client Management System*™, delivers a business-building campaign using e-mail, letters, faxes, and phone scripts designed to generate quality referrals from all the players in a loan closing.

"My goal in every transaction," said Frost, "is to replace the loan in process before it closes with another loan application." Real estate professionals can take a lesson from the many results-tested ideas Frost has perfected with the help of renown direct-marketer Jay Abraham. Or better yet, diversify and become a loan originator, too.

Here are 13 referral sources Frost cultivates in every transaction with his successful system:

1. *Buyer* (referral bird dog)
2. *Buyer's selling agent* (loan updates and meal invitation)
3. *Buyer's coworkers* (fruit basket to office with referral cards)
4. *Buyer's employer* (referral cards for all employees)
5. *Selling agent's sales manager* ("Pleasure to work with . . .")
6. *Coborrower* (referral bird dog)
7. *Coborrowers coworkers* (fruit basket to office with referral cards)
8. *Coborrower's employer* (referral cards for all employees)
9. *Home seller* ("You'll be needing a loan soon.")
10. *Home seller's listing/selling agent* (loan updates and meal invitation)
11. *Seller's employer* (referral cards for all employees)
12. *Listing agent's sales manager* ("Pleasure to work with . . .")
13. *Local top agents* (Mission: "To find, prequalify, and refer buyers to our REALTOR partners.")

Action Planner for a Lifetime Customer E-Strategy

The following checklist and Figure 15.1 are designed to be an Action Planner for developing a lifetime customer retention campaign. Ask yourself and your team for each of the check-off steps, "What are we doing?" and "What can we do better?" Assess what you have accomplished. Put quantities and accomplishments after each checkbox. Then develop an action plan for the future because the competition is always moving your cheese. (More on planning your e-strategy in Part Four.) This Action Planner was inspired by a chart provided by Bigfoot Interactive, an e-mail communications provider headquartered in New York City, as reported by Bruce McCracken in Part 3 of

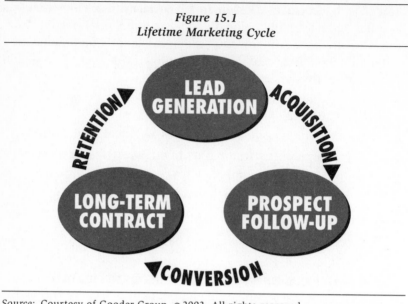

Figure 15.1
Lifetime Marketing Cycle

his series "Targeted e-mail: From Spam to Choice," published in eCRMguide.com, February 3, 2003.

Test yourself—and brainstorm solutions—for the following questions:

Lead Generation (Acquisition)

- ☑ Opt-in programs?
- ☑ Soft-sell offers? (information)

Follow-Up (Conversion)

- ☑ Auto-response or postal fulfillment?
- ☑ E-mail drip campaign?
- ☑ Website revisits?
- ☑ Hard-sell offers? (Service)
- ☑ Appointments?

Long-Term Contact (Retention/Loyalty)

- ☑ Good service?
- ☑ Newsletters/market updates?
- ☑ Profile-driven offers?
- ☑ Loyalty programs?
- ☑ Satisfaction surveys?

Win-Back (or "Aged-Prospect Viagra")

- ☑ Usage stimulation? (Rate Alert/Refi/CMA)
- ☑ Referrals and repeat? ("By the way, if anyone you know...)
- ☑ Win-back offers? (especially for change of address contacts)

Costly Mistake to Avoid When Preparing Your Referral Campaigns

Mistake: Sending Too Much E-Mail Too Often

How often should I send e-mail? I don't want to be pushy or annoying, but I don't want my prospects and customers to forget me either. What is the optimum frequency?

SOLUTION

There's no single right answer. One good rule of thumb: The less timely the content, the less often it should be sent. If your e-mail is follow-up tied to an event, such as an open house visit, a prelisting appointment, or a purchase anniversary, then the relevance is obvious—and welcome. Like an overpriced listing that gets traffic but doesn't get offers, watch for signs that indicate the just right frequency for your e-mail. One sign is a surge in opt-out requests. That may mean you're sending too often—more commonly, the content is not pertinent to the prospect—or their preferences have changed. Another rule of thumb: The content itself gives you a clue. Listing updates may be daily; buying tips may be weekly, whereas a newsletter is often best monthly or bimonthly. Best of all, let your prospects indicate their preferences on your opt-in website response forms (Daily updates? Monthly newsletter?).

16

Building a Trophy E-Mail Database

OLD RULE

Internet games are diversions for kids.

NEW RULE

Kids who first played Internet games
are now prime first-time buyers.

Build Your Trophy E-Mail Database to Achieve Financial Freedom

If your exit strategy is to sell your e-practice some day, then the most valuable asset you can build is a permission-based, e-mail enhanced, Trophy Database. The value a buyer of your practice will place on your database comes from its quality and size. Ultimately the buyer will pay more for a high-quality, well-maintained, information-rich database—the larger the better. Building a Trophy E-Mail Database is achieved with three simultaneous strategies over time:

1. *eRainmaker Strategy #1:* Maximize Database Growth by capturing e-mail addresses from new consumers and business sources.

2. *eRainmaker Strategy #2:* Fill The Database Gap by enhancing existing customer and contact records with e-mail addresses.

3. *eRainmaker Strategy #3:* Practice Database Hygiene by constantly maintaining your invaluable list.

eRainmaker Strategy #1: Maximize Database Growth

"When the consumer perceives real value, there is no hesitation in giving their e-mail address," said Joe Valenti (CBSHOME.com), president and CEO of CBSHOME Real Estate, a leading brokerage in Omaha, Nebraska. Valenti says making it a rule to provide service—not just generate leads and "be there"—is the best route to collecting e-mail addresses. "The secret is to offer 'Real Value' to the prospect or client," said Valenti. "Often this is perceived as 'full service.' The consumer wants to make decisions and be a part of the process of buying or selling. We strive to have our CBSHOME sales associates help every step of the way."

Here are several tips to maximize your database growth.

Website Collection

If collecting e-mails is your goal, you can do better than sending your prospects to your general home page. Instead, give them a direct link to a response form with a relevant, must-have offer. Add multiple response form(s) to your website to capture voluntary submission of visitor's contact information. Successful variations of this registration technique include:

☑ A popup form that requires registration to access specific information on website is called a *gateway*. Prospects must enter information in the required fields. This technique is similar to a virtual office website (VOW) that requires registration, but without the disclosure forms and acceptance by mouse click.

☑ Guest Book voluntary sign-up.

☑ "Forward to a Friend" forms capture the sender's name and e-mail, as well as the recipient's name and e-mail address.

☑ Customer only or member only section that requires e-mail address to gain access.

Offline-Online Combinations

Similar to website collection but with twist: No website is needed. Set up situations where prospects can get information only by providing their e-mail address. You might, for example, offer a special seller's kit or investor's kit by mail in your real estate magazine ads. To get a kit, the prospect has to e-mail you at a particular e-mail address. Set up a special "mailbox" to receive the e-mail requests. It makes tracking your advertising effectiveness a snap!

As we have said before, include your e-mail on everything you distribute—your business cards, ads, flyers, promotional giveaways, and so on. Use your print, broadcast advertising, and yard signs to invite prospects to register by e-mail for promotions. Prospects must register by e-mail, which captures their e-mail address. ("Winners notified by e-mail.") Don't forget to ask everyone who gives you a phone number for an e-mail address. Ask sign calls, ad calls, open house visitors (include e-mail registration on all paper forms allowing plenty of space), model home, broker opens (get agents' e-mails, too!), and even casual conversations where you exchange business cards. For prospects (or clients) in a hurry, provide the ability to send an instant text message direct to your pager wherever you are. Add the text-pager form to your website (Figure 16.1).

Include e-mail in your voice mail. Make sure your voice-mail message includes your e-mail address (and your website address too). Again, add a special giveaway here and ask people to e-mail you to receive it. "Press 1 for today's e-mail giveaway." The giveaway online must exchange something that fills a customer need in return for contact information.

Here are some proven response techniques (more in Chapter 8):

☑ Sign-up for an e-newsletter subscription.

☑ Register for new listing updates.

☑ Request recent sales information or market updates.

☑ Offer a sweepstakes or prize drawing (Figure 16.2).

☑ Provide an "Open Soon" list of upcoming open houses.

☑ Promote "Open All Week" lists of past open houses with links to property information (if you missed it).

☑ Feature free e-reports ("Seven Costly Mistakes Even Smart Sellers Make—and How to Avoid Them").

Figure 16.1
Capture More E-Mail with Text "Page Me" Service

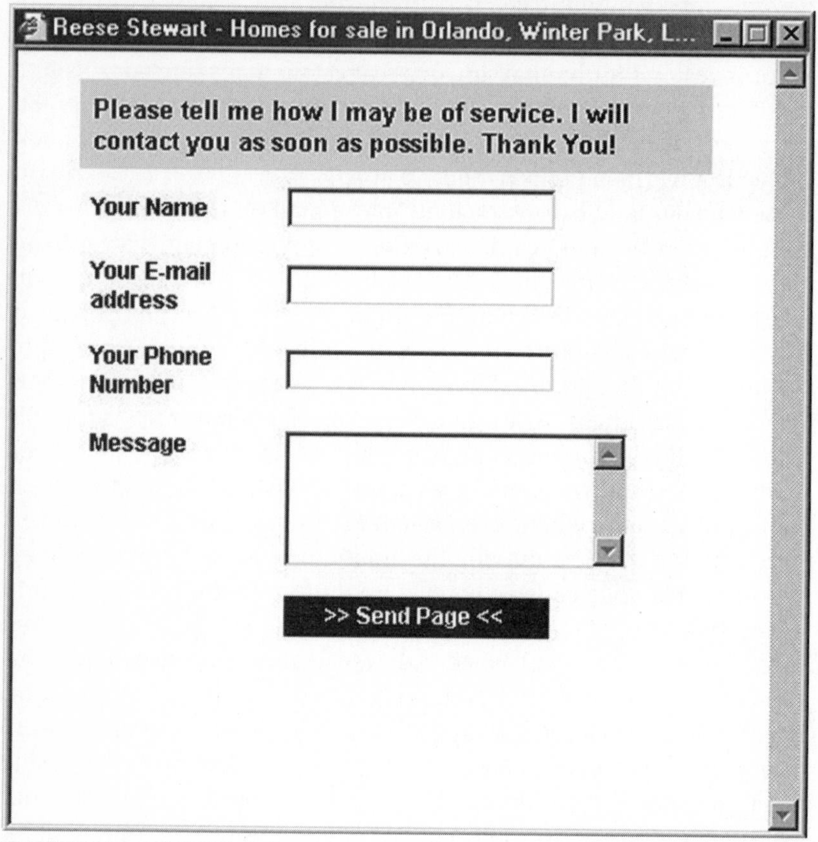

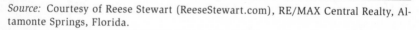

Reese Stewart - Homes for sale in Orlando, Winter Park, L...

Please tell me how I may be of service. I will contact you as soon as possible. Thank You!

Your Name

Your E-mail address

Your Phone Number

Message

>> Send Page <<

Source: Courtesy of Reese Stewart (ReeseStewart.com), RE/MAX Central Realty, Altamonte Springs, Florida.

☑ Offer price opinion ("Free, Quick Home Evaluation by E-Mail").

☑ Request home-for-sale property information ("Any home, any broker, any time.").

Build a Geographic E-Farm

One of the first discoveries eRainmakers make about collecting e-mail addresses is that contacts are scattered across town. How do you get

Figure 16.2
Capture E-Mail with Sweepstakes for $18,000 Mortgage Payments

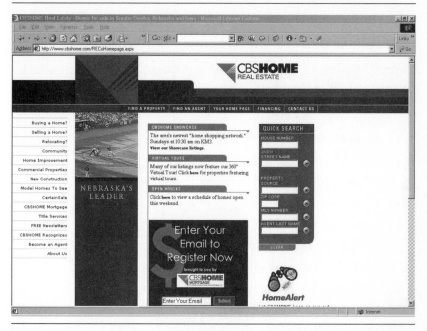

Source: Courtesy of Joe Valenti (CBSHOME.com), CBS Home Real Estate, Omaha, Nebraska.

the e-mail addresses of people who live in a specific area? Accurate neighborhood house-to-house e-mail lists don't exist commercially (unlike postal addresses in crisscross phone directories), especially in the small numbers of a prospecting farm area. The return on your effort comes from assembling a one-of-a-kind asset.

One technique is to use one of several services that provide a ready-made community website where residents can visit and learn more about their neighbors. As the area real estate specialist, the eRainmaker sponsors and promotes the site (your photo typically is on every page with an e-mail and website link). As a sponsor, you may be allowed to e-mail residents that sign up for the neighborhood site and its services (policies vary). Neighbors typically can login and check event calendars (or add their own event), post classified ads, publish photos or exchange recipes, to name a few features the community can share. By being the sponsor of a community website, eRainmakers can become the "neighborhood specialist" to their e-farm even in cyber-space (eRainmaker.com: Client/Community Pages).

Assemble a B2B E-Mail Network

Beyond consumers, experienced eRainmakers also build Business-to-Business (B2B) networks of e-mail partners (Figure 16.3). Here are several idea starters:

☑ Agents in your office.

☑ Agents in your company.

☑ Co-op agents you have worked with locally.

☑ Top agents in your area.

☑ Franchise colleagues in area or region.

☑ Nationwide referral contacts.

☑ Acquaintances at real estate meetings and conferences.

☑ Local transaction-related service providers.

☑ Area home-service providers.

☑ Professional referral sources locally.

☑ Relocation managers at area corporations.

Figure 16.3
Leverage Your B2B Network on the Net

Source: Courtesy of Elite 20 Network and Paulette Greene, Ebby Halliday Realtors, Dallas, Texas.

All of these B2B contacts should be cultivated with regular e-mails. Content can range from a friendly "Hello, haven't talked with you recently" to evidence of your success (just listeds, just solds, sales awards, public appearances) to market updates and reminders "We're never too busy to handle your referrals." You can include links to useful market updates and to your website of rich, deep, quality consumer-oriented content. Growing your Trophy E-Mail Database with B2B contacts will be a big moneymaker in two ways. First, these business contacts will come into contact with a stream of potential buyers and sellers, representing far more transactions over time than the average consumer can provide. Second, most of your local B2B contacts will be homeowners themselves who will need your services when they move up or invest or acquire a second home.

The need for consumers to be serviced by a network of cooperating local real estate professionals was clear in the Dallas, Texas, market in 1990. That is when 20 of the top-producing agents who specialized in the "Golden Corridor" of North Dallas and Collin County formed the "Elite 20." Not only does the group hold a monthly tour of properties listed by members of the group, but they also have established an "all call" 24-hour messaging network. The network allows members to announce to all members with one call information such as new listings or requests for homes matching specific buyer needs. To find out more about the Elite 20 ("Call One for the Power of Twenty"), one member to contact is Paulette Greene (PauletteSellsDallas.com), the Number-One Individual producer in 2002 with Ebby Halliday Realtors.

eRainmaker Strategy #2: Fill the Database Gap

The *database gap* is the difference in size between an offline/direct mail database (your mailing list) and an online/e-mail database (your e-farm). For example, if you have 1,000 records in your direct mail database but only 200 records have e-mail addresses, your database gap is 80%.

The reverse database gap is an *e-mail only* record that doesn't have a postal address. The reverse syndrome is an equally vexing problem, especially for active eRainmakers who generate substantial leads from their websites where prospects may not give postal addresses. Mega-agent Mike Hyles (Hyles.com), one of the top 10 RE/MAX agents in the world with RE/MAX 1st Choice in Pleasanton, California, turns this reverse gap to his advantage by using an automated service to update his Microsoft Outlook address book with complete contact information (eRainmaker.com: Address Book Updates). The first time Hyles sent out an update request he had numerous responses from past clients. "I even had a couple that wrote back," Hyles said, " 'By the way . . . we have a friend that is looking to buy a house. Can we forward him your information?' Getting my name in front of hundreds of people pays off, and the best part is the service is free."

The goal of every eRainmaker should be to ensure every possible database record is complete with postal address *and* e-mail address. Remember, all three Trophy Database strategies in this chapter are at work simultaneously. By working together, every effort maximizes its effectiveness. For example, past clients as well as new prospects will respond to the same website form, thus adding their e-mail address to your Trophy E-Mail Database.

Here are several tips to close a database gap.

Ask Them for Their E-Mail Address

Get into the habit of asking your past customers and sphere of influence contacts for their e-mail address. Ask during calls and casual conversations. Be sure to clearly say what the e-mail address will be used for, how the customer will benefit, and let them know that the person can remove their e-mail address at any time. You'll discover some people actually prefer to give you their "arm's length" e-mail rather than their phone number. This "ask them" habit becomes second nature and is very effective because you already know the contacts. Naturally every mailing piece you send to your database should suggest they reply by e-mail or visit your website.

Here are two successful database gap techniques. In a special mailing, announce you publish a free online newsletter, tell them what the benefit is to them and ask them to e-mail you if they want to receive the latest edition. CYBERSTAR® Leslie McDonnell of RE/MAX Suburban in Libertyville, Illinois, sent Allen Hainge this tip for his newsletter: "For those having a holiday client-appreciation party, replace 'Regrets Only' by asking them to RSVP by e-mail to your e-mail address. Great way to capture those e-mail addresses you don't have!"

E-Mail Append

This process matches e-mail addresses to a currently existing contact database. (A variation is the "reverse append" that matches street addresses with e-mail records.) Although a growing number of firms provide e-mail append, the technique typically is used for large customer databases—often in the hundreds of thousands or millions (eRainmaker .com: E-Mail Append). Here's how it works. The database owner sends in their customer list in an electronic file. The service matches the name and street address against their database, and appends or enhances as many records as possible with an e-mail address. Match rates run the gamut. Consumer lists (B2C) match rates range from 10% to 30%, while business lists (B2B) match rates range from 8% to 15%, depending on the quality and quantity of the service provider's database. Often, the service sends an initial opt-out message allowing recipients to unsubscribe if they don't want to receive an e-newsletter or promotional offers. The enhanced database is then returned to the owner. Typically, the owner pays per match of a deliverable e-mail address.

eRainmaker Strategy #3: Practice Database Hygiene

E-mail addresses have a discouraging rate of attrition. Reports range between 20% and 40% address changes annually. That means more than 2% to 3% of e-mail addresses go dead every month. Worse still, few e-mail accounts bother with a change of address forwarding service. In a nutshell, e-mail addresses change five times faster than postal addresses, which change occupants at a glacial rate of 5% to 7% per year on average, according to the e-mail append service Acquire Now that is based in Richmond, Virginia. In addition, the U.S. Postal Service still delivers first-class mail regardless who lives in the home.

Your customer database is one of your most valuable and expensive assets. To let it waste away at a rate of 20% to 40% per year is not a viable way to do business. The best "attrition insurance" for this fact of e-marketing life is a good offense—which means gathering e-mail addresses at every opportunity. Just as online marketing is a slice of your total marketing pie, e-mail addresses are a slice of your total contact information. A complete contact record is the goal of every Trophy Database.

Call or Write

When e-mail goes bad, your first step is to contact your customer or prospect by phone or mail (postcard, letter) to ask for their new e-mail account. Without your postal database to back you up, your e-mail database will soon degrade in value. That's why the e-maxim says, "An e-mail address without a postal address is ultimately worthless." Successful eRainmakers who take the time to reach out to e-mail account changes are always pleased with the retention effect this has on the customer relationship. Often, customers are impressed you are paying close enough attention to notice the change ("We recently sent you an important e-mail and see your e-mail address has changed."). In the end, bounce-back e-mail is simply another reason to stay in touch. Calling undeliverable e-mail customers is also a great task to outsource to a buyer's agent or delegate to staff.

E-Mail Change of Address

Another solution is an e-mail change of address (ECOA) service that matches your bounce-backs (nonworking, invalid e-mails) against the service provider's database to reconnect you with your customers. Match rates vary. Some providers claim a typical successful match rate between 2% to 10% on initial runs, or as high as 20% on consumer lists and 30% on business lists. Nonetheless, even a 30% recovery rate means you've lost e-mail contact with 70% of your database. The only practical way to reduce your attrition is to contact your bounce-backs personally—and that requires a street address and phone number.

Keeping Your E-Mail List Fresh with Guaranteed Database Hygiene Techniques

Web-savvy eRainmakers give special attention to establishing a routine system of list maintenance and e-mail database hygiene (cleaning your trophy database) to keep their Trophy E-Mail Database up to strength.

Here are some key issues to watch as your e-mail list grows:

☑ *Undeliverables:* Returned e-mails that were not deliverable have typically gone bad and are no longer usable. One exception is "soft bounce-backs" caused by a temporary server problem (hard bounce-backs are permanent bad addresses). An easy solution is to resend undeliverables a second or even third time to confirm they are truly dead. Inactive (returned several times), bogus (example: test@test.com or sflsiud@jfljfoe.com) and duplicate addresses should be deleted periodically to make it easier to track your response rates.

☑ *Opt-ins:* Once your system of lead capture is running on all cylinders, you may be flooded with web inquiries. Take the example of Vern and Audrey English (TampaBayAreaRealEstate.com, TheEnglishes.com), superstars with Keller Williams Realty in Palm Harbor, Florida, who earn about $75,000 a year from their websites. By linking 40 real estate domains that capture keywords and niche markets, their two principal websites generate about 15,000 to 16,000 unique visitors every month. From that traffic the Englishes capture 500 opt-in e-mails a month on average using a guest book, e-coupons and club membership incentives. "Our biggest secret to conversion is a first-response e-mail that is personalized based on the prospect's comment in the remarks box," Vern English said. Their next step is to put in place a system to auto-register opt-in signups into a database and launch an automated drip follow-up series to maximize conversions and minimize their workload.

☑ *Double opt-in:* This technique requires users to enter their e-mail address twice to check that the e-mail address is typed correctly. A simpler device is for you to respond or fulfill the offer by e-mail. For example, for an e-report or e-newsletter, the prospect must enter an e-mail address to receive the information. This encourages the prospect to enter their e-mail address correctly. You may want to compose a "Thank You" or "Welcome" auto-responder e-mail message to confirm the request was registered.

☑ *Opt-outs:* Remove or unsubscribe requests are a good gauge of customer loyalty, but can sometimes run 2% to 4% or higher. Typically, opt-out requests are lower on relationship lists of people you know. Take-me-off-your-list requests, just like opt-ins, can be a burden if handled manually. One technique used by busy eRainmakers is to create a special response form that is sent to a specific e-mail address that your rules wizard routes to a subfolder for easier handling. Consider composing a "Good-Bye Message," such as a saved signature file, confirming that the contact's request has been processed. Also, some people, after receiving the good-bye message, may have a change of heart and resubscribe, so be sure to include a box for a message or an option to sign up again.

☑ *Double entry:* To avoid sending multiple e-mails to the same contact who is registered more than once in your database, use their e-mail address as the unique identifier, *not* their name. Having an automated e-mail system that checks for an existing e-mail match before populating a new record is a godsend for eRainmakers. Remember, searching by last name and scanning for duplicates is an easy way to purge contacts with multiple e-mail addresses.

☑ *Automate your list management:* To automate your list management, you can subscribe to an automated e-mail service (eRainmaker.com: Automated E-Mail). Other options include buying professional list management software (eRainmaker.com: List Management), renting the list management service from an ISP, or subscribing to a ListServ service that maintains and sends mass e-mail for you (eRainmaker.com: ListServ).

---

eRainmaker Tip

Opt-Out but Don't Delete: If you receive an opt-out request, stop sending automated e-mail, but do keep the contact in the database. Remember, you may still send them postal mail, and someday they may come back. *Caution:* Some people send an unsubscribe request from a different e-mail address than the one on your list. When they do use a different e-mail, lookup of additional e-mail accounts is only possible if you also have the person's name and postal address. That's another reason why your database must contain full contact information.

PART

FOUR

DEMYSTIFYING
INTERNET
MARKETING

17

E-Marketing Plan: Six Steps to Effective Online Marketing

OLD RULE

Internet users aren't like you or me.

NEW RULE

Internet users are you and me.

Six Simple Steps: E-Goals, E-Benchmarks, E-Objectives, E-Customers, E-Strategies, E-Budget

Here are the six steps, in brief, to creating an effective online marketing plan. For an expanded description of preparing a marketing plan complete with worksheets and exercises, see the six chapters in Part Five of my book *REAL ESTATE RAINMAKER®* (John Wiley & Sons, 2000) titled, "Writing a Marketing Plan in Six Easy Mornings."

Step #1: E-Goals

E-goals are a blueprint to your exit strategy. Write down your primary Goal, your ultimate reason for being in this business. You may find you have more than one. Consider giving your practice a *SWOT Analysis.* Ask yourself these four questions: What are the **S**trengths, **W**eaknesses, **O**pportunities, and **T**hreats facing my business? Take an honest look. Know thyself. Imagine you are a prospective buyer of your practice with a bird's eye view asking what should be done differently. Pretend you're a start-up again. Go back to basics. Watch for that Big "Aha!" idea that will help you renew and refresh your e-marketing plans. Often, the simplest goal can have the biggest, most far-reaching impact on your bottom line. Having an e-marketing plan at all may be one super-size "Aha!"

Your goal will shape your entire plan. For example, if your goal is financial freedom, then making more money (and keeping it) is the path to that goal. To reach that goal there are two options: Decrease costs and/or increase sales. The bottom line in either direction is greater profits. The e-goals in your online marketing plan will help you reach your ultimate business goal in multiple ways. Here are some e-goal examples:

- ☑ Increase new business from offline marketing.
- ☑ Minimize lead-generation costs.
- ☑ Reduce costs of marketing.
- ☑ Deliver marketing message to a wider market.
- ☑ Boost B2B marketing and referrals.
- ☑ Maximize conversion of prospects into clients.
- ☑ Improve customer satisfaction and long-term retention.
- ☑ Build a valuable, sellable brand.

Step #2: E-Benchmarks

E-benchmarks are the figures that give you a snapshot of your practice. Keep records. Track trends. Improve. These numbers may include sales figures, such as Internet generated units, gross commission income from web leads, average online transaction price, number of listings and sales closed from Internet prospects, and so on. Benchmarks can also include marketing figures, such as average monthly website visitors, e-mail addresses in database, marketing e-mails sent per year, prospects captured from website response forms, units closed from B2B referrals, and more. Connecting the benchmarks year after year in a record-keeping document, such as your accumulated annual online marketing plans, will be a very useful tool to verify the value of your practice to a prospective buyer.

Step #3: E-Objectives

E-objectives are targets. Put several objectives on paper and you have a road map of action steps to reach your destination. Objectives must be measurable and dated. That means, when you write an objective it must be quantifiable in money, units, e-mail addresses, opt-outs, bounce-backs, e-mails sent, percentages, responses, calls, listings, appointments, closings, and the like. Also, every objective must have a date. Thus, some sample objectives read: *Increase the e-mail addresses in my database from 500 to 1,500 by December 31, 20XX. In year 20XX increase number of transactions generated by my website by five more than previous year. Expand Internet-generated commissions to be 20% of total gross income for fiscal year 20XX.*

Step #4: E-Customers

E-customers are target markets with which you want to do business. Naturally, customers include home buyers and home sellers. The purpose of this step during your planning is to put a finer point on *exactly* what kind of consumers you want to target. Among buyers, some possibilities include first-time buyers, move-up buyers, relocation buyers, investor buyers, military buyers (Figure 17.1), second-home buyers, new-home buyers, condominium buyers, waterfront buyers, golf-property buyers, luxury-home buyers, or others. You can substitute the word "sellers" for "buyers" in all these target groups except first-time buyers and new-home buyers. Among sellers, some additional possibilities include builders, seniors, inherited estates, college parents (investors), divorcing couples, relocation third parties, and so on. These are the target customers you want to do business with. Write down the customers you want to target with your online marketing.

PROPERTIES AND B2B

We all know what a customer is. Or do we? Beyond buyers and sellers, sophisticated eRainmakers also target two other "customer" types: actual properties and business-to-business contacts.

Treat the home as a customer. Concentrate on past listings listed by you, your office, or your company. Regardless of who lives in the property, if you listed and sold the property before, no one is in a

Figure 17.1
Military Prospects Power an Effective E-Customer Plan

Source: Courtesy of Darrell Hutson (SolanoSearch.net), Gateway Realty, Fairfield, California.

better position to market that property next time. Target your marketing to the address—and the owners will become your next client. If you weren't the listing agent (and the listing agent is no longer with the office), launch a "win-back campaign" and assign yourself to be the exclusive "account executive" for that property. Marketers call this an "orphan campaign" because it is designed to recapture past-customer properties that have been abandoned and are not being serviced.

Multiply referrals with a B2B network. A rich database of opportunity exists among professional providers of transaction services, homeowner services, financial services, as well as agents locally and outside your service area. Remember, not only does this network hear of upcoming transactions continuously, but almost all individual "bird dogs" are homeowners themselves.

CUSTOMER VALUE

Another insightful way to look at customers is to define their lifetime customer value. After all, one-time transactional customers are worth far less than a lifelong relational customer. Similarly, sources of repeatable referrals are of much more value than a single-purchase consumer. You may want to focus on customers that offer the greatest lifetime customer value. One way to assess customer value is to estimate their gross commission value either from past transactions or future price range. Some successful eRainmakers give themselves a raise by setting a minimum gross commission income (GCI) value for prospective clients. Customers below the minimum value are referred.

Step #5: E-Strategies

E-strategies are projects that achieve the objectives on the road map to your goal. Every strategy provides a To Do List of activities to accomplish. Think of strategies as the stepping stones along the path to success. Exactly how you do that, and exactly what strategies you develop vary with every eRainmaker—that's one of the reasons this industry is so endlessly interesting. Strategies are the marketing ideas you've marked as you read this book or pickup by buttonholing your peers at seminars or create yourself to add to your marketing program. Here are some fundamental e-strategies for every eRainmaker practice:

1. Register a brand domain.
2. Buy a destination website (either an advanced personal site or custom site).

3. Enrich website with direct response content and offers.

4. Promote the website offline and cultivate strategic link partners online.

5. Build a Trophy E-Mail Database.

6. Follow-up website prospects and nurture contacts with automated e-mail (Figure 17.2).

7. Hire a techie or virtual assistant to implement your e-strategies.

Step #6: E-Budget

E-budgets show you the money. Budget setting is like batting practice: At first it makes your hands hurt because it's much more like work than play—but the ultimate payoff is worth every swing. If you're

Figure 17.2
Exclusive Buyer Agency Puts Sharp Focus on E-Strategy

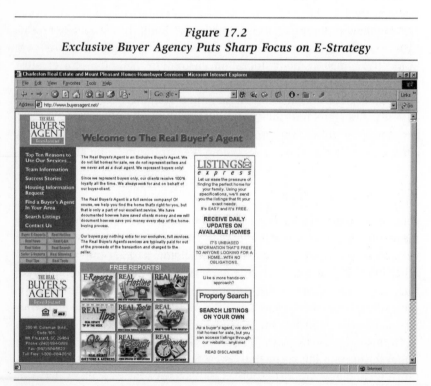

Source: Courtesy of David Kent (BuyersAgent.net), The Real Buyer's Agent, Mt. Pleasant, South Carolina.

going to hit a home run, you must have a budget. So, roll up your sleeves and start swinging.

In almost 25 years of real estate marketing, trying to find accurate industry budget figures for real estate professionals is like trying to reach Nirvana. I have faith the figures are out there, but I'm still searching. The best we have is a recent compilation by Gary Keller, founder and board chairman of the Keller Williams organization. In Keller's best-selling and highly acclaimed book, *The Millionaire Real Estate Agent,* written with Dave Jenks and Jay Papasan, the authors publish their findings in a "Budget Model" (Figure 17.3). The figures were the result of compiling the income and expense reports of scores of top producers, using a chart of accounts developed over several years.

What Gary Keller discovered is that top producers spend about 10% (9.2% to be exact) of GCI on lead-generation marketing. (Divide by 12 to get a monthly marketing budget figure.) The 10% figure is right on the money with every survey and analysis and estimate I have ever seen. By the way, out of 100% GCI, the surveyed Keller Williams mega-agents spend about 30% on Cost of Sales (listing specialist salary and commissions, and buyer specialist commissions), roughly 30% on Operating Expenses, including about 20% on all other Expenses, and about 10% on Marketing. Overall, Keller discovered top producers spend about 1.5% of GCI on technology in general, in addition to the 10% on lead-generation marketing. Thus, the bottom line, on average, is net income in the 40% range of CGI for those millionaire agents, according to Keller's figures.

It's an important footnote to Gary Keller's findings to understand exactly what items the Keller Williams study includes in a marketing budget, and what items the study leaves off the budget. Budgeted lead-generation expenses include: all advertising for newspaper, general magazine, proprietary magazine, radio, TV, billboard; Internet expenses for design work, website maintenance, home page/access/e-mail and other Internet costs; giveaway items, business cards, signs, flyers, direct mail (production, printing, postage), telemarketing, 800 number, hot-line interactive voice response (IVR) technology, and other miscellaneous advertising expenses.

Noteworthy "technology" expenses that are *not* included as marketing are: contract labor (virtual assistant, programmer, virtual consultant), technology support (such as staff salaries for website or network administrator), computer equipment purchase, rental or maintenance, or high-speed Internet access phone line.

Figure 17.3
The Budget Model of the Millionaire Real Estate Agent

There are two key areas of expenses:
1. Cost of Sales*
This is the cost of acquiring the income and includes the salary and commission of a listing specialist and the commission of buyer specialists.

Seller Specialist	4.4%	$100,000
Buyer Specialists	24.8%	$600,000
Total Cost of Sales**	29.2%	$700,000

2. Operating Expenses*
This is the cost to generate leads and run the business. Key categories here are:

1) Salaries	**12.0%**	**$288,000**
2) Lead Generation	**9.2%**	**$220,000**
3) Occupancy	2.0%	$48,000
4) Technology	1.5%	$36,000
5) Phone	1.0%	$24,000
6) Supplies	1.0%	$24,000
7) Education	1.0%	$24,000
8) Equipment	1.0%	$24,000
9) Auto/Insurance	0.5%	$12,000
Total Expenses	29.2%*	$700,000

The Big Two (Salaries and Lead Generation) make up 72.6% of Operating Expenses!

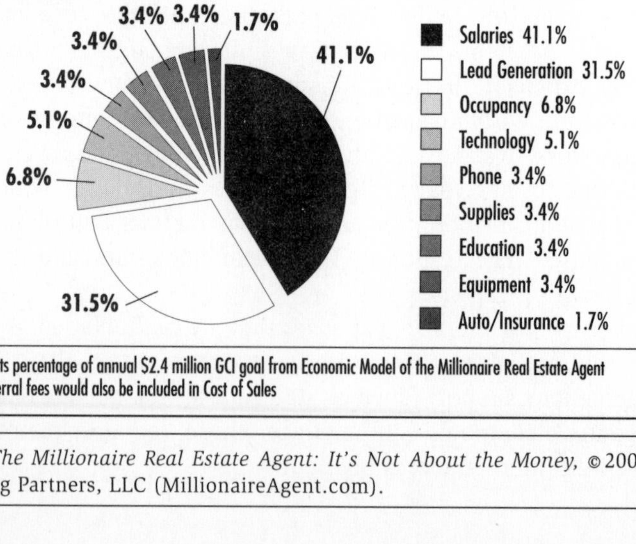

Salaries 41.1%
Lead Generation 31.5%
Occupancy 6.8%
Technology 5.1%
Phone 3.4%
Supplies 3.4%
Education 3.4%
Equipment 3.4%
Auto/Insurance 1.7%

*Reflects percentage of annual $2.4 million GCI goal from Economic Model of the Millionaire Real Estate Agent
** Referral fees would also be included in Cost of Sales

Source: The Millionaire Real Estate Agent: It's Not About the Money, © 2003 Rellek Publishing Partners, LLC (MillionaireAgent.com).

Marketing Budget Rules of Thumb

No one rule fits all. Different online marketing plans call for different budgets. Here are some simple marketing budget rules of thumb I recommend based on my experience:

☑ Use 10% of gross commission income (GCI) for marketing in a mature practice, that is, in a "maintenance" budget situation or referral-only business.

☑ Use 15% of GCI for marketing if you are new, plan to expand into a new territory, or want aggressive growth.

☑ Use 20% of GCI for a one-year marketing blitz if you have intense (entrenched) competition, expect significant initial expenses, such as a custom website, or have purchased another practice and anticipate transitional expenses.

☑ Consider a "Transaction-Based Budget" instead of a "Percent of Income" budget. Determine your average marketing cost per transaction from last year (divide your total marketing expenses by total transaction sides). Then, multiply that average marketing cost per unit times the number of transactions in your goal for the year. The advantage of this approach is that it uses your "real" numbers that reflect your average price, your market conditions and your business model, and the budget is easy to apply transaction by transaction. Remember, use this approach as a supplement to your profit-and-loss accounting, not as a replacement.

More Marketing Rules of Thumb

Here are some additional marketing rules of thumb (ratios) that can be used for budgeting purposes as well:

☑ Generally, the ratio of appointments to closed transactions is 2:1. That means, on average it takes two appointments to land a listing or buyer representation that leads to 1 closed transaction. (According to Gary Keller's findings: For sellers, 80% of appointments lead to a seller listing taken, and 65% of those listings sell. For buyers, 65% of appointments lead to a buyer listing taken, and 80% of those buyers close.) This is true of web-generated appointments as well as offline lead generation. (Skillful qualification screening and closing skills will improve this general ratio.)

☑ On average, for every six contacts in your personal database (people you know), you should expect to generate one sale or one referral per year.

☑ On average, for every 50 contacts in your farm database (people you don't know), you should expect to generate one sale per year.

☑ Overall, listings and sales hold a 1:1 ratio. For every listing sold, if marketed well, expect to generate one sold buyer side, and vice versa. Top producers have a simple saying, "Replace every current client with a new client."

☑ How well does e-mail work? Some of the best statistics on conversions come from retailers and catalogers who use e-mail to drive consumers to their online stores where a purchase averages $110. For every 1,000 e-mail pieces sent, the average conversion is 2.35 purchases which is an e-mail-to-sales ratio of about three-tenths of 1%, according to *Q1 2003 E-mail Trend Report*, copyright DoubleClick, Inc. (Figure 17.4).

Five Easy Principles

There are five simple eRainmaker principles for preparing your e-marketing plan.

Principle #1: Find a Quiet Place to Plan

To give yourself permission to focus on the big picture, find a quiet place to plan. This may mean staying out of the office every morning for a week after setting your e-mail on "out-of-office assistant" and the phone on voice mail, or locking your office door after telling everybody you'll be out of town, or actually going out of town. Do whatever it takes to get away from distractions. No phones. No e-mail. No faxes. No clients. No family (planning is business, not a holiday). In some cases, you may want to have your staff join you for input and feedback—especially those who will be responsible for implementing the online marketing plan. You also may want to have some records and accounting numbers handy. You'll be glad you took time away

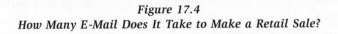

Figure 17.4
How Many E-Mail Does It Take to Make a Retail Sale?

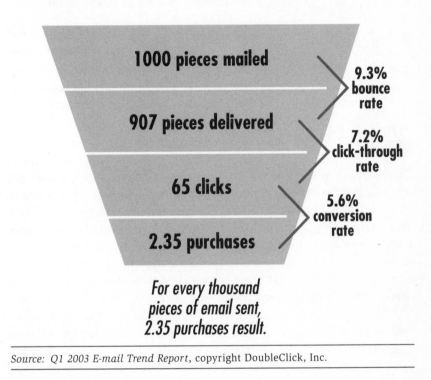

RETAIL E-MAIL CONVERSION FUNNEL

1000 pieces mailed

9.3% bounce rate

907 pieces delivered

7.2% click-through rate

65 clicks

5.6% conversion rate

2.35 purchases

For every thousand pieces of email sent, 2.35 purchases result.

Source: *Q1 2003 E-mail Trend Report*, copyright DoubleClick, Inc.

from work for this special time of year to recharge and focus. Remember, this is business, not busyness.

Principle #2: Begin with the End in Mind

In the words of Stephen R. Covey, author of *The 7 Habits of Highly Effective People,* " 'Begin with the end in mind' is based on the principle that *all things are created twice.* There's a mental or first creation, and a physical or second creation to all things." Setting the right goal is your first step. Remember, your goal is the endgame, the Big Idea, the Holy Grail at the end of the quest—in short, your exit strategy.

Where do you want to be when the dust settles at the end of the day? That goal is your vision.

Principle #3: Keep It Simple

Relax. You're not writing a blockbuster film script or the Great American Novel. All you want to do is put your ideas down on paper. Entire books have been written on goal setting and preparing complex marketing plans. This is not one of them. Keep your online marketing plan document simple. Keep it short. Keep it actionable where anyone on your team could read it and know what needed to be done next.

Principle #4: Implement One Bite at a Time

The Internet is not a mystery. Yet, the task of understanding e-marketing can seem to be so big, some real estate professionals are paralyzed with inaction. It bears repeating: If someone else knows something about technology you don't know, they just got started first. Everybody learns about technology by doing. The secret to understanding the Internet is the same secret to eating an elephant: Take it one bite at a time. The solution is no more complicated than making a list. As my Grandfather Leslie M. Gooder was fond of saying, "Bite it off and chew 'til you swallow." Select a big payoff idea, implement it, move on to the next idea. Grandpa Gooder had another favorite saying: "If you chase two rabbits, both are likely to get away." He was right. When it is time to look back at the accomplishments you make during the coming year, you'll be amazed how far you have come.

Principle #5: Repeat the Process Every Year

Every year you will measure your results. Adjust your old plan. Implement your new plan. Measure your benchmarks again. Repeat the process every year. Ultimately, when the time comes to execute your exit strategy, you will need proof of value for your practice. Nothing establishes value better than a track record of marketing plans, assessments, benchmarks, accomplished objectives, and a proven Trophy Database that keeps on generating business for your buyer. The tangible record of your achievements will be presented in your collected marketing-plan documents as well as financial records. Taken

---

eRainmaker Tip

———

Tools of the Trade: A number of marketing plan software are available on the market. The best ones are designed for e-marketing to help you use worksheets, forecasting, measurement and analysis tools to generate a budget, compare campaigns and profitability for e-mail, website, banner ads, lifetime customer value, e-mail list sales growth, and so on. Some come with snazzy PowerPoint templates and presentation documents (using Microsoft Office 97 or later is required), which may be overkill for most eRainmakers. If you need help putting an unorganized hodge-podge into an organized system, software may be for you (eRainmaker.com: Professional Growth).

---

together, these documents are a guide to how you ran your business, how your buyer can keep the good times coming—and an opportunity outline for the new buyer to improve the system with a new plan.

eRainmaker Bonus Strategy: Saving Your Business in a Down Market with Lower Cost E-Marketing

E-mail is not free, but it is cheap. That's because, even though the delivery of e-mail is very low-cost (compared to direct-mail postage and printing), the acquisition and maintenance of addresses in your Trophy E-Mail Database require substantial investment (compared with street addresses, which rarely change and are generally free). Also, websites often cost more to maintain over the years than to create.

Yet, the bottom line is that e-marketing can reach more prospects more often with more interactive response offers and value-added services for less cost than offline marketing. The secret is being prepared. Put a website in place. Build a substantial opt-in permission-based e-mail database. When the inevitable market fluctuations send your gross commissions south, tightening your budget belt may mean restricting new spending, but it doesn't necessarily mean restricting the e-marketing you already have in place.

Tracking Results from Your Online Marketing Dollars with 10 Savvy Techniques

To be sure you get the most for your marketing dollars, savvy eRainmakers refine their record-keeping system to track critical statistics. The bottom line to working smarter, not harder, is to *stop* doing what you are doing that produces the same old results and reinvest your money in techniques that work better or try promising new approaches worth testing.

Keeping records is critical. As every parent (and child psychologist) knows: "What is rewarded is improved." In a business context, as the legendary management consultant Peter Drucker once said, "If you can't measure it, you can't manage it." Put another way: That which is tracked gets done.

1. *Cost per acquisition (CPA):* This can be acquisition of an e-mail address, lead/prospect inquiry, or appointment. (See below, Cost Per Action.)

2. *Cost per sale (CPS):* Divide marketing expense by total transaction sides to determine your CPS as a dollar amount.

3. *Return on investment (ROI):* Divide gross commission income/sales revenue (return) by marketing cost (investment); percentage is the bottom line on how successful marketing was in terms of sales (returns) stated as a percent of money spent (invested). (Example: $500,000 revenue divided by $50,000 marketing cost equals 1,000% ROI, or 10 times the investment.)

4. *Pay per sale (PPS):* Payment of referral fee for closed transaction, typically a percentage of sales price, such as HomeGain model (requires service provider have a broker's license).

5. *Customer lifetime value (CLV):* From experience, determine how many repeat transactions and closed referrals your Trophy Database produces on average (Example: If 120 past clients are the source of 20 sides per year on average or .17 sides per client per year at an average GCI of $2,500 per side, then a 10-year CLV is 1.7 sides per client or $4,250—well worth staying in touch!).

6. *Customer value (CV):* Estimate average GCI a specific home price will produce from a single transaction; especially useful to set objective to increase your average GCI per unit (Example: $500,000 property × 1.5% commission split = $7,500 GCI).

7. *Cost per click (CPC):* Cost per click-through; also "pay-per-click" if buying the service, often from search engines or directories, or "pay-per-view" if paying for ads on larger websites, such as portals or search engine sites (Example: $200 marketing cost divided by 400 click-throughs is a $0.50 cost per click).

8. *Cost per action (CPA):* Cost to get visitor to take specific action beyond clicking on ad, such as subscribe to your newsletter or submit response form (Example: $0.50 cost per click times 30 click-throughs to get one prospect to register in guest book is $15 cost per action).

9. *Cost per lead (CPL):* Cost to get enough prospect information for follow up; also "pay-per-lead" if buying the service (similar to CPA).

10. *Cost per thousand (CPM):* Price for one thousand ad views ("impressions").

18

E-Operations Plan: Streamlining with Virtual Assistants

OLD RULE
All this tech-talk is just Geek to me.

NEW RULE
You should definitely hire a virtual assistant.

Using Virtual Assistants to Build Value into Your E-Marketing Systems

Steven Sinofsky and Eric Rudder are not household names—unless you work for Microsoft. Before each was appointed head of a Microsoft division (Sinofsky is senior vice president, Office, and Rudder is senior vice president, Servers and Tools), they worked as Bill Gates' personal technical assistant in the 1990s. Their job (among other things) was to explain the Internet and new technologies to Bill Gates—and along the way help shape Microsoft's .Net strategy. Simply put, even Bill Gates needs a tech assistant. If you could learn everything you need to know about e-marketing and technology, it doesn't mean you should. Considering how ever-expanding technology arrives relentlessly, few of us take much convincing about the value of getting help.

One savvy solution for real estate professionals is to hire virtual assistants (VAs), who work like regular assistants except they sit somewhere else and use the Internet, phone, fax, and instant messaging to do their job. Some VAs work by the hour or the project, while others are paid by the transaction. Hiring a VA may mean you don't need another full-time assistant or your onsite assistant can focus on "in-office" hands-on tasks.

Remember, every VA has strengths and specialties. To learn how specific VAs can help almost any aspect of your practice, visit the websites of several VAs. Here are some tasks concerning marketing that VAs do routinely for clients:

☑ Prepare virtual tours with photos and data you provide.

☑ Maintain drip e-mail follow-up campaigns.

☑ Update e-mail lists and send a monthly online newsletter.

☑ Enhance online listings with additional photos.

☑ Website maintenance or work with web designer.

☑ Create electronic property flyers for e-mail.

☑ Submit your website to search engines.

☑ Create e-stationery for Outlook.

☑ Research Internet on assigned topics, such as e-marketing tools.

☑ Monitor website traffic logs, reports, and more.

☑ Mail a monthly printed newsletter.

☑ Print and mail Just Listed/Just Sold postcards.

☑ Produce custom CMAs, seller, and buyer laptop presentations.

☑ Prepare presentation handouts, overheads, flipcharts, or Power-Point slideshows.

☑ Send post-closing and referral thank-you gifts and notes.

☑ Develop relocation packages.

☑ Accomplish virtually any administrative task you have.

Some of the best VAs have been certified by software providers like REALTOR.com and Gooder Group (look for Gooder Group's "Rainmaker Certified" seal shown in Figure 18.1) with special training and testing to be proficient on the providers' programs—so you don't have to be. For a list of real estate specialist VAs, visit eRainmaker online resource center (eRainmaker.com: Virtual Assistants).

Figure 18.1
Rainmaker Trained Virtual Assistant

Checklist of FAQs about Real Estate Virtual Assistants

Here are 13 essential "Frequently Asked Questions" that should be asked by anyone considering a virtual assistant:

1. *What is a virtual assistant?* VAs are independent contractors who provide administrative support or specialized business services from outside your office. VAs may be sole practitioners or have a staff. VAs don't so much work "for" you, as "with" you, often developing a very close collaborative partnership. Also, VAs network extensively and can call on other VA colleagues to help on a big project or during a busy time. VAs work in almost every industry. Yet, in real estate the demand is so great for VAs and the fit so natural (78% of REALTORS have home offices, according to 2003 *REALTOR Magazine* survey), many VAs have specialized in helping real estate professionals.

2. *How much does one cost?* Rates vary. Hourly rates range between $15 to $55 an hour, typically $30+ per hour. Most VAs have a fixed hourly rate for all work. Some work on a fee based on monthly closings. Others have an hourly rate scale for different types of work. Some VAs discount their hourly rate, perhaps 5% to 20%, if you retain them for a regular block of hours, say, more than 5 hours a week or 20+

hours a month. Be sure to clarify what work costs and get estimates for large projects. As a relationship develops, it's not uncommon for a retainer to replace piecework, project-work, or overflow-work. Transaction coordination is often a separate arrangement priced per closing. Be sure to discuss any surcharges for rush jobs and work outside normal business hours.

3. *What are some things a VA does not do?* Although most VAs have some outstanding specialty skills, generally a VA is a highly experienced, very efficient executive assistant. Services are administrative. Typically, VAs are not consultants or business coaches, ad agencies, speaker booking agents (some arrange travel), tax advisors, accountants (some do bookkeeping), web developers (some can design or maintain your site), technology consultants, or receptionists (some answer e-mail).

4. *Does a VA need to have a real estate license?* No, not if the VA is not promoting the sale of real estate property. Basically, as long as the VA is doing general office tasks that do not involve direct customer contact (like phones and original property-oriented e-mail), and tasks that do not involve sending specific property information to specific consumers, you typically do not need a licensed VA. Be sure to check your real estate commission's rules pertaining to unlicensed personal assistants, as rules vary by state. For example, here are some guidelines adopted by the state of Illinois: An unlicensed assistant may not (1) interpret information on listings, titles, financing, contracts, closings, or other information relating to a transaction; (2) explain or interpret a contract, listing, lease agreement, or other real estate document with anyone outside the licensee's company; (3) negotiate or agree to any commission, commission split, management fee, or referral fee on behalf of a licensee; or (4) perform any other activity for which a license under the Act is required.

5. *When is hiring a VA a bad idea?* To answer that question, let me quote from an article by Stacy Brice (AssistU.com), *The Top 10 Things to Know about Professional Virtual Assistants,* which originally appeared on TopTen.org in January 2002. Thanks to Kim Hughes (KimHughes.com), a founding member of Real Estate Virtual Assistant Network, who introduced me to Brice's article. In Brice's words:

> If you are controlling, need to micro-manage, have trust issues, aren't online, can't understand how or why this would work, live in the urgent, procrastinate, rush to deadline, aren't organized, want someone at your beck and call, have a huge ego and can't work in partnership with

others, don't understand the power created in a relationship with a fantastic assistant, aren't open to learning new ways of working and communicating, or if you work in a high-pressure field where things run you instead of the other way around, you probably need an in-person employee, not a VA.

6. *Is the VA on my payroll?* No. VAs are independent contractors. You are not responsible for withholding taxes or benefits or insurance or OSHA or ERISA requirements. Plan to send your VA an annual 1099 tax form indicating total payments for previous tax year. Remember, a VA is a business owner, not your employee.

7. *How do I know what I am paying for?* Ask for an itemized invoice or supporting documentation (time sheet) that indicates hours worked on specific projects. Some VAs require a deposit upfront to begin a large project. Once a relationship is established, most VAs send monthly invoices. Out-of-pocket expenses, such as postage, overnight delivery, shipping costs, long-distance phone, and printing through an outside source are reimbursable; be sure to identify upfront what is a business expense for the VA and a client-expense for you.

8. *How do I find a VA?* Ask other real estate professionals for referrals. Visit eRainmaker.com for a list of Rainmaker Trained Virtual Assistants. Go to the International Virtual Assistants Association website (IVAA.org) and click through VA Directories > Real Estate Support Specialists (RESS) for a long list by state. Another source is the International Association of Virtual Office Assistants (IAVOA.com) for a worldwide directory organized by country, state, then city. There is a very helpful organization, Real Estate Virtual Assistant Network (REVANetwork.com), where any real estate professional can register and exchange Q&As with VAs anonymously and get assistance for specific tasks.

9. *What are some tips to select a VA?* Not all VAs are equal. Most VAs have special strengths, whether working with a specific software program or doing certain tasks. Ask about their specialties. Itemize the tasks you want a VA to do for you. Some tasks are technology driven; others are hard-copy administrative tasks that can be done anywhere. Look for a VA that has strength specifically in what is most important to you.

10. *How do I get started with a VA?* After you have interviewed and selected a VA, let them guide you. Many new clients ask the same questions. Some VAs have specific "start-up" procedures, such as a no-fee, one-hour consultation. Consider mutually developing a specific list of tasks or projects to minimize misunderstandings. Think of the start-up

as an exercise in writing a job description for a tech assistant or a marketing assistant or transaction coordinator. Consider selecting a medium or small size "get to know each other" stand-alone project to accomplish before moving on to large projects—hold off the new website or listing presentation or converting from one database software to another until later—or before entering into a permanent retainer relationship.

11. *What kind of equipment do I need?* Beyond phone, fax, and e-mail (not AOL), consider what tasks the VA will be doing. Communicating by instant messaging is a plus. If they need access to your desktop computer (which allows file sharing but keeps the files in one place), you will need remote-access software, such as GoToMyPC (web based) or PCAnywhere (desktop based). If you want them to work any time on your computer (or network server), your hardware must stay on. Being connected with "always on" high-speed Internet access is best. A toll-free number is ideal, especially for transaction coordinating. If you have large files that require collaboration and syncing to separate desktop hard drives, or if you need your own intranet to manage a group of VAs, there are web-based services that provide shared Internet workspace for teams and groups working remotely (eRainmaker.com: Dispersed Workgroups). There are also web-based large-file transfer services for multimedia presentations and large closing documents (eRainmaker.com: Large Files). Again, ask your VA, who has been around this track often.

12. *Can my VA work with such-and-such a program?* Ask. Generally, VAs are very technological, detail-oriented, experienced individuals who make it their business to serve remote clients. Being experienced in your database software is a plus, but most VAs can learn it quickly if need be. Consider upgrading your own system to bring it in line with a VA's state-of-the-market software.

13. *Do I have to commit to a long-term contract?* Although tasks and projects paid hourly are typical, a commitment of time helps both you and the VA plan the workflow. Most clients and VAs agree to a reasonable notification period to call it quits, such as 30-day or 60-day notice. (By the way, VAs fire clients, too.)

Have High-Speed Modem, Will Telecommute

Michael Russer (aka, Mr. Internet®) is one of the leading technology trainers and a founding member of the Real Estate Virtual Assistants

Network. Russer has written extensively about virtual assistants and even has a special section of his informative website (ePowerNews.com) devoted to a "VA Corner." With his permission, here is an excerpt from an article that appeared in *Realtor* magazine, December 1999. Look for Russer's groundbreaking book, *Transform Your Business Using Virtual Assistants*, co-authored with Christine Durst and Michael Haaren (StaffCentrix.com, 2002). The book is chock-full of eye-opening insights into hiring and working with VAs.

Before you start looking for and hiring these digital gunslingers, it is important that you are very clear about the following issues:

☑ *Job description:* When working with someone at a distance, you don't have the luxury of being vague or general about what needs to get done. You are much better off being *very* explicit and exact (in writing) about what needs to be accomplished.

☑ *Position versus project:* Does the job require someone who will work with you on an ongoing basis or just on a project-by-project basis?

☑ *Proximity:* Is it important that your virtual assistant be located in a particular geographical region? Will face-to-face meetings occasionally be needed? These requirements can *severely* limit your search.

☑ *Autonomy:* Most virtual assistants are used to working autonomously. The question is: are *you* ready to let someone take a project and run with it, without the ability to hover over them?

☑ *Benchmarks and milestones:* Since with a virtual assistant you will not have arbitrary access to work in progress, it is important that you lay out specific expected timelines, benchmarks, and milestones for any work that needs to be completed. Remember, it can be difficult to work through misunderstandings with someone who is 2,000 miles away.

☑ *Fees:* Know what fee range you are willing to pay.

"Keep in mind that," Russer adds, "unlike traditional on-site assistants who are typically trained to be a Jack (or Jane) of all trades (and hence, master of none), Virtual Assistants are hired for their specialty. This way you only hire 'Masters' for each function which eliminates much of the training and management issues associated with typical on-site assistants."

19

E-Action Plans: Becoming an eRainmaker

Simple Objectives to Color

Simple solutions are the best solutions after all. Years ago, just out of college, one of my classmates at Beloit College in Wisconsin, Nic Paley, who is still a close friend, sent me one of his paintings. More than 25 years later I look at that painting every morning in my library. The title is "Simple Objects to Color." Using nothing more than a black line on white paper, a story full of memories is captured, from a flying fish and lighthouse to two connected cherries, to a derby hat, to a mitten-with-shovel. Every object is simple—like a child's coloring book. Every morning over my tea, the painting makes me smile. The more I look at the painting, the more I get out of it.

Starting an effective online marketing plan is also simple; yet getting the most out of your system takes time. Most real estate professionals don't have time to read every supplier's website, penetrate every product; find the diamonds amidst the slag. In the words of Michael Russer, "The real estate industry suffers from an embarrassment of riches with respect to having many powerful solutions to help you do more with less. That is if (and it's a big 'if') you can implement and use them consistently."

There's the rub. First, the choices must be narrowed. Then, the solutions need to be implemented. As I've said before, the basic plan to becoming a successful eRainmaker has three simple strategies:

1. Create a branded, customer-focused, destination website and promote it.
2. Build a permission-based, e-mail enhanced Trophy Database and automate the system.
3. Delegate technology tasks to virtual assistant(s) or staff so you rarely touch a keyboard (except for e-mail).

Often in my workshops, the first question I ask participants is: "How many e-mail addresses do you have in your database?" Just knowing that one fact—or not—is revealing. Then I pose the question: "What would it take to have 10 times as many?" Once I have their attention, I lay out the challenge. Your first step is a content-rich website designed to capture responses from visitors. Those responses—combined with your e-mail-enhanced direct-mail list—will become your Trophy E-Mail Database with targeted addresses. Next you send e-mail—with your contacts' permission and at a frequency they approve—containing links back to valuable information of interest to the customers on your site. Able and willing customers click-through or call for appointments when they are ready. All you do is close.

The plan is simple—as the best solutions always are. This chapter is designed to show you a simple blueprint and to outline some simple objectives to color. The coloring of them—in your own choice of colors and in your own time—is up to you and will define your online presence along the path to building a profitable eRainmaker practice. Happy coloring!

Your eRainmaker Technology Shopping List

If you are wondering where to start and what you need to take your existing e-marketing to the next level, here is a simple eRainmaker shopping list. Focus on a single item. Implement it. Move on to the next. No one builds a complete e-marketing system overnight. The best ones take time. Most real estate professionals complete one stage before moving on to the next, but items are in no particular order within a stage. Be sure to visit eRainmaker.com for specific eRainmaker recommended suppliers. Here are the major "infrastructure" milestones along the way:

Stage One: Basics

- ☑ Desktop and/or notebook computer (high speed, large capacity).
- ☑ Brand name domain (web address, URL; protect it with variation URLs).
- ☑ Broadband Internet access (Cable, DSL, T1).
- ☑ Professional e-mail software to send and manage messages.
- ☑ Contact management software to store your enhanced Trophy E-Mail Database.
- ☑ Anti-virus and backup software to protect your data.

Stage Two: Continuing

- ☑ Personal website (eRainmaker.com: Website Buyer's Guide).
- ☑ Automated e-mail program that's web-based with nothing to install or download.
- ☑ Digital camera and virtual tour capability for enhanced electronic advertising.
- ☑ Enriched plug-in website content (for buyers/sellers, e-newsletter, schools, demographics, mapping, etc.).

Stage Three: eRainmaker

- ☑ Virtual assistant or on-site assistant to manage e-marketing.
- ☑ Custom website or redesign makeover of aged initial personal site.
- ☑ More plug-in website content with response forms and customer service tools.
- ☑ Strategic links pages to build link popularity.
- ☑ Search engine placement software to get more traffic for less work.

Sales and General Technology

Beyond your e-marketing to generate and follow-up leads, other general and sales-oriented technologies will also enhance your business. Several are mentioned here to give you an idea of additional tools you will use once you are working with a client or that your staff will use to run the business.

- ☑ Palm Pilot or other portable digital assistant (PDA).
- ☑ Presentation software.
- ☑ Desktop publishing software.
- ☑ Color printer (laser or inkjet).
- ☑ Portable printer.
- ☑ Scanner.
- ☑ Financial analysis software.
- ☑ Online transaction management subscription.
- ☑ Online settlement processing service.

Top 12 Tools for Your Online Marketing Toolbox

One of the leading custom real estate website designers in the nation is Sandy Teller (SizzlingStudios.com) in Naples, Florida. Visiting the Sizzling Studios site is an excellent exercise for either the newbie or the advanced user. Check out Teller's insightful articles on how to get started, legal issues, search engines, marketing your site, spam, and a host of other topics.

Spend some time to understand Teller's description of her company's template websites, and then check out her custom website pricing (the more features you get, the more the sites cost). You will come away with a sophisticated understanding of the elements of all websites. You'll discover where to begin, how to build your online marketing toolbox, what you get with a template versus custom website, and how to enhance your site with add-on content or "bells and whistles," as Teller calls them. With Teller's permission here is a copyrighted excerpt from the Sizzling Studios' site (SizzlingStudios.com: Site Map > Your Toolbox):

Top 12 Tools for Your Online Marketing Toolbox

To be fully web functional, you need a few tools. If you don't have them, get them now! Even if you do have some or all of them on your computer, you may not have the latest versions. Check out the tools and make sure your toolbox is up-to-date.

(Please note: all of the products listed below are included for your convenience only. Sizzling Studios offers no guarantee or warranty whatsoever, and Sizzling Studios accepts no responsibility should you choose to download any products. Download addresses and links are available at SizzlingStudios.com. Be sure to read Sizzling Studio's *Terms of Use* disclaimer before you take any action.)

1. *Your Browser:* Microsoft Internet Explorer is head and shoulders above Netscape. It's free.

2. *A "Real" ISP:*
   - ☑ A real ISP means *NO AOL.*
   - ☑ A real ISP is one that does not use SpamCop as their source for blacklisted ISPs. (See Sizzling Studio's page on e-mail spam for more info on SpamCop.)
   - ☑ A real ISP is one that supplies full disclosure to you about any e-mail filtering they may be doing and gives you a choice of whether to filter or not filter your mail.

3. *Your E-mail Program:* When you use Outlook Express, you can send messages in color and with embedded photos. It's free and part of the Microsoft Internet Explorer browser. *AOL subscribers cannot easily use Outlook Express. If you want to know why AOL e-mail is not compatible with Microsoft Outlook or Outlook Express: It's AOL's decision—not Microsoft's!* If you want the concise version of why you shouldn't be subscribing to AOL:
   - ☑ You can't easily use a full-featured third-party e-mail program like the one we use (Outlook Express).
   - ☑ You can't easily include the received message in your reply. This is a horrible shortcoming for a businessperson

(continued)

who needs to include a complete record of all e-mail exchanges in every e-mail on the subject.

☑ You should be using you@yourdomain.com as your reply to address—not SuziQ@aol.com. It's very hard for a tech savvy person to take any e-mail seriously when the sender is an AOL subscriber.

☑ In the interest of full disclosure, there are some things you can do to use third-party mailing programs and services when you are an AOL subscriber. Links to information can be found at SizzlingStudios.com.

4. *e.Fax Messenger:* This program turns any printable document into an e-mail attachment. It is a free utility. (Do not confuse the paid program e.Fax Messenger Plus with the free program e.Fax Messenger!)

5. *A Zip Program:* You need a program for compressing and decompressing files, especially if you send and receive e-mail attachments. We use WinZip. *This is not a free program but you can try it free.*

6. *A Virus Checker:* There is nothing worse than giving or receiving a virus. We use the Norton Antivirus Program from Symantec because it 'pushes' new virus definitions to you automatically when you subscribe to LiveUpdate. *This is not a free program but you can try it free.*

7. *Macromedia Flash Player:* The player allows you to view flash animations in your browser. It's free.

8. *RealMedia Player:* The player allows you to experience Real-Audio and RealVideo. Make sure you are downloading the free version unless you want to purchase a fancier version.

9. *Adobe Acrobat Reader:* You must be able to read .PDF files (Portable Document Format files). It's free. If you want to produce .PDF files, download the full Acrobat software program, which is not free.

10. *A Firewall:* Prevent hackers from accessing your computer via Trojan Horses, worms, and spyware. We use Zone Alarm. Search for the free version unless you want to purchase the Pro version.

11. *An AdWare Eliminator:* We use Spy Bot Search and Destroy. It will remove those nasty unwanted popups and cookies placed on your computer by the companies that proliferate adware. This program is free, although the author accepts donations.

12. *A Broadband Internet Connection:* You have no idea, if you've never experienced it, how much difference a fast connection makes. Don't mess around with a dialup (phone-line connection). Get:

☑ Cable modem connection, or

☑ DSL connection, or

☑ *Direct PC* connection, or

☑ ISDN line connection, or

☑ T-1 connection.

☑ The above options vary from about $40/month to a few hundred dollars a month for a T-1. You must do something that gives you a faster connection than a dialup. Remember, your customers are most probably far more techno-literate than you are. Don't throw away business because you are scared of technology or too cheap to invest in your success! How much do you lose out on by just one lost commission?

☑ If your broker doesn't provide a broadband (fast) connection at your office, scream bloody murder. Demand the tools that will lead to your success. Your broker has an obligation to you to help you be productive.

When you have all of the above, you're fully equipped for web success! Downloading and installing is not enough. You won't be fully web-literate until you learn how to use your tools.

Your eRainmaker E-Marketing To Do List

As you acquire the hardware and software tools for your website and e-mail infrastructure, you will also check off strategic items from your E-Marketing To Do List. Again, don't expect to accomplish the entire list immediately. Plan to pace yourself. Focus on one task, implement it, and move on. Start by doing it yourself; which puts a solid foundation under your understanding of e-marketing and technology. Later, you will be able to delegate tasks and monitor accomplishments better. That's how you build an effective eRainmaker marketing system that increases production, maximizes profit, and exits with top dollar for your practice.

Stage One: Basics

Remember, learning about technology is totally a matter of exposure—then repeating that exposure until you remember it easily:

- ☑ Find a "techie" to advise you on e-marketing needs (even consider tech-savvy family and friends to start). Pay with food.
- ☑ Enter all contacts in database software (do-it-yourself or outsource; ideal assignment for temp employee).
- ☑ Register your own domain. Buy variations: .NET, .ORG, .BIZ (Chapter 3).
- ☑ Learn to use e-mail.
- ☑ Buy a personalized low-cost website.
- ☑ Promote website domain in all marketing to increase traffic and brand.
- ☑ Launch effort to collect e-mail addresses (Personal list, B2B, Website leads, Strangers).
- ☑ Create first-response routine e-mails saved as signatures.
- ☑ Evaluate sites of your local real estate competitors. Save their e-mail addresses in your B2B database.
- ☑ Become a student of online marketing, including spam for effective techniques to beat it.

Stage Two: Continuing

- ☑ Hire local "techie" you can learn from, ask questions; someone whose answers grow as your questions grow, and who can respond in an emergency. Pay by the hour or project.
- ☑ Integrate your offline and online marketing to maximize response and minimize cost.
- ☑ Add plug-in content to your website, emphasize lead-capture offers and web forms.

☑ Subscribe to automated e-mail software and enter at least 100 opt-in contacts.

☑ Launch drip marketing e-mail campaign to permission database with monthly e-newsletter.

☑ Generate virtual tours for your listings (do-it-yourself or hired). Link to website.

☑ Create virtual tours for your staff and area communities or specialty markets.

☑ Send regular e-mail announcements to B2B network of local top agents and co-brokers.

☑ Evaluate top agent sites nationwide. Save their e-mail addresses in B2B database and URLs in favorites.

Stage Three: eRainmaker

☑ Hire full-time techie "coach" or retain virtual assistant for administrative tasks. Pay by salary or retainer.

☑ Hire web designer to create a custom "destination" website. Update with specialized content, consumer tools and optimize with search keywords and titles regularly.

☑ Launch corporate identity campaign to maximize brand recognition using consistent logotype, symbol, and slogan.

☑ Create separate content sections on main site or inexpensive specialty sites to attract targeted prospects (new homes, luxury homes, seniors, second/vacation homes, investors, waterfront, condominiums, subdivision, and so on).

☑ Buy multiple specialty domains to point to sections of your destination site that your traffic analysis indicates have appeal to consumer needs. Advertise domains.

☑ Create transaction management "extranet" where current buyers, sellers, and service providers have 24/7 access to their transaction.

Stage Next: Ongoing

☑ Plan and budget major destination site revision approximately every two to three years.

☑ Be a student of the Internet. Regularly visit supplier and competitor websites with a specific purpose in mind. Attend e-marketing seminars and conferences. Network with other eRainmakers. Continuously add new tools to your online marketing toolkit. Ask your tech advisor, "How'd they do that?" Don't be afraid to say, "What does that mean?" when cyber-babble doesn't make sense.

15 Absolute "Musts" for Every eRainmaker E-Strategy

Promote Listings

1. Display your own listings.
2. Display MLS listings (IDX, VOW, or framed).
3. Add virtual tours of your listings.
4. Install links to maps for all your properties for sale.
5. Use listing manager software that makes it easy to manage and load your listings (if not provided by MLS).

Capture Website Leads with Plug-In Content

6. Link to in-depth articles for buying, selling, relocating, financing, homeowning.
7. Add rich content on your specialties: First-Time Buyers, Seniors, Investors, Condos, Second Homes, New Homes, Renting, Waterfront, and so on.
8. Embed multiple response forms and prospect-capturing offers.
9. Link to local information, useful sites, "About You" pages.
10. Install e-loyalty pages for past customers with photos of "Solds," testimonials, business directory, newcomer services, and so on.

Build Trophy E-Mail Database

11. Add auto-registration into database of response form inquiries from website.
12. Add automatic e-mail follow-up drip marketing campaigns.
13. Cultivate a consumer referral database (advocates).
14. Cultivate a real estate professional referral network database (local and nationwide).

15. Cultivate local business-to-business database for reciprocal referrals.

Turning the Internet to Your Unfair Advantage in One Hour a Week

The secret to avoiding *Internet information overload* is to stay focused on real estate. Here are seven easy steps to become an eRainmaker. But remember, the Internet is addictive. Try to avoid mousing off Hobbit-like into the never world of Planet Internet, link-by-seductive-link, never to return in time to list and sell. Just say no. Stay focused on real estate. Limit your study time. Understand that the Internet wasn't built in a day, and you won't understand it in a day:

1. *Get high-speed Internet access.* Get high-speed access (also, "broadband") with a digital subscriber line (DSL) or cable modem. Study time becomes a pleasure, instead of a frustration.

2. *Shop like a consumer.* Spend 15 minutes once a week searching with a purpose (not "surfing") as if you are a home buyer or seller on the Internet. Pretend you're local one week, and then pretend you're moving to a distant market the next. What do you appreciate? What is annoying?

3. *Check out the competition.* Spend 15 minutes once a week visiting real estate websites. Start with local competitors' websites (get URLs from homes magazines, classifieds, and signs). Graduate to the hundreds of top websites listed in the eRainmaker.com Great Websites section. Bookmark (save) favorite sites. One extraordinary change the Internet has brought is your ability to experience the online marketing strategies of real estate professionals in any market, not just your local competitors.

4. *Change your default homepage.* Once a week, change the default homepage (also, "start page") on your Internet Browser to open to a different real estate page. Try competitors, company sites, portals, search engines, resource sites (see eRainmaker.com). Experience what your customers' experience.

5. *Tap the best tips.* Subscribe to free or membership e-newsletters for real estate professionals, such as Allen F. Hainge's *CYBER-STAR® News & Views* (AFHSeminars.com), Jack Peckham's *Real*

Estate Cyber Tips (RECyber.com), Michael Russer's *Mr. Internet's ePower News* (ePowerNews.com), Steven M. Canale's *Tips & Tricks Newsletter* (Canale.com), or Risa Saltman's site *Risa's Web Tips* (RealEstateWebPro.com).

6. *Chat and post.* Study what's happening on the street by visiting "for real estate professionals only" forums in chat rooms, bulletin boards or news groups, such as Real Talk (RealTalk.com), Real Estate Cyber Society (RECyber.com), or your franchise, designation, or National Association of REALTORS (REALTOR.org).

7. *Find someone smarter.* Cultivate people who know more than you do and who can answer simple "What does that mean?" and "How did they do that?" questions. Ask a kid (yours or someone else's), staff technology person, or virtual assistant. Buttonhole colleagues. You don't need a "geek for hire," just someone who can point you in the right direction.

Delivering High Touch through High Tech

When Ira Serkes (BerkeleyHomes.com), a CYBERSTAR and top producer in the Berkeley, California, market, says he delivers "high touch through high tech" you can believe it (Figure 19.1). Here are some of Ira and Carol Serkes' top tips:

- ☑ Focus on content and community, not just homes. Homes are very important, but unless you give the consumer a compelling reason to linger at your site, just having homes for sale doesn't differentiate you from anyone else.

- ☑ Content is king. That's why we get such detailed messages from buyers and sellers who come to our website.

- ☑ The corporate sites tend to focus on their own listings, or making loans. The successful personal real estate professional sites focus on what the consumer wants and needs. Stay tuned to station WIIFM: What's In It For Me.

- ☑ We strongly feel your website should be designed assuming someone is accessing it using AOL on a dialup line . . . because they probably are.

- ☑ FLASH rarely conveys information. Flash is generally done for ego gratification. We recommend having a non-Flash page be

Figure 19.1
Focus on Content and Community, Not Just Homes

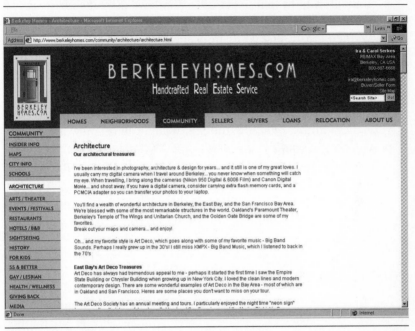

Source: Courtesy of Ira and Carol Serkes (BerkeleyHomes.com), RE/MAX Executive, Berkeley, California.

your default page, and let people click on the Flash link if they want to see Flash. You can certainly have fancy stuff on your site. I love the EGG virtual tours, but it is bandwidth intensive, so we put it as a separate link so it doesn't slow down photo loading on the property page. Same thing for pop-ups, applets, anything out of the ordinary.

☑ We just spent a large amount of time and money on our web re-design . . . and I think we successfully kept it to state-of-the-art. The only exception is the JavaScript effects on the navigation, but I felt okay that even old browsers could handle it.

☑ Oh . . . and set the default to "sound off." All my computers have the sound off. Except my laptop which has the volume turned down to one of the lowest settings. Nothing irritates me more than going to a site and getting music. It would really irritate me if I were surfing the web from work!

☑ Learn how to create Adobe Acrobat files from digital documents or scanned disclosures. We create Acrobat originals from digital contracts and have also set up a Windows machine for scanning multipage documents to Visioneer PaperPort (Visioneer.com). We then create PDF Files from the scans, and upload to one of our server sites. We also receive all faxes on the Windows computer, which makes it easier to forward them, create PDF Files, or multiple copies.

☑ Learn how to upload files to a server and e-mail the link to your client, without e-mailing the file, which can be very large.

☑ We've programmed our web inquiry form so that the inquiries go to my e-mail, Carol's e-mail, and each of our cell phones. There's nothing like the Wow of calling a client to say, "Hi . . . I received your e-mail a little while ago and just wanted to get back to you." . . . and having them say, "My finger is still on the send button!"

Rule #1: Be There!

When I asked Tim Kinzler what specific advice he would give to novice and experienced agents to improve their online marketing, Kinzler (TimKinzler.com), a leading agent with Coldwell Banker in Delray Beach, Florida, and a CYBERSTAR, thought of one of his favorite movies: "Being There," starring Peter Sellers. "Rule #1: Be there!," said Kinzler. "The consumer is spending more time on the Internet than TV. Identify the target you wish to reach. Understand what is important to them and how they access the Internet. Find products that help put you on the Net. Then tell everyone you know, and want to know, how to find you. Use other media to drive the customer to your site, including bumper stickers, postcards, voicemail, business cards, print media, the works."

Costly Mistake to Avoid When You're New to the Internet

Mistake: Surfing the Net and Not Having Anything to Show for It

The Internet is a "pull" medium (in contrast to e-mail, which is a "push" technology). In other words, the Internet is endlessly fascinating, infinitely connected, and very addicting—it literally pulls you in. One link leads to another, then another and another. Pretty soon you're hooked. Lost in the 3W world. Consumed. Overloaded. Zoned. How do you keep from becoming an Internet junkie?

SOLUTION

Put yourself on an Internet diet. Remember, the web is a huge repository of information as well as a doorway to interactive communities. Avoid the temptation to take a quick, purposeless plunge "just to get your feet wet." Instead, approach the Internet as one big cyber-tradeshow. Sit for a moment outside the show and develop a plan. Make a list of target URLs as a guide. Take it aisle by aisle. Moderation wins the race. Have a purpose, particularly a business purpose. Search, don't surf. Limit your time. (My research Diva uses an egg timer to limit a search session to 6 minutes.) Discipline yourself to produce an "outcome" from your time: take an action, send e-mail, or write a document.

Learn how to use advanced search options on major search engines such as Google, Yahoo!, MSN, AOL, Ask Jeeves, AllTheWeb. Most have concise explanations. Some tips:

- ☑ Increase number of results shown in a page from the default (often 10) to 50 to 100 or more ("preferences" in Google, "advanced search" in Yahoo).
- ☑ Find related sites (handy for comparison shopping when researching products) by typing supplier URL and searching for "pages similar to this page" (Google).
- ☑ Be specific. A phone number will return name and address in Google. Search an address and get a map. Zip code and "weather" give you temperature and forecast in Yahoo. Type zip code and "electrician" or "Red Lobster" and get a Yellow-Pages listing.
- ☑ Refine your advanced search query with "and," "or" and "not" which is called "Boolean" logic. Consult the "Help" section of the search engine to learn what type of Boolean terminology (full, implied, or template) the search engine employs and what each type looks like in the search site's form.
- ☑ Search for images instead of words ("pictures" in AllTheWeb, "images" in Google).

Become a Student of the Internet

The Internet is an entire world unto itself—part communication tool, part mass media, part store, part library, part classroom, part to be determined. It is made up of a gazillion tiny communities so vast it touches most of the modern world in some way all without taking a breath.

Become a student of the Internet. Experience how your prospects use the web. Check out how your competition uses the Internet. Study the Internet enough to put your key in the ignition and take off. The more you drive your mouse, the more ideas you will discover.

Exit Strategies: Branding an E-Practice to Sell

Branding Your Practice Value from Domain to E-Dentity

Not only does your e-strategy fit into your overall marketing plan and business strategy, but your e-strategy also should fit into your exit strategy. In its simplest form, an exit strategy is the ultimate goal— the goal that answers the fundamental question: "Why am I doing this?" Put another way, your exit strategy is your final step in a series of milestones to reach your *Big Goal*.

Some eRainmakers plan to retire. Others anticipate a move to another market and will need cash to establish a practice in a new hometown. Still others plan to leave their practice to an adult child.

The ultimate exit strategy is to prepare for a spouse to take over the business if the owner dies. Whatever your motivation, the road map to reaching your goal is the same, an e-strategy. Your e-strategy will play a very significant role in any exit you plan to make.

Alice Held (Come2AZ.com) is a top agent in Phoenix/Scottsdale, Arizona, with RE/MAX Excalibur and an Allen F. Hainge CYBER-STAR®. She wrote an excellent article, "Exit Strategies: What's Yours?" for the International Real Estate Directory (IRED.com) in its Web-Biz section. Held said,

> I began to consider the exit strategy question as an opportunity to educate myself about what was truly needed. I began to see my exit strategy less as a termination and more as a logical part of the goals I had set for both my business and myself. While I may, at some point in my career, sell, exit, merge, and so on I will be more prepared.

Take a tip from this industry leader: Held recommends, "Write your exit strategy down. Have a road map with a start and a finish. Track and account for your business from start to finish, monthly and yearly. You need to justify and provide concrete evidence to ensure that a new buyer can come in and duplicate your income based on your account. Being prepared for any eventuality, any surprise, health, move, or desire, provides you the highest value for your business. Know how to answer the 'What is your exit strategy?' question, but also know that you're really answering the 'What are your vision and goal?' question. And realize that, through identifying your exit strategy, you have a chance to preserve and control your own entrepreneurial nirvana."

Developing Systems Your Buyer Can Step into and Run without You

Warren Buffett, the renown investor and chairman of Berkshire Hathaway, once said, "You need a moat in business to protect you from the guy who is going to come along and offer [your product] for a penny cheaper." A moat, or "barrier to entry," is a barrier to competition that keeps competitors at bay. In a nutshell, a moat is a successful business asset other real estate professionals cannot copy easily. A moat could be a unique way of doing business (Whole Foods, the organic grocery store) or huge research and development investments (drug companies) or patents (manufacturers) or technology (Microsoft) or a brand (Coca Cola). Ask yourself what your practice delivers better than anybody else—and build your own moat.

For Carol and Jim Chamberlain (CarolandJim.com), CYBERSTARS and top producers with Preferred Home Brokers in Brea, California, one of the most valuable e-assets they have developed is a completely automated property update system. "This is a good source for sellers not just buyers," said the Chamberlains. "Sellers want to know what they can buy before they put their house on the market."

"IDX with our MLS has given us a great source for new leads," the Chamberlains said. "IDX gives the consumer all the properties in the MLS to look at. We use a splash page (GotListings.us), which requires a first name and e-mail address to do their own searches. After we have captured the e-mail address, we send an e-mail to invite the consumer to use our automated home search (ForHomeInfo.us). The system allows the buyer to enter search criteria and automatically sends the properties to their inbox before most other agents see the listings. Once entered into the automated system, the potential buyer will receive a series of automated e-mails giving information to help in the buying process. The last sentence of the e-mail tries to get the client to engage by calling or e-mailing us for more help ('Dear John: Over the last week you have received 35 properties that fit your criteria. Would you like to see any of these properties?'). About 75% of those who have signed up at the first site also accept our invitation to the second site with the automated home search in the first 48 hours. The complete system is automated from beginning to end. Until the prospect engages us, we haven't spent any of our time."

Best of all, the Chamberlain's branded property update is completely transferable to a buyer of their practice without missing a beat.

Creating a Network of Contacts Your Buyer Can Take over Easily

You get a sense of Ken Deshaies' unique talent for promotion when you learn he is author of the book, *How to Make Your Realtor Get You the*

Best Deal, and that he is trademarking his favorite line: "When you're lucky enough to live in Summit County, you're lucky enough.™" Deshaies is a top agent with RE/MAX Properties of the Summit in Silverthorne, Colorado, and a CYBERSTAR.

"I consider the Summit Social Club our most valuable e-asset," said Deshaies. "It's an online group I formed of our past, present and future clients. It's a place where members can share and collaborate, where they ask for and receive recommendations for plumbers, electricians, house cleaners, water engineers and restaurants. We post social calendars and encourage members to join together for events. We've had as many as 35 members of the Club show up at an outdoor concert, many of whom had never met before. Membership has gone beyond clients, and members request membership for their friends and neighbors. As long as they are not licensed in real estate, we let them in. For people relocating to our community," Deshaies said, "it's a great way to help them acclimate and make friends."

"The Club has taken on a life of its own," Deshaies continued. "For example, one member, in 2001, suggested we have a Christmas party. We simply watched the messages as members planned the event (a pot luck), and we offered our home. Over 50 people showed up. At the beginning of 2002, a member proposed starting some cooking classes. One person researched a location. Another found a traveling chef. The event, food and all, cost $20 per person, and 14 members attended."

"While we do not advertise listings or our services blatantly, we do occasionally post Market Updates, and I have a signature on all my posts reminding everyone what I do. Just today, I received an off-list message from a member with whom I've never done business, referring three executive friends to us. This mechanism has been a great way to stay in the top of the minds of members," said Deshaies, "without constructing reasons to have a sales pitch with every communiqué."

"Keep in mind this is an online forum," Deshaies added, "and that it is free. Do not confuse it with setting up a website or bulletin board that people have to visit online in order to post messages. There are several places on the Internet where you can set up a group for free (two sites are: Topica.com and YahooGroups.com). Be sure to get permission from all your contacts to add their e-mail addresses to the group. Once you do that, you are in business. Any message sent to the forum automatically gets sent to all the e-mail addresses in the group.

Members only need to hit 'Reply' to respond to any message. Simple and effective," Deshais concludes.

Building a Track Record You Can Bank On

Since 1995, when Pete Doty began building his e-practice with a personal domain (PeteDoty.com), he has not looked back. Doty, a CYBER-STAR and broker/owner of Pete Doty & Company in Highlands Ranch, Colorado, owns eight domain names as of this writing. The three principal domains have websites behind them (DenverRelocation.com, PeteDoty.com, and DenverHomeSource.com), and five secondary domains redirect traffic to DenverRelocation.com. The personal "name" site is particularly useful, Doty says, for agents across country to find him and send referrals. Doty also "leases" domain/sites through subscriptions and dues with organizations like Howard Brinton's Home-Agent and Allen F. Hainge's CYBERSTAR site, which generate additional traffic to his "stickiest" site, DenverRelocation.com. Every e-mail identifies which site the initial request comes from and "we watch our traffic closely via WebStats," said Doty.

"My most valuable e-assets," Doty explained, "are the domain names and the sites behind them. All our web activity generates over $60,000 per year in GCI for the company. Sometimes, a REALTOR from out of town will find us on the web and refer a client. Other times, the lead might come from the PeteDoty.com site—whose job it is to be found and send prospects to DenverRelocation.com."

What is Doty's formula for success? "My e-practice started in 1995 with PeteDoty.com. Still, it is by far the most findable site. Yet, the depth of information on DenverRelocation.com combined with the quality of that name and DenverHomeSource.com—which tell what we do and where we do it—plus the proven track record of the sites make them very valuable indeed."

Building Brand Value with a Symbol

Great brands are transferable to another eRainmaker. One of the best ways to make a brand memorable is with a symbol. Ideally symbols tie-in to your practice in multiple ways, such as your website, your

Figure 20.1
Maryland Crab Symbol

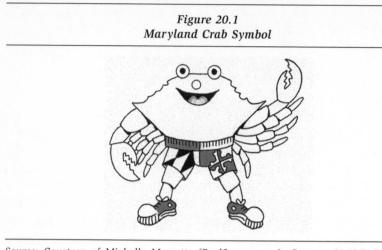

Source: Courtesy of Michelle Margetts (RealSource.com), Century 21 H.T. Brown, Laurel, Maryland.

URL, your location, your specialty, your slogan. Figures 20.1 through 20.5 include some outstanding brand symbol examples.

Beating the Crowded Resale Market for Domain Names

We all know how much used computer equipment and software is worth in an asset sale . . . pennies on the dollar. What are

Figure 20.2
Friendly Cactus Character

Source: Courtesy of Alice Held (Come2AZ.com), RE/MAX Excalibur Realty, Scottsdale, Arizona.

Figure 20.3
Snow Place Slogan

Source: Courtesy of Ken and Mary Deshaies (SnowHome.com), RE/MAX Properties of the Summit, Silverthorne, Colorado.

truly valuable among the assets of an e-practice are the items of *intellectual property* (IP) that you have invested in over time. Together they make up a significant portion of your "brand." Among your e-dentity assets are:

- ☑ Brand name, logotype, and symbols/icons (ideally trademarked or copyrighted).
- ☑ Website(s).
- ☑ Slogan(s).
- ☑ E-mail address(es).
- ☑ Domain name(s).

Figure 20.4
Home Team Expert Brand

Source: Courtesy of Bruce Jay Breger (HomeTeamExpert.com), RE/MAX Gold Coast, Thousand Oaks, California.

Figure 20.5
Chester B. Chatsworth Official Spokesdog

Source: Courtesy of Judy McCutchin (DallasHomes.com), RE/MAX Preston Road North, Dallas, Texas.

The domain name resale market is exploding. For example, before acquiring the Afternic name in December 27, 2002, the Afternic domain name exchange had about 18,000 domains listed in less than a year. After acquiring the Afternic name, five months later the site had more than 250,000 domain names listed, according to Michael Collins, vice president of marketing for Afternic (Afternic.com), one of the leading sites for selling and buying domain names based in Ft. Lauderdale, Florida. The number of domain names in Afternic's Real Estate category alone (Business > Real Estate) was more than a thousand, as of this writing. One feature Afternic offers on its site is a list of recent sales prices that give real estate professionals an idea of comparable values.

"Like the real estate industry, knowing comparable prices helps both parties have confidence in their price," Collins said. "Our appraisal service uses sales comparables from other sources besides just our own site in determining appraised value. I would put almost no value to asking prices in this market. Asking prices in the domain name market are often unrealistic."

> **eRainmaker Tip**
>
> ---
>
> **Domain Names and Appraisals:** You can get an instant appraisal of your domain name's value (or your competitor's domain) for free online by completing a quick form (SwiftAppraisal.com). For sales price comparables, several sites provide recent sales (notice how some domains feature value-adding URL logotypes). Other sites specialize in available real estate domains. Still other sites will perform a researched appraisal for a small fee for your specific domain—a smart move for eRainmakers with a practice to sell (eRainmaker.com: Domain Appraisals).

Ultimately, resale prices establish value, not asking prices. Just like real-world real estate, where value is driven by property improvements and comparables, the resale market for domain names is similar. A domain with a developed website (and perhaps a domain logotype) is far more valuable. One of the biggest competitive and depressing factors on prices of resale domains is the ability to build new domains without buying resale (why buy when you can build cheaper?)—as it is with new homes and resale property prices.

Eight Secrets to Domain Name Value

Here are eight factors that affect the value of your domain name:

1. *Business brand:* Domains are the most valuable when they are used as a brand, a redirect URL, a promotion campaign address, and are associated with a business, product, or service. The bigger the market area, the bigger the domain value. A state (ComeToPennsylvania.com) is worth more than a city (ComeToPhiladelphia.com), which is worth more than a neighborhood domain (ComeToSouthPhily.com).

2. *Website:* Domains with a developed website are worth more than a simple domain by itself. Always have your domain pointed somewhere, even if it is only to a web page with your contact information or your main site.

3. *Intuitive:* An intuitive domain, that is descriptive and is exactly the same as your practice name, trumps hard-to-remember URLs. Your personal name as a brand domain has almost no value to a buyer (although it's in a buyer's interest to require that a personal name domain be included in the sale and redirected to the new buyer's site). A transferable toll-free number has value (For example: 800NowSold.com).

4. *Extension:* .COM wins over everything in the resale market, even .NET, .ORG, and the new .BIZ. Two sought-after extensions, .INFO and .US, have been popular because they add a memorable ring to the right domain name (For example, ResidencesForSale.info and DreamHomeFinder.us were both available at press time). Once you have the domain, you can also use it for your e-mail accounts with an internet service provider (ISP), such as: BuyNow@ResidencesForSale.info or QuickSearch@DreamHomeFinder.us.

5. *Length:* Shorter is better; unless it is so cryptically short it becomes an undecipherable virtual license plate. One word is best; two or three words are okay; four words maximum (abbreviations and acronyms count as a word). Few multiword domains command high resale value because it's often easy to create a new one for the cost of registration.

6. *Spelling:* Easy spelling and common words that are hard to mistype add value. Domains already misspelled hurt value (Homz4Sail.com). Avoid hyphens (two or more hyphens are virtually worthless) and underscores (invisible when active link is underlined). Try to resist the temptation to use easily mistyped substitutions and abbreviations: "EZ" for easy, "4" for for, "10" for ten, "2" for to, "U" for you.

7. *Trademark:* Validate that you own a sellable asset. Register an entity or product as a trademark or slogan as a service mark (See the Patent & Trademark Office at USPTO.gov). Register copyright (See the U.S. Copyright Office in Library of Congress at LOC.gov). Without proof of ownership, a buyer may discount the value.

8. *Legal:* Domains that infringe on others trademarks are worse than worthless; they can be a costly liability, as we mentioned before (Examples: WorldsGreatestRealtor.com; TopReMaxAgent

.com; Century21SuperStar.com). The Trademark Cyberpiracy Protection Act, signed November 29, 1999, sets statutory damages up to $100,000 for registering a domain with bad faith intent that is the same or confusingly similar to a registered trademark or living person's name. Even though the law is on the trademark owners' side, suing "cyber-squatters," unfortunately, can be costlier than buying them out.

Building Brand Value with Website Logotypes

One of the simplest and most powerful techniques to build your brand is to transform your website address into a URL logotype. Use the logotype in offline advertisements as well as on every page of your site. As time goes on a website logotype brand will far surpass a "personal logo" in resale value because it owns a piece of your customers' minds and directly generates business through website traffic. Figures 20.6 through 20.9 include some leading real estate website logo examples.

How to Sell Your Practice

Begin now to prepare your practice to sell years from now. For one thing, ideally you will want to show a three-year or five-year track record of profitable financial statements. These figures are the basis of the valuation of your practice (plus your active listings and buyer agreements), and the record makes it possible for a buyer to put a fair value on your practice. To sell your practice, you may want to

---

Figure 20.6
DallasHomes.com

Source: Registered service mark of Judy McCutchin (DallasHomes.com), RE/MAX Preston Road North, Dallas, Texas.

Figure 20.7
Duckin.com

Source: Courtesy of Rick Miner (Duckin.com), Coldwell Banker Bain Associates, Seattle, Washington.

prepare a formal marketing document (what business brokers call a *Sale Prospectus* and investment bankers call an *Offering Memorandum*). The document outlines the information that interested buyers will need to evaluate the practice. Much of the work you have put into your E-Strategy Plan will be directly applicable for your Sale Prospectus. Broadly, a prospectus often includes sections about:

1. Company history (beginnings, milestone dates);
2. Operations (systems, administration, business philosophy);
3. Competition (real estate professionals, builders, local economy, etc.);
4. Assets (equipment, software, intellectual property, real estate, if any);

Figure 20.8
LakeGenevaProperty.com

Source: Courtesy of Bob Webster (LakeGenevaProperty.com), Keefe Real Estate, Lake Geneva, Wisconsin.

Figure 20.9
BerkeleyHomes.com

Handcrafted Real Estate Service

Source: Courtesy of Ira and Carol Serkes (BerkeleyHomes.com), RE/MAX Executive,
Berkeley, California.

5. Marketing practices (corporate identity, slogan, track record, promotions portfolio, so on);

6. Customer database (software, quantities, segments, e-mail percentage);

7. Personnel (employees, VAs, job descriptions);

8. Owners (biographies, titles, responsibilities);

9. Liabilities (debts, legal matters); and

10. Financial statements (five-year history, three-year projections).

An invaluable basic resource about buying or selling a business in general can be found on the Internet at Capital.com, even though the site specializes in helping middle-market companies raise capital from financial institutions. Particularly, check out the site's section on "Sell a Company" with its straightforward explanations on the basics, team, work plan, time line, and checklist to sell your company.

Tips for Selling Your Practice or Buying Someone Else's Business

Blanche Evans, a nationally recognized real estate journalist, is publisher of *Agent News* and the associate editor of *Realty Times,* one of the Internet's largest independent real estate news services. Evans' outstanding books, *The Hottest E-Careers In Real Estate* and *homesurfing.net: Insider's Guide to Buying and Selling Your Home Using the Internet* (Dearborn Financial Publishing), have set milestones for many real estate professionals and consumers. Here, with permission of *Realty Times,* are Evans' tips for selling a real estate practice that originally appeared in REALTOR magazine in September 2001.

If you are interested in selling your business here are a few tips:

1. Make sure your client/customer list is current. The more accurate and up-to-date the information is, the more valuable it is.

2. Beef up the content on every contact. A buyer is going to want extensive information, not just the phone number.

3. Make sure you have the names and birth dates of the clients, their children, and all relevant information on the home they bought. The more data fields you have completed in your contact management software the more valuable it is.

4. Inform your sphere that you are retiring or moving, and introduce your buyer as someone you handpicked to take over the business. Make sure that the client understands that your replacement was chosen because their business philosophy closely matches your own.

5. Allow the clients to contact you if they wish.

6. Make sure your replacement is techno-literate because they will be using the database you create for him/her.

7. Only sell to people with a solid track record for doing business, so that you will know that your clients are being serviced the way you want them to be.

8. Decide whether you want to maintain a license and whether you would like to contribute occasionally to the business. Make sure the replacement is compatible with your new goals.

9. Get it in writing.

What's Your Practice Worth?

The marketplace ultimately determines the value of a real estate practice, like real property itself, at time of sale. What a buyer will pay is
the true test. "There is no rule of thumb that I have been able to determine other than putting all the facts through our computer program and getting good estimates," said Bob Bohlen Board Chairman
of PreviewProperties.com in Brighton, Michigan. Bohlen is one of the
leading brokers of private real estate practices in the country with 39
sales completed since 1996, as well as having bought or sold 90 companies himself as principal in Bohlen & Associates, an international
company that brokers real estate, medical, and legal businesses. For
10 of 11 years from 1990 through 2000, Bob Bohlen was the number
one sales agent for the entire Prudential real estate network worldwide. Bohlen also has personally coached more than 40 real estate
agents living in 4 different countries.

"Real estate practices have sold from just under $50,000 to over $1
million," Bohlen said. "There are no rough formulas. Several years
ago I developed a computer software program to evaluate the value of
a practice. To determine the value of a seller's practice, I run a *pro
forma* financial statement that consolidates the practice for sale with
the purchaser's business to determine combined values."

The key valuation factors in Bohlen's experience are:

- Pending contracts,
- Listing inventory,
- Expired listing ratio,
- Average commission,
- Buyer contracts,
- List-to-sell price ratios,
- Volume of past customers and clients on database,
- Market absorption rates (also, "turnover" or annual percent of
  homes sold in market),
- Velocities ("time on market" or pace of sales), and
- Personal property, such as computers and desks.

"The sales proceeds have varied," Bohlen said, "from cash upfront to no cash and payments over seven years. Common is a three- to

five-year payout based on database productivity with a 20% to 30% upfront payment."

Another approach used by other sellers is the "book of business" model where a referral fee percentage, often 20% to 30%, is paid on sales and referrals from a registered client list over a period of time, often three to five years. The key is a tightly written contract. Be sure to get professional help to spell out specific responsibilities and a relatively large upfront payment. As time passes, sellers typically stay in touch with their business, and buyers appreciate the ongoing client relationships, as the seller phases out of the business.

Other ways to structure a sale include: a multiple of the last three years average annual cash flow, sometimes in the range of 3 to 5 times EBITDA (Earnings Before Interest, Taxes, Depreciation, and Adjustments); a percentage of the most recent year's profits and a smaller percentage of the two previous years, perhaps 50% and 20%; a unit price for every verified past client in the database, such as $100 to $250 per client; or a combination of structures.

What is the ideal approach? "It's easiest to sell to someone in the same firm," Bohlen said. "Obviously, when we tender for bids, the more bids, the higher the value. The most offers I have ever received on one practice was nine. My best advice is plan a year in advance and work hard as heck until the practice is sold. The biggest mistake most sellers make," Bohlen said, "is slowing down their practice and letting their listing and buyer inventory slip while—or before—they make a decision to sell."

One of the most successful real estate practice sales Bohlen brokered was a mega-practice where the seller averaged 174 transactions a year with an average commission of $5,580. "The annual GCI of the seller was more than $970,000, and the buyer averaged $750,000 in annual commissions in a hot market where properties were selling fast, sometimes over listing price," Bohlen said. "It was a perfect match." Sale proceeds exceeded $980,000 to the seller, and the buyer paid off the sale from additional profits within four years. "It's certainly a record that can be broken," predicted Bohlen.

20 New Rules of Online Marketing

From websites to e-mail databases to virtual assistants every real estate professional today can build an eRainmaker practice. The productivity

these principles release, from #1 New Rule of Online Ma Internet changes everything except the rules of business. Rule ("Retirement means selling your e-practice to th der."), allows entrepreneurial eRainmakers to realize pro unheard of 10 years ago.

Put an eRainmaker system in place and you will b valuable your business will become to a future buyer. amazed at what fun it is to take your practice to the ne end of the day, putting together your own eRainmaker p way to suit your own e-strategy is the purest form of the

Make it Rain!®

Resources

eRainmaker
www.eRainmaker.com

Online Resource Center

In the Introduction, I promised a guide to *doing* as well as *thinking*. Nothing works better to find out more about online marketing than the Internet itself. To help you we have created a companion website for **REAL ESTATE RAINMAKER: Guide to Online Marketing.** You can find the Online Resource Center site at **eRainmaker.com.**

    REAL ESTATE RAINMAKER: Guide to Online Marketing is a book about marketing, not sales or technology. That is why the Online Resource Center focuses primarily on e-marketing tools, not soup-to-nuts general technology. To maintain its cutting edge, **eRainmaker.com** (no hyphen) is regularly updated and expanded. Naturally, the great advantage of eRainmaker.com as an Online Resource Center is the active links direct to featured suppliers' websites and e-mail, as well as the current phone numbers, addresses, and expanded descriptions.

291

Contact information often changes on the site. Be sure to check with product and service providers directly for their latest information. If you uncover any changes that need to be made to the eRainmaker Online Resource Center, please e-mail your suggestion to **Resource@eRainmaker.com.** We are always happy to hear from readers.

Here are the main categories at the eRainmaker.com Online Resource Center:

☑ *Website Buyers Guide:* For the first time anywhere, we have assembled a list of website providers that specialize in real estate. The combined list of website providers offers scores of real estate website packages. Websites and providers are grouped by a ballpark price of first-year website cost (initial design and one-year operating expense) into four budgets: under $1,000; $1,000–$2,500; $2,500–$5,000, $5,000 or more. Custom and broker/company website specialists are also listed.

☑ *Link Index:* An easy-to-use directory of real estate online marketing tools is cross-referenced to the page numbers and chapters of **REAL ESTATE RAINMAKER: Guide to Online Marketing.** In addition, every item is organized into the "Natural Order of Marketing™." This unique naming scheme was inspired by a similar classification system established by Swedish naturalist Carolus Linnaeus (1707–1778) for classifying plants using shared characteristics. Every online marketing tool is classified from "Kingdom" (Marketing), down through "Division" (Advertising), "Class" (Direct & Electronic), "Order" (E-Mail & Internet), "Family" (Sub-Groups), and "Genus" (Categories) to "Species" (Product or Service) and "Author" (Company).

☑ *Resource Guide:* In these invaluable time-saving entries, we preview the main features of outstanding e-marketing products in a concise eRainmaker summary. The Resource Guide gives you a short description plus links to complete contact information to drill into specific products that exactly fit your needs.

☑ *Great Websites:* What makes a great website a site to behold? To answer that question, we reviewed hundreds of real estate websites, plus many more non-real estate websites. To earn the designation as a REAL ESTATE RAINMAKER® Great Website a site must:

- Be customer focused with a rich offering of content found through easy navigation.

- Feature multiple opportunities for visitors to opt-in and identify themselves through direct-response offers.

- Provide an environment designed for prospects to revisit and convert them to customers.

- Create a cyberspace that welcomes past clients back with useful after-sale information and services.

- Be a core business asset that delivers a significant portion of production to the eRainmaker's practice.

☑ *GeekSpeak Glossary:* For novices and experts alike, talking the talk can go a long way toward walking the walk. In our unique GeekSpeak Glossary, we define hundreds of online marketing terms to put a finer point on your understanding of the Internet—and how to put it to work for you.

☑ *New Additions:* Watch the site regularly for new additions, updates, and special features to help you do a better job with your online marketing. By all means, if you have suggestions, please e-mail us at **Resource@eRainmaker.com** with both your rants and your raves. We welcome your feedback.

Shelf Help

REAL ESTATE BOOKS

Dominate! Capturing Your Market with Today's Technology, by Allen F. Hainge. Reston, VA: Allen F. Hainge Seminars, 2001, 275 pp., spiral bound. Direct from Allen F. Hainge seminars at (800) 695-3794 or AFHSeminars.com.

ePowerPro™: Online Success Strategies for Real Estate Professionals, by Michael Russer. Santa Barbara, CA: Russer Communications, 2001, 236 pp., spiral bound. Direct from Russer Communications, 1124 Las Olas Avenue, Suite 100, Santa Barbara, CA 93109; Toll Free (877) 977-1188 or ePowerPro.com.

Internet Marketing in Real Estate, by Barbara Cox and William Koelzer. Upper Saddle River, NJ: Prentice Hall, 2001, 245 pp., paperback. ISBN: 0-13-011547-9.

Next Generation Real Estate, by J. Lennox Scott with Shelley Rossi. Crete, NE: Dageforde Publishing, Inc., 2002, 80 pp., paperback. Direct from Dageforde Publishing, Inc., 128 East 13th Street, Crete, NE; (800) 216-8794, Dageforde.com. ISBN: 1-886225-6.

Rich Buyer, Rich Seller! The Real Estate Agents Guide to Marketing Luxury Homes, by Laurie Moore-Moore. Dallas, TX: The Institute for Luxury Home Marketing, 2003, paperback. Direct from Institute for Luxury Home Marketing, 1409 South Lamar, Suite 355, Dallas, TX 75215; (214) 485-3000, LuxuryHomeMarketing.com. ISBN: 0972600108.

Secrets of the CyberStars®: Making Money with Today's Technology, by Allen F. Hainge. Reston, VA: Allen F. Hainge Seminars, 2004, 275 pp., spiral bound. Direct from Allen F. Hainge seminars at (800) 695-3794 or AFHSeminars.com.

Terri Murphy's e-Listing and e-Selling Secrets for the Technologically "Clueless," by Terri Murphy. Chicago: Real Estate Education Company, 2001, 1996, 233 pp., hardcover. ISBN: 0-7931-3548-6.

The Eight New Rules of Real Estate, by John Tuccillo. Chicago: Real Estate Education Company, 1999, 200 pp., hardcover. ISBN: 0-7931-3166-9.

The Hottest E-Careers in Real Estate, by Blanche Evans. Chicago: Real Estate Education Company, 2000, 232 pp., hardcover. ISBN: 0-7931-4256-3.

The Millionaire Real Estate Agent, by Gary Keller with Dave Jenks and Jay Papasan. Austin, TX: Rellex Publishing Partners, 2003, 362 pp., paperback. Direct from MillionaireAgent.com. 40% discount on case (14 books). ISBN: 0-9702941-0-7.

Use What You've Got, and Other Business Lessons I Learned from My Mom, by Barbara Corcoran with Bruce Littlefield. Portfolio (a member of Penguin Group United States), 2003, 256 pp., hardcover. ISBN: 1591840023.

Your Successful Real Estate Career, by Dr. Kenneth W. Edwards. New York: AMACOM, 2003 4th edition, 240 pp., paperback. ISBN: 0814471609.

RELATED MARKETING BOOKS

Convergence Marketing: Strategies for Reaching the New Hybrid Consumer, by Yoram (Jerry) Wind, Vijay Mahajan with Robert E. Gunther. Upper Saddle River, NJ: Prentice Hall, 2002, 336 pp., hardcover. ISBN: 0-13-065075-7.

Effective E-Mail Marketing, by Herschell Gordon Lewis. New York: AMACOM, 2002, 288 pp., paperback. ISBN: 0-8144-7147-1.

E-Mail Marketing: Using E-mail to Reach Your Target Audience and Build Customer Relationships, by Jim Sterne and Anthony Priore. New York: John Wiley & Sons, 2000, 303 pp., paperback. ISBN: 0-471-38309-0.

Guerrilla Marketing Online: The Entrepreneur's Guide to Earning Profits on the Internet, by Jay Conrad Levinson and Charles Rubin. Boston: Mariner Books, 2nd edition, 1997, 336 pp., paperback. ISBN: 039586061X.

Internet Marketing for Dummies, by Frank Catalano and Bud Smith. Foster City, CA: IDG Books Worldwide, 2001, 317 pp., paperback. ISBN: 0-7645-0778-8.

Loyalty.Com: Customer Relationship Management in the New Era of Internet Marketing, by Frederick Newell. New York: McGraw-Hill, 2000, 325 pp., paperback. ISBN: 0-07-135775-0.

101 Internet Marketing Tips for Your Business, by Jeff Davidson. Newburgh, NY; (800) 421-2300, SmallBiz Books.com. Entrepreneur Press, 2002, 199 pp., paperback. ISBN: 1-891984-34-9.

Permission Marketing: Turning Strangers into Friends, and Friends into Customers, by Seth Godin. New York: Simon & Schuster, 1999, 255 pp., hardcover. ISBN: 0-684-85636-0.

Planning Your Internet Marketing Strategy: A Doctor Ebiz® Guide, by Ralph F. Wilson. New York: John Wiley & Sons, 2002, 256 pp., paperback. ISBN: 0-471-44109-0.

Streetwise® Low-Cost Web Site Promotion: Every Possible Way to Make Your Web Site a Success, without Spending Lots of Money, by Barry Feig. Holbrook, MA: Adams Media Corporation, 2001, 368 pp., paperback. ISBN: 1-58062-501-0.

The Big Red Fez: How to Make Any Web Site Better, by Seth Godin. New York: Simon & Schuster, 2001, 111 pp., paperback. ISBN: 0-7432-2790-5.

The 22 Immutable Laws of Branding, by Al Ries and Laura Ries. New York: Harper Business, 2002, 254 pp., paperback. ISBN: 0-06-000773-7.

Index

Action plan, 201
Action planner, 215–217
Adobe Acrobat Reader, 262
Advanced Access, 51
Advertising, 78–80
Afternic, 280
Allen F. Hainge CYBERSTARS®,
    35, 49, 51, 121, 150, 161,
    166, 197, 198, 205, 210, 211,
    274
AllTheWeb, 271
AOL, 191, 101, 271
Apple, 99
Appraisals, 281
Ask Jeeves, 271
Assist 2 Sell Buyer & Seller
    Realty Center, 35, 154
Assist 2 Sell Reality, 17
AT&T, 113
Atacan, Antonio, 22
Attachments, corrupted,
    181–182
Auto-responders, 196

Automated marketing system,
    200
   B2B network, 201
   creative content, 201
   ideal, 200–201
Automated property updates, 116
Automation software, 101–102
Avis, 159

Bad e-mail/bounce back rate,
    179–180
Banner ads, 129
Bells and whistles, 58
Benchmark, 47
Berger, Bruce Jay, 35–36
Berkshire Hathaway, 274
Best Image Marketing, 103, 150
Blockbuster, 159
Bohlen, Bob, 287–288
Bohlen & Associates, 287
Bolin, Alexis, 148
Bookend technique, 19–20
Book of business, 288

Bottom-Up Marketing (Reis and Trout), 31
Brand domains, 30–32
Brand mistakes to avoid, 36–37
Brand value, 37–39
Brice, Stacy, 252
Brochureware, 7, 43
Broker price opinion, 116
Broker reciprocity, 134
Browser page, 55
B2B, 235, 237
    contacts, 212
    e-mail network, 224–225
    network, 201
    referrals, 234
Budget:
    e-budget, 238–239
    marketing, 241
    model, 239
    percent of income, 241
    transaction based, 241
    website designing, 47
Buffett, Warren, 274
Buffini, Brian, 210
Burnham, Jay, 121
Business brand (domain name), 281
Business@ the Speed of Thought (Gates), 5

Canale, Steven M., 268
CBSHOME Real Estate, 22, 220
Century 21 Properties Plus, 20, 103
Chader, Steve, 132
Chamberlain, Carol, 275
Chamberlain, Jim, 275
Channel enhancement, 176
Click-through rates, 179
"Client only" page, 162–164

Coca Cola, 275
Coldwell Banker, 270
Coldwell Banker Residential Brokerage, 121, 197
Collins, Michael, 280
Competitive market analysis (CMA), 149–150, 188
Consumer-centric, 33
Contacts, creating a network of, 275–277
Content:
    creative, 201
    customer-focused, 51
    of search engines, 103–104
    of website, 48
Control panel tool, 44
Convergence, 18
Convergence Marketing (Wind and Mahajan), 6
Copywriter, 44
Corcoran Group, 71–72
Cost per acquisition (CPA), 246
Cost per action (CPA), 247
Cost per click (CPC), 247
Cost per lead (CPL), 247
Cost per sale (CPS), 246
Cost per thousand (CPM), 247
Covey, Stephen R., 243
Credit report, 119
Cross-channel marketing, 18
Cross-selling referrals, 214–215
Customer(s):
    focus on, 16–17, 48
    organize your target, 47–48
    prequalifing, 20–21
    relationship, mistakes to avoid, 166–167
    service tools, 56
        bells and whistles, 58
        interactive, 56–58

Customer lifetime value (CLV), 246
Customer relationship management/marketing (CRM), 158–160, 210
Customer value (CV), 237, 246
Cyber-customer, 5

Database:
  gap:
    closing, 226–227
    filling the, 225–227
  growth:
    B2B network, 224–225
    e-farm, 222–224
    offline-online combinations, 221–222
    website collection, 220
  hygiene, 227–230
Dead hyperlinks, 181
Deshaies, Ken, 166, 275, 276
Deshaies, Mary, 166
Destination website, 45
  domain, 33
DiGennaro Real Estate, Inc., 20
Direct-mail marketing, 172–173
Direct marketing, 160
Direct navigation, 59
Direct-response e-offers, 20–21, 138
Ditto, Gary, 213–214
Divorce and real estate, 152
Domain(s):
  destination, 30–31
  names, 40–42, 278–282
  register, 188, 190
  selecting, 29–42
  syntax rules, 42
  user-friendly, 32–34

Dominate! Capturing Your Market with Today's Technology (Hainge), 62
Doty, Pete, 277
DoubleClick, Inc., 10, 173
Double deals, 148–149
Double entry, 230
Double opt-in, 229
Drewien, Kathy, 124
Drucker, Peter, 47, 246
Durst, Christine, 255

Earning money with search marketing, 110–111
Earthlink Web Mail, 191
Ebby Halliday Realtors, 225
E-benchmarks, 234–235
EBITDA, 288
E-customers, 235
Edwards, Jim, 125
e.Fax Messenger, 262
Effective E-Mail Marketing (Lewis), 209
E-goals, 233–234
Eight-Level Scale, 209–210
E-leads, 113
E-loyalty, techniques to maximize, 164–166
E-mail, 10–12
  append, 227
  automating, 21–22
  change of address (ECOA), 228
  content, 173
  filters, 11
  follow-up, first response, 195–200
  list, things to watch, 229–230
  marketing strategy, 171–172
    effective principles, 177–178

E-mail *(Continued)*
  e-marketing engine,
    176–177
  mistakes to avoid with AOL,
    181–182
  opportunity/challenge,
    173–175
  responses, 178–180
  results, 172–173
  mistakes to avoid in
    preparing, 194, 206–207
  permission-based, 22–23
  responses:
    first impressions, 184–185
    high-impact graphics, 191
    market analysis, 188–191
    mistakes to avoid, 194
    text, 192–193
    tips, 185–188
    writing no-fail e-mail,
     183–184
  templates, 199
E-marketing, 17–18
  permission based, 175
  plan:
    budget, 241
    principles for preparing,
     242–245
    rules of thumb, 241–242
    six steps, 233–239
  to do list, 263–266
  word-of-mouse, 209–210
English, Audrey, 229
English, Vern, 229
Enhanced electronic advertising,
  132–134
Entrance page, 55
E-objectives, 235
E-practice, building a self-
  sustaining, 24–25

ERA Old South Properties,
  148
E-reports, 115–116
E-strategies, 237–238
E-strategy, 61
  integrated, 176–177
  "musts," 266–267
  plan, 284
E-techniques, 210–211
Eudora 5.0, 191
Evans, Blanche, 286
Exit page, 55
Exit strategies, 29–30, 273–274
  developing systems, 274–275
  domain names, 278–282
  logotypes, 283
  network contacts, 275–277
  online marketing, 288–289
  selling the practice, 283–285,
   286
  symbols, 277–278
  track record, 277
Expired listings, 151–152
Extension (domain name),
  282

Federal Express (FedEx),
  159–160
File transfer protocol (FTP),
  102
Financial calculators, 16
Firewall, 262
1st Signature Homes/GMAC Real
  Estate, 47
First Team Real Estate, 18, 96,
  167
Follow-up, 138–140, 216
  seller:
    attracting, 145–147
    domains, 148

generating listings, 154
mistakes to avoid, 155–156
techniques to capture,
148–154
buyer, 131
Fonville-Morisey Realtors,
202–203
Forms, website, 48
Forrester Research, 172
Forward rate, 180
Free reports, 115
French, Pete, 199
Frost, Greg, 214–215
Frost Mortgage Banking Group,
214

Gates, Bill, 5, 249
Gateway, 220
Geographic e-farm, 222–224
Goldstein, Neal, 6
Gooder, Leslie M., 244
Gooder Group, 3, 119, 250
Google, 9, 19, 101, 271
Graphics in e-mails, 191
Gray Direct, 173
Greene, Matt, 87
Greene, Paulette, 225
Gross commission income (GCI),
157), 241
Guest book, 123–124, 220

Haaren, Michael, 255
Haas, Galand, 35
Hainge, Allen F., 35, 49, 62,
267
Henderson, Ron, 20, 103
Hertz, 159
Hiers, Brooke, 96–97
Hiers, Richard, 18–19, 38, 96–97,
167

"High tech" marketing, 19
"High touch" follow-up, 19
Home Finder, 204
Home page, 55
HomeGain, 95–96
*homesurfing.net: Insider's Guide
to Buying and Selling Your
Home Using the Internet*
(Evans), 286
Horse Sense (Reis and Trout), 31
Hotmail, 22
Hotspot images, 126
*Hottest E-Careers In Real Estate,
The* (Evans), 286
Howard Brinton Star, 35
*How to Make Your Realtor Get
You the Best Deal*
(Deshaies), 275–276
Huey, David, 139
Hughes, Kim, 252
Hyles, Mike, 225–226
Hyper text markup language
(HTML), 191–193
Hyperlink, 83, 128

Identity, brand (corporate),
31–32
IDX, 134, 139, 275
Initial public offering (IPO), 22
Intellectual property (IP), 279
Interactive customer service
tools, 56–58
Internet:
changing, 15–16
customer, 5–6
and finding a real estate agent,
6–7
and gathering information, 6
information overload, 267
mistakes to avoid, 270–272

Internet data exchange (IDX), 17, 123
Internet Explorer, 99, 172, 261
Internet protocol (IP) address, 33, 102
Intuitive (domain name), 282
Iowa Realty, 87
Issues, privacy and security, 113

Jacklin, Gary, 139
Jacovini, Frank, 20
Jenks, Dave, 239
Johnston, Geoff, 61
Jupitar Research, 10

Keller, Gary, 8-9, 158, 239
Keller, Jerry, 51
Keller Williams, 239
Keller Williams Integrity First Realty, 132
Keller Williams International, 8
Keller Williams Reality, 33, 161, 229
Kenkel, Scot, 195-196
Keywords, 107
King, Don, 150
Kinzler, Tim, 270
Komack, Adam, 173

Landing page, 55
Last-chance trigger, 204-205
Lateral search, 108
Lead generation, 216
Legal (domain name), 282
Length (domain name), 282
Levin, Lori, 72
Lewis, Hershell Gordon, 209
Link popularity, promoting, 85-89
Links, types of, 108

List management, 230
Listings, 150
  capturing, 153-154
  generating, 154
  promote, 266
Long & Foster Real Estate, Inc., 67, 142-143, 153, 213
Long-term contact, 160, 217
Lotus Notes 5.0, 191
Loyalty, 157-167

Macromedia Flash Player, 262
Mahajan, Vijay, 6
Market analysis, 188-191
Marketing:
  basics, 99-111
  budget, 241
  online, 113-115
  statistics, 179-180
  strategy, 131
Marketing Warfare (Reis and Trout), 31
Marshall, Gary, 17, 35, 154
Mathes, Dick, 34, 105, 106
Mayer, Ethel, 67
McCracken, Bruce, 174, 215-216
McDonald's, 31
McDonnell, Leslie, 226
McGarry, Peter, 202-204
McGinnis GMAC Real Estate, 198
Metatags, 104
  description, 105
  keyword, 106-107
  title, 105
Microsoft, 22, 99, 249, 275
Microsoft Hotmail, 191
Microsoft Outlook, 191, 196, 199, 226

Millionaire Real Estate Agent, The (Keller, Jenks, and Papasan), 8, 239
MLS, 16, 22, 139, 275
MORE Company, The, 35, 125
Mosaic, 172
Most valuable customer (MVC), 158
"Mousetrap," 100
Mozilla, 172
MSN, 101, 271
Mueller, Heidi, 95–96
Multi branding, 34–36
Multimedia, 191
Multiple listing system (MLS), 133
Mythunderstandings (six), 8–9

National Association of REALTORS (NAR), 3, 5
National car rental, 159
National Do-Not Call Registry, 174
Navigation labels, 117, 118, 120, 121
Navigation menu, 126
Netscape, 22, 172
Newsletters, 212–214
Nielsen/NetRatings, 100
Norton Antivirus Program, 262

Offering memorandum, 284
Offline-online combinations, 221–222
O'Hara, Stephen, 96
One-to-one e-mail, 176
One-to-one surveys, 160
Online agent, 162
Open Directory Project, 88
Open house, 141–143, 154

Open rates, 179
Opinion of value, 116
Opt ins, 10–11, 229
Opt outs, 229–230
  link, 206
  unsubscribe rate, 180
O'Rourke, Kathy, 213
Overture, 19, 96

Paige, Satchel, 10
Paley, Nic, 257
Panorama technique (virtual tour), 137
Papasan, Jay, 239
Pareto, Vilfredo, 157
Pareto's Law, 157
Parking, 33
Pasmanick, Zac, 68
Pay per sale (PPS), 246
Pay per click, 91, 92–93
  search engines (PPCSE), 92
Pay per closing, 92, 94–96
Pay per lead, 91–92, 94
Pay per performance (PPP), 84, 90–92
Pay per view, 91, 92
  ads, 100
Peckham, Jack, 267
Percent of income budget, 241
Permission-based e-mail, 10–11
Permission-based e-marketing, 175
Permission marketing, 24
Pete Doty & Company, 277
Pinto, John, 139
Pointing, 33
Pop-ups, 128–129
Position, branding your, 47
Positioning: The Battle for Your Mind (Ries and Trout), 31

Practice:
  selling your, 283–285
  value of, 287–288
Preferred Home Brokers, 275
PreviewProperties.com, 287
Price estimate/market value, 116
Prudential California Realty, 95
Prudential Fox & Roach, 22
Prudential real estate network,
  287
Prudential Wilmot Whitney, 213
"Pull" technology, 17
"Push" technology, 17

Randall, Tom, 70
Real Estate Rainmaker, 233
Real Estate Virtual Assistant
  Network, 252, 254–255
RealMedia Player, 262
Realty World John Pinto &
  Associates, 139
Reciprocal links, 84
  partners, 87
Redirecting, 33
Referral campaigns, mistakes to
  avoid, 217
Referrals, 157–158
Referring URLs, 83
Relationship driven, 160
Relocation, 150
  kits, 119
RE/MAX, 96, 152, 225–226
RE/MAX Central, 212
RE/MAX Central Reality, 16
RE/MAX Distinctive Real Estate,
  210
RE/MAX Equity Group, 25
RE/MAX Executive, 66
RE/MAX 1st Choice, 226

RE/MAX Gold Coast, 35
RE/MAX Greater Atlanta, 68
RE/MAX Integrity, 35
RE/MAX Mainstreet, 152
RE/MAX Olson & Associates, 51
RE/MAX Premier, 73
RE/MAX Professionals, 205
RE/MAX Properties, 276
RE/MAX Properties of the
  Summit, 166
RE/MAX of Rancho Bernardo,
  150
RE/MAX Real Estate Center, 70
RE/MAX Real Estate Services, 96
RE/MAX Realty Enterprises, 150
RE/MAX Suburban, 226
Renaud, Bill, 21–22
Renaud Otten Team, The, 21–22
Response form, 126
Response rates, tracking,
  178–179
Results, tracking, 246–247
Return on investment (ROI),
  246
Richardson, Nadine, 47
Ries, Al, 31
Ries, Laura, 31
Ries & Ries, 31–32
Roche, Thierry, 73
Rome, Margaret, 67, 197
Rudder, Eric, 249
Russer, Michael, 47, 199,
  254–255, 257, 268
Safari, 99, 172
Sale prospectus, 284
Saltman, Risa, 268
Sanford, Walter, 165
Schwab, Charles, 6
Search directory, 100

Search engine(s), 60
  placement, 84
    tools, 102–103
  strategies to maximize, 100–111
Search marketing, 100
Sears, Ed, 143
Sellers, capturing online,
  148–154
Seller's package, 116–117
Selling Your Home Alone
  (Edwards), 125
Serkes, Carol, 268
Serkes, Ira, 66, 268
*7 Habits of Highly Effective
  People, The* (Covey), 243
Shade, Gary, 150
Signatures, 196–199
Sinofsky, Steven, 249
Site, promoting your, 59–81
Sizzling Studios, 260–263
SOAR Automation, 139
Soesbe, Linda, 198–199
Spam, 10, 175
  killers, 11
Spelling (domain name), 282
Splash page, 55
Stewart, Reese, 16–17
Strategic links, 59, 83
  approaches to, 84
  foundation, 84–85
  mistakes to avoid, 89–90
Streaming video (virtual tour),
  138
Street, Ron, 212
Stumpf, Joe, 210
Success:
  strategies for:
    #1 Focus on the customer,
      16–17

#2 Understand e-marketing,
  17–18
#3 Maximize results, 18–20
#4 Direct-response e-offers,
  20–21
#5 Automate e-mail, 21–22
#6 Cultivate permission-
  based e-mail, 22–23
#7 Virtual assistants,
  23–24
#8 Build e-practice to sell,
  24–25
Sutton, Dianne, 210–211
Symantec, 262

Teaser (softener), 19
Tech-and-Touch (TnT), 18,
  176
  customer, 5, 6
  prospect, 132
  services, 29
Techniques to capture prospects,
  204–205
Technology, 29
  truths:
    #1 Most customers contact
      only one real estate
      agent, 3–5
    #2 Tomorrow's Internet
      customer will drive the
      train, 5–6
    #3 Only 6 percent of
      customers find their
      real estate agent on the
      Internet, 6–7
    #4 Brokerages and mega-
      teams have declared
      war on your customers,
      7–8

Technology *(Continued)*
#5 Six mythunderstandings
that stand between you
and high achievement,
8–9
#6 The Internet pressures
every website to be
better today than
yesterday, 9–10
#7 The honeymoon is over-
e-mail is not for the
unsophisticated
anymore, 10–12
#8 The rules of the online
marketing game are
constantly changing,
12–13
Teller, Sandy, 62, 260
Template website, 44
Top level domain (TLD), 40
Trade-ins, 152
Trademark (domain name), 282
Traffic, tracking, 79, 80–81
Transaction-based budget, 241
Transaction driven, 160
*Transform Your Business Using
Virtual Assistants* (Russer),
255
Trophy database, 158
Trophy E-Mail Database, 23, 91,
160, 176, 238, 244, 245,
258, 266–267
building, 219–230
Trout, Jack, 31
Tryggeseth, Steve, 205–206
Turnkey (virtual tour),
137–138
*22 Immutable Laws of
Marketing, The* (Reis and
Trout), 31

Two-click rule, 48
Two-from-one, 89
Tyler, Beth, 153–154

Undeliverables, 229
Unique selling proposition
(USP), 47
U.S. Postal Service, 159
Universal resource locator
(URL), 129
Updates, automated listing,
138–140
URL, becoming a household,
59–62

Valenti, Joe, 22, 220
Vertical search, 108
Viral marketing, 124, 180
Virtual assistants (VAs), 23–24
building value, 249–250
checklist, 251–254
telecommuting, 254–255
Virtual office website (VOW),
123, 134–136, 139, 220
Virtual tours, 15, 16, 136–138,
211–212

Wallace, Dave, 33–34
Walters, Todd, 152
Wanamaker, John, 78
Wasserman, Mollie, 161–162
Web appeal, 54–55
Web Centric, 62
Web-centric marketing model,
146
Web designer, 44, 46–48
Web developer, 44
Website:
checklist to buy, 46
collections, 220–221

custom, 45–46
customer centered:
  buy or build, 44–46
  creating, 48–49
  critical strategies for making
    money, 49–55
  customer service tools, 56–58
  simple strategies, 43–44
  web designers, 46–48
domain name, 283
five musts to creating, 48–49
lead capture, 126–129
logotypes, 284
and making money strategies,
  49–55
personal, 45
response offers, 115–126
template pages, 44–45
traffic, boosting, 62–78

Weichert Realtors, 211
Weismann, Barbara, 211
Welcome page, 55
Whole Foods, 275
Willanger, Adrian, 153
Williams, John F., 35, 125
Wilser, Patti, 25
Wilser, Tom, 25
Win-back, 217
Wind, Jerry, 6
Windermere Real Estate, 153
WinZip, 262
With, Peter, 150
Woods, Gary, 84, 166
Woods, Laury, 84, 166
Word of mouse, 124

Yahoo!, 88, 101, 191, 271

About the Author

Dan Gooder Richard is the creator of the *RAINMAKER LEAD SYS-TEM*® now in use by thousands of real estate professionals nation-wide. Dan is a publisher, consultant, and speaker. He and his wife, Synnöve Granholm, founded GOODER GROUP® in 1983 and still man-age the Fairfax, Virginia-based publisher of marketing materials for real estate and mortgage professionals.

GOODER GROUP currently publishes five monthly printed newsletters and two e-newsletters for prospecting and an extensive series of marketing tools including RAINMAKER E-CENTRAL® (comprised of lead-capture website content and automated drip e-mail), handbooks, brochures, postcards, print ads, marketing letters, and more, all de-signed for lead generation, prospect follow-up and long-term contact. More than 12,000 real estate and mortgage salespeople in the United States and Canada use GOODER GROUP marketing products every year. Annually, GOODER GROUP's customers purchase and distribute more than three million units of GOODER GROUP products.

As one of the real estate industry's leading authorities in marketing and lead management since 1979, Dan has decades of experience at "making the phone ring" for real estate professionals. With a master's degree in journalism from the University of Missouri (Columbia), Dan began his marketing career in 1979 as the first director of marketing for Long & Foster Real Estate, one of the largest real estate brokerages in the country. In five years with Long & Foster, he directed the corporate marketing effort and helped the company grow from 900 agents to 2,400 agents, from 30 offices to 59 offices, and from $859 million in sales to $2.4 billion in sales. (In 2002, total sales for all Long & Foster Companies exceeded $23 billion.)

Dan's middle name comes from his maternal grandfather, Leslie MacDonald Gooder, who was a publisher in Chicago from the early 1910s through the 1950s. Dan is carrying on the family name in publishing. Born in Davenport, Iowa, in 1947, Dan now lives in Arlington, Virginia, with his Finnish-born wife, Synnöve Granholm.

Dan Gooder Richard can be contacted at:

GOODER GROUP
2724 Dorr Avenue, Suite 103
Fairfax, VA 22031-4901
(703) 698-7750
(703) 698-8597 (Fax)
Leads@GooderGroup.com
GooderGroup.com